JACKBOOT
THE STORY OF
THE GERMAN SOLDIER

Battle Standards Military Paperbacks
from David & Charles

BATTLE STANDARDS

JACKBOOT
THE STORY OF
THE GERMAN SOLDIER

JOHN LAFFIN

A DAVID & CHARLES MILITARY BOOK

British Library Cataloguing in Publication Data

Laffin, John
    Jackboot.
    1. Germany. Heer, history
    I. Title
    355'.00943

    ISBN 0–7153–9458–4

First published 1965 in hardback by
Cassell & Company Ltd. This paperback
edition published 1989
by David & Charles Publishers plc
and printed in Great Britain
by Redwood Burn Limited, Trowbridge, Wiltshire
for David & Charles Publishers plc
Brunel House   Newton Abbot   Devon

Distributed in the United States by
Sterling Publishing Co. Inc,
2, Park Avenue, New York, NY 10016

Cover pictures
Front: German postcard of 1941, featuring soldier
        of 1918. (*Peter Newark's Military Pictures*)
Back: 1939–45 Nazis. (*Topharn Picture Library*)

To the greatest German
soldier of them all—
Colonel Paul von Lettow-Vorbeck,
the only undefeated German
leader of the Great War and
a very gallant gentleman.
He died in Hamburg on
9 March 1964, aged ninety-three.

John Laffin is one of the world's best known writers on war and military history; more than 50 of his 100 books are on these subjects. He is a contributor to most military and defence journals and he frequently lectures about war. Dr. Laffin served in the infantry throughout World War II and he is an observer at contemporary conflicts. He and his wife, Hazelle, who is his assistant, have their own unique private battlefield museum. They have personally dug their thousands of artefacts from modern battlefields.

Acknowledgements

I feel it necessary to explain that because I have tried to analyse the German soldier in an impartial way this book is bound to cause controversy equally among staunch pro-Germans and strong anti-Germans. Even before publication it excited critics, pacifists and neo-Nazis in one way or another. To obviate petty criticisms which could result from violent reaction, I point out that because so much variation and confusion exists in the names of people and places I have adopted that which appears to have been most widely used; for example, General Seidlitz rather than Seydlitz and Auerstadt rather than Auerstädt or Auerstedt. Again, it is always difficult to obtain accurate figures relating to casualties, strength of formations and numbers of weapons, so I have used those given in official histories or by reliable authorities. Description of life in the German Army at various periods is based on the experiences and recollections of men who served in it; better evidence would be difficult to find. I am specially grateful to Major Klaus Winkel, formerly of the Africa Korps, for his help in translation and in checking details. If any errors do exist, they are mine alone. I have dedicated my book to Colonel Paul von Lettow-Vorbeck rather than to him as a general—which rank he did eventually reach —because it was as a colonel that he was generally known and preferred to be known. I am grateful to Jonathan Cape Ltd. for permission to quote extracts from *In the Lines* by George Bucher and to Chatto & Windus Ltd., for extracts from *Storm of Steel* by Ernst Jünger. Some of the material on Frederick the Great is derived, by permission, from the article in Chambers's Encyclopaedia by Dr. George Peabody Gooch, O.M.

By the Same Author:

Military

Middle East Journey
Return to Glory
One Man's War
The Walking Wounded
Digger (The Story of the Australian Soldier)
Scotland the Brave (The Story of the Scottish Soldier)
Jackboot (The Story of the German Soldier)
Tommy Atkins [The Story of the English Soldier)
Jack Tar (The Story of the English Seaman)
Swifter Than Eagles (Biography of Marshal of the Royal Air Force Sir John Salmond)
The Face of War
British Campaign Medals
Codes and Ciphers
Boys in Battle
Women in Battle
Anzacs at War
Links of Leadership (Thirty Centuries of Command)
Surgeons in the Field
Americans in Battle
Letters From the Front 1914–18
The French Foreign Legion
Damn the Dardanelles! (The Story of Gallipoli)
The Australian Army at War 1899–1975
The Arab Armies of the Middle East Wars 1948–1973
The Israeli Army in the Middle East Wars 1948–1973
Fight for the Falklands!
The War of Desperation: Lebanon 1982–85
The Man the Nazis Couldn't Catch
On the Western Front
Brassey's Battles: (3,500 Years of Conflict)
Holy War (Islam Fights)
War Annual 1
War Annual 2
War Annual 3
The Western Front 1916–1917: The Price of Honour
The Western Front 1917–1918: The Cost of Sacrifice
World War 1 in Postcards
Greece, Crete & Syria 1941
British Butchers and Bunglers of World War 1

General

The Hunger to Come (Food and Population Crises)
New Geography 1966–67
New Geography 1968–69
New Geography 1970–71
Anatomy of Captivity (Political Prisoners)
Devil's Goad
Fedayeen (The Arab-Israeli Dilemma)
The Arab Mind
The Israeli Mind
The Dagger of Islam
The Arabs as Master Slavers
The PLO Connections
Know the Middle East

And other titles

Contents

CONTENTS

War is for the privileged, combat the ultimate honour.
Frederick the Great, 1760.

It is noble for a Prussian to die for his country; an individual death is merely following the laws of perfection which preserve the whole, if necessary, by the loss of a part.
Thomas Abbt, professor at the University
of Frankfurt on the Oder, 1761.

The Prussian Army is the best disciplined and the readiest for service at a minute's warning of any now in the world or perhaps that ever was in it.
John Moore, M.D., an English traveller, in 1779.

German war is an affair of the intellect; the intellect is stronger than any other force.
The inscription on the white statues of Prussian soldiers
beside the temple in Unter den Linden, Berlin, in the 1820s.

Deutschland, Deutschland über alles, über alles in der Welt.
Hoffmann von Fallersleben, 1841.

The beautiful idealism of war, which lies indestructible in the blood of every proper German. . . .
Heinrich von Treitschke, 1858.

The Army is the most outstanding institution in every country, for it alone makes possible the existence of all civic institutions. . . . Perpetual peace is a dream and not a very beautiful dream at that.

Field-Marshal Helmuth von Moltke, 1869.

War knows of only one method: force. There is no other; it is destruction, wounds, death, and this employment of brute force is an absolute rule. As to international law, which all lawyers are so full of, it imposes on the object and the law of war only insignificant restrictions; in effect, none whatever.

To introduce into a philosophy of war a principle of moderation would be an absurdity. War is an act of violence pushed to its utmost bounds.

Karl von Clausewitz.

A war requires enormous sacrifices of blood and property from the German people, but we will show our adversaries what it means to attack Germany and I now commend you to God. Go to church. Kneel down before God and ask him for help for our brave army.

The Kaiser, August 1914.

The attack was terribly beautiful. The most beautiful and at the same time the most terrible thing I have ever experienced. . . . The attack was glorious.

Alfred Vaeth, German infantryman, 13 October 1915.

One does not make war sentimentally. The more pitilessly war is waged, the more it is fundamentally humane; for it will come to an end so much the quicker. The methods of war which bring peace most quickly are and remain the most humane methods.

Field-Marshal von Hindenburg, 1915.

The voice of national conscience tells us what German militarism really is: the best item in our political, national and ethnical development.

General Ernst von Bülow, 1916.

We must give lead soldiers as gifts to our children; that is how we shall be working for the German future.

General von Seeckt, 19 September 1927.

Time only strengthens my conviction that it (war) was a good and strenuous life, and that the war, for all its destructiveness, was an incomparable schooling of the heart. The front-line soldier whose foot came down on the earth so grimly and harshly may claim this at least, that it came down cleanly.

Ernst Jünger, Lieutenant, 73rd Hanoverian Regiment, 1929.

It is impossible to build up an army and give it a sense of worth if the object of its existence is not preparation for war. Armies for the preservation of peace do not exist; they exist only for the triumphant exertion of war.

Adolf Hitler, 1930.

The best type of German, the type which determines soldier-ship, is no particular friend of absolute security and the ensuing quiet. Although his conscientiousness protects him against reckless play, he feels all the same attracted to a 'dangerous life'. Nothing has proved more clearly that soldier-ship is the very kernel of German nature, than the fact that the newly established comprehensive and general way of German life had to originate from the spirit of soldiership.

Münchener Neueste Nachrichten, 8 October 1940.

'Gentlemen, you have chosen the most wonderful profession on this earth. You have before you the highest aim there can ever be on this earth. We teach you here how to reach that aim. You are here in order to learn that which alone can give the life of each of you its ultimate significance. You are here in order to learn how to die.'

The customary address made by the commandant of Lichterfelde Cadet School to new cadets, aged ten and eleven.

Although twelve years have passed the German people have neither yielded nor reconciled themselves to the situations imposed upon them.

Franz Amrehn, acting mayor of Berlin, July 1959.

I would exchange an arm for twenty-four hours in battle for my country.

A German student in London to the author of this book, 1964.

INTRODUCTION

The German Destiny

On the highest point of the steep cliffs overlooking Tobruk is the memorial the Germans built to commemorate their soldiers who died in the North African battles of 1940–3. It is one of the most impressive, soldierly memorials I have seen— and in my travels in the steps of armies I have seen many. Square, built of blocks of white stone and with great double doors, it looks like an outpost fortress. It is manned, too—by 6,000 dead German soldiers, all buried under the paving stones of the barracks-like courtyard. The names of those who could be identified are inscribed on black marble around the interior walls of the fort. Wreaths are sometimes sent to the memorial; once I saw one from Frau Rommel, widow of the great general.

The fort—I cannot help thinking of it more as a fort than as a memorial—impresses me deeply; it is so martial, so masculine, unlike the war memorials of some other countries. So many French monuments look like a woman's work, while the hand of the professional sculptor can be seen in British memorials. I appreciate any monument to soldiers, because to me fighting soldiers are the most genuine and worthwhile people who have ever existed. But there is some extra quality about a German monument. Whenever I am in Lindau, the German holiday town on Lake Constance, I am drawn to the old garrison church, on whose walls are inscribed the names of dead soldiers. The only object in the church is a slab of marble on which reclines, larger than lifesize, a German soldier, booted and helmeted, in brown marble. I have seen Germans, supposedly an insensitive race, moved to tears by this figure. The Tobruk fort probably has the same effect.

When I was last at the fort I met a former German soldier, a member of the Afrika Korps, a man of my own age, a fellow soldier.

He rescued me from a distressing situation. A German woman visitor, seeing my name and nationality in the visitors' book, approached me calmly enough and asked if I had been a soldier. When I replied that I had she became emotional and practically accused me, personally, of having killed her son, now buried in the fort. The former Afrika Korps man intervened, soothed the woman and when she had gone back to the town we sat in the hot sun and talked about war and soldiering. We have talked many times since, for we became good friends. That first day I told him that I wrote books about wars and soldiers and that one day I intended to write a study of the German soldier.

'How will you finish it?' he asked.

'Probably at the end of the war in 1945.'

'I don't mean that,' he said. 'What will you prophesy for the future?'

'I shall say that one day the Germans will march again.'

He looked at me seriously. 'You are right,' he said slowly. 'We are not finished with our jackboots yet.'

No, the Germans are not finished with war. For every German, peace is a suspension of the state of war. The German breathes war, he is imbued with it, he glorifies it. Other nations have glorified it, too, in external trappings. Britain has excelled all others in this respect—in her military traditions, her pomp and ceremony, her near reverence for the military caste, though, as we shall see, much of Britain's glorification of war was inherited from Prussia, which moulded the entire German race into soldiers.

The difference between Germany and other nations is that German veneration for war is not merely in external forms; it is internal as well. The German, every German, is a born soldier. He has the virus quality of aggression and fortitude in his blood. Like soldiers of other nations he needs to be trained but the material is there already, not base clay, but refined material.

A few comparisons to bring out the point. For sheer dash, *élan* and initiative no soldier of modern times has equalled the Australian; for dogged persistence and obedience to orders no race can touch the English and Welsh; for fighting fury I nominate the Scots; for the ability to plan, for method and for thoroughness the American is superb; for fanatical courage and endurance I commend the Japanese; for the capacity to suffer and still keep fighting who can excel the Russian?

But the troops of all these races, fine though they are in their various ways, are not complete soldiers. They fight because circumstances make it necessary for them to fight. Even the Australian, who often fights with a grin on his face, hates it.

The German is a complete soldier, because war to him has a religious quality. It is almost a holy thing. Almost? To many Germans, past and present, it *is* holy. There is nothing fanatical about this reverence for war, as there is with the Japanese. The Japanese soldier sees glory in death in battle. The German no more wants to die than any other soldier of any other nation, but he accepts death more philosophically. The complete soldier fully realizes that his only logical end is death; that this is a soldier's only privilege. The German knows this.

Napoleon's soldiers are the only troops in modern times with whom the Germans, in a limited way, can possibly be compared, but this comparison is only valid for the short period Napoleon commanded them. Before that time and especially after it their quality was poor, though inept leadership is more to blame for this than lack of quality in the men.

Any soldier who has fought against the Germans will concede, even if grudgingly, that 'the Huns are bloody good soldiers'. But because they have twice been beaten in the last fifty years there is a popular misconception that they can always be beaten. There was never a more mistaken idea. When lecturing about Napoleon, I am always prepared to acclaim him as the greatest general in history, and inevitably somebody will say smugly, 'Wellington defeated him'. There is no more logic in this than in saying that because the Germans have been beaten the troops who beat them are therefore better troops.

The Prussians and Germans never did consider themselves beaten in any conflict up to 1918 and while they could hardly fail to admit defeat in 1945, the significant point in both wars is that they held out for so long. At the end of the 1939-45 war they fought against impossible odds, virtually encircled by enemies, pounded day and night by thousands of bombers, losing not mere divisions but whole armies, whole industries, entire cities. And when the Allies were convinced of near victory the Germans made their fantastic, final counter-attack in the Ardennes in the winter of 1944-5—the Battle of the Bulge. In the end this spirited thrust was defeated, but it will for ever remain a magnificent feat of arms. It was the Germans' psychological approach to the battle, not their weight of arms which produced this astonishing last ditch battle. As we shall see, psychology has always played a big part in German military affairs.

It is important to remember that it is only in fairly recent years that we can speak of the 'German soldier' as such, for it is less than a century since the Germanic peoples—the Prussians, Saxons, Hanoverians, Bavarians and the others—became united. For many centuries they were quite disunited and even as recently as the first half of the nineteenth century the relationship of certain Germanic countries was strained to say the least.

Despite Germany's relatively recent emergence as a nation with a national army, the German soldier is unique—as unique in his way and in his time as the Roman legionary, the Saracen horseman and the Zulu warrior. To understand the reason for this we must go back to the first half of the eighteenth century. We could, indeed, go back much further, but it was at this period that Prussia began to crystallize her military qualities.

At present, and for a time longer, the Germans are licking their deep wounds. They have been scarred by defeat and so many families lost fathers, sons and brothers that the Germans now profess to dislike war. The older Germans are still groping for some acceptable reason for defeat—some deeper reason than the merely superficial one of being physically pounded to pieces. The younger Germans, genuinely revolted by stories of the Nazi concentration camps, say, 'It will never happen again.'

They may well be sincere, but the German can never evade his destiny; he does not really want to evade it. He is a soldier. A soldier fights.

John Laffin

Halland,
Sussex,
England.

CHAPTER I

The Army—Frederick the Great's Inheritance

The soldier who was to impress, startle and terrify Europe sprang from a country which, in the early eighteenth century, was one of the most backward countries of Europe. Prussia was landlocked and her soil was hard and barren; she had no cities worth the name, little industry and less culture, while her people were poor and largely barbarous.

Among the few ambitious families were the Hohenzollerns, as old as any of the noble families of Europe, but until only a short time before the accession of Frederick II mere feudal lords of a relatively small area, Brandenburg. They knew, however, that land and military strength were the keys to power. First they bought territory, then they acquired more by service to the Holy Roman Emperor; all the nobles and Electors of Germany were subjects of the Emperor at this time. Finally the Electors of Brandenburg gained land by might and then they wrung from the Emperor the right to be called kings of Prussia.

Frederick William, who was twenty-four when he came to the throne in 1713, did much to establish Prussia as a rising power. He was a vigorous, violent and often frightening man.

'I do not want this vermin,' he said, referring to pacificist sects, 'their children do not become soldiers.'

He put the finances of the kingdom in order and raised the army to a strength of 89,000 by conscripting the officers and impressing or kidnapping the men. Foreign observers admired the discipline and training of the army more than its size. Many of his troops were foreigners. In a period of twenty-eight years Frederick William impressed or enrolled, outside his dominions, more than 40,000 men, many of them English.

Frederick William had a mania—collecting tall soldiers for his Potsdam Giants, otherwise known as the Great Grenadiers or the Big Prussian Blues. 'He who sends me tall soldiers,' Frederick William often said, 'can do with me whatever he likes.'

This confession was unanimously accepted at its face value and emperors, kings, queens, princes, nobles and foreign ministers hastened to pay their court through giant recruits. In 1714 Peter the Great of Russia, for instance, sent a contingent of eighty Muscovites 'notable for their stature' and from then on, every year until his death, the Tsar sent eighty to two hundred Russians rounded up from the corners of his dominions.

In March 1720 the British Minister in Berlin forwarded to the Earl of Stanhope the measurements of the tallest man then in the Great Grenadiers; a giant 7 feet 6 inches tall. 'If it be possible to find any men near that size,' he wrote, 'I am sure it would be the most valuable present His Majesty (George I) could make.' Within a few months a squad of fifteen very large Irishmen arrived in Berlin under military escort.

Frederick William saw some very tall men on parade when he visited the King of Poland and so pestered his host that the Polish king finally handed over twenty-four of them.

His agents, hundreds of them, scoured Europe buying or kidnapping tall men. Some of these agents were shot or hanged, but Frederick William paid so well for giants that few of his agents were deterred by casualties in their ranks. Even men of good family and rank were abducted and once they were forcibly enlisted in the Great Grenadiers no power on earth could get them out. Nobody was safe. An Italian priest was sandbagged while celebrating mass and dragged away.

No man in the regiment measured less than 6 feet without his boots; some men were reported as being nearly 9 feet tall and a mitre-shaped hat added another 12 or 15 inches to this spectacular height.

Between 1713 and 1735 a grand total of 12,000,000 thaler or nearly £1,750,000 was sent abroad for recruits. James Kirkland, a colossal Irishman, cost his captors £1,260 before he was safely lodged at Potsdam. The annual review in May was in part a sale of tall men, for then officers brought along men they had enlisted during the year to sell them to the King. At the review of 1731 the King bought sixty men for 145,100 thaler.

Maintenance of the regiment of Giant Grenadiers—which at its peak had 3,030 men in its ranks—equalled that of eight ordinary regiments of the line. In the matter of rations they were treated better than princes of the blood. But this was probably the only benefit; in all other respects the Grenadiers lived miserably and hopelessly, coveted playthings to be marched and drilled and exhibited and never left alone. Illustrious visitors were routed from their beds at unearthly hours of the morning and in all weathers to see the drowsy, shivering giants put through their paces.

No drillmaster in the army was more exacting than the King. His sight was so keen he could instantly detect the slightest irregularity in the swing of the longest line. Officers and men went in fear of his merciless cane. Suicides were not uncommon and twice groups of grenadiers mutinied. Mutiny was punishable by death, but Frederick William could not afford to lose valuable property, so he selected a single likely-looking ringleader and had him executed.

As a man the King was mean, unpleasant and crude and though he had fourteen children he gave none of them any love. His fourth child was christened Frederick, known to history as Frederick II and, more aptly, Frederick the Great, born in 1712.

That he rose to be great was not due to his father's encouragement. Frederick William hated his son. The boy was educated by a French governess and tutor and developed a devotion to French culture which continued all his life. He despised the German language and was not interested in German literature. His only playmate was his sister Wilhelmina, three years his senior and the only woman he ever loved.

Father and son differed in looks, and manner, too. Frederick William, abrupt and loud-mouthed, looked coarse and not particularly intelligent or interesting. Frederick had a sensitive face and reflective eyes and an arresting handsomeness. His manner was quiet and he rarely raised his voice.

Young Frederick loved music, art and literature, all vices in his father's eyes. The King tried to strangle him with a cord, later had him whipped and gaoled. He swore at him and personally beat him frequently. Life became so hideous that Frederick, who was taken into the army at seventeen, deserted with a close friend, Katte, and tried to leave the country.

Both were arrested and gaoled. Only fear of Austria's reactions stopped the King from executing his son, but nothing could save Frederick's friend; he was executed while Frederick was forced to watch.

Frederick found gaol preferable to his father's company and when he was released he was better able to stand his tyranny. He had realized that submission to his father was the price of freedom, and in 1732 he was appointed colonel of a regiment at Ruppin. He had hoped to marry his cousin Amelia, daughter of George II (Frederick's mother was George II's sister) but at the age of twenty-one he reluctantly accepted his father's choice and married Elizabeth Christina of Brunswick, whom he respected but did not love, and after his accession they separated.

The next seven years were the happiest of his life, for his father gave him Rheinsberg, a pleasant estate near Ruppin. He did not neglect his military duties but he devoted himself to poetry and became a close friend of the great French writer, Voltaire.

He wrote some essays. One, revised by Voltaire and published anonymously in Holland in 1740, proclaimed that the ruler must be the first servant of his estate and that war was permissible if demanded by its interests. This was a significant statement in the light of Frederick's later acts.

When Frederick William died on 31 May 1740, he left his son nothing personally, but he did hand down a secure, prosperous country and, what was more, a magnificent army, the best trained in Europe. It was untried in battle, for Frederick William was afraid of war.

It was popularly believed, at home and abroad, that Prussia under Frederick would now become militarily weaker and domestically more tranquil. Important people who had suffered from the scourge of Frederick William's tongue and irrational behaviour expected the new king to be docile and malleable. He would live in semi-seclusion and let the nobles run the country. But overnight Frederick gave up many of his interests and became a warrior, intent on creating a mighty Prussia. A dictator, he was his own commander-in-chief, prime minister, foreign minister, chancellor of the exchequer.

But in most ways he did not follow in his father's footsteps. He ended—at least for a time—the harsh methods of recruiting, for instance, although he did keep a guard of 2,000 picked, big men. However, they were all volunteers.

He investigated the ability of his troops to manœuvre and was not satisfied. He wanted the infantry to move faster. His ideal was the superiority of fire of the infantry. They already

4

fired rapidly and well from their original position, but to change over to another formation—to a square, for example—took too much time, and the intervals between fire were too long. There was no flexible arrangement of riflemen at the time and soldiers fired only when given a direct order—or were supposed to. Frederick wanted changes made but initially he was concerned with Prussia's strategical weakness.

She had no natural land frontiers and she was surrounded by aggressive neighbours. As Frederick saw it, to remain strong Prussia had to expand. His House had ancient claims to three of the duchies which formed part of the Austrian province of Silesia, but he would have to take them forcibly. He needed a pretext for war. He was ready to fight, too, for he was no mere parade ground soldier like his father. The pretext cropped up in the matter of the Austrian Succession.

In 1711 the Emperor Joseph had died without male issue and his brother Charles succeeded him as Emperor Charles VI. Charles also had no son and a family compact, the 'Pragmatic Sanction', was agreed upon. Under this arrangement, Charles's daughter, Maria Theresa, gained priority of succession to the Habsburg empire over Joseph's daughter, Maria Amalia, the wife of Charles Albert of Bavaria. After much negotiation the compact was accepted by every important court, except Bavaria. Then, on 20 October 1740, Charles VI died.

Frederick had been on the throne only a few months but he was a born opportunist. Knowing that Austria was unprepared for war and that European politics were confused and unstable, he recognized Maria Theresa's succession and offered her military assistance if she needed it, in return for which he proposed to occupy Silesia. The Austrians emphatically denied his claim to Silesia, so Frederick marched his army across the Silesian frontier, thus beginning the War of the Austrian Succession.

The guarantors of the Pragmatic Sanction did not at once help Maria Theresa and did not stir themselves until the Prussians badly defeated the Austrians at Mollwitz in April 1741. Yet Frederick's personal military career in the field began ignominiously at Mollwitz. He was incapable as a commander and even appeared to lack courage as a soldier.[1] He had the sense to leave the field and the battle to Field-Marshal von Schwerin, who won it for him. Frederick was intelligent and he

[1] Frederick admitted in his *History of My Times* that no general had ever committed as many faults as he did in the First Silesian War.

learned quickly. This man, who said he hated war, never made the same mistake twice.

The conflict now became general. Charles Albert of Bavaria invaded Bohemia; the French came in as Bavaria's ally. The Saxons and Savoyards attacked Austria, while England and Holland indirectly supported Maria Theresa by preparing to attack France. The English policy consisted in awkwardly balancing the respective claims of two Powers—Austria and Prussia, which were at war with each other, but were both in alliance with England, and of continuing her war with France who was also an ally of Prussia. In steering clear of these entanglements England helped Maria Theresa against France but would not help her against Prussia.

Frederick defeated the Austrians at Chotusitz and reached agreement with France. Maria Theresa, prompted by England, ceded Silesia to Frederick, who withdrew from the war.

It was about this time that he gave orders to melt down one of the heaviest guns in Europe. Built at the beginning of the century this gun, called Asia, weighed 33 tons and fired cannon balls reputedly weighing 1,000 lb. But the range did not exceed 550 yards and 56 lb. of powder was used to fire each shot. Frederick thought this was too expensive; it was one of the many lessons he learned about artillery.

Following Austrian successes, Frederick re-entered the war in September 1744 and again invaded Austria. But he was forced out and a year later the two countries came to terms. Silesia and Glatz were ceded to Frederick and he recognized the Pragmatic Sanction. He had won 16,000 square miles and another million people to his realm. He needed them; Prussia had only 2,500,000.

It is hardly an exaggeration to describe Frederick's occupation of Silesia as bare-faced robbery, though perhaps Frederick justified it to himself as revenge for the gross dishonesty Austria had shown towards all three of his immediate predecessors in the matter of territories. No power could throw stones at Frederick on the score of treachery, for all had broken pledges at one time or another in the first forty years of the eighteenth century. Frederick's *coup* met with the success which morally it was far from deserving. The people of Silesia cared little whether they were attached to the Austrian or the Prussian crown; they probably preferred the Prussian.

Encouraged by his success, ruthless in his ambitions and his methods—he had no use for the forms of international law—

Frederick now set out systematically to raise Prussia to the status of a first-class power—far above her true level. He did this with a singleminded intensity that has rarely been equalled. Prussia became so much of a military state that even civil administration was merely a minor department of the army. Five-sixths of the country's resources went on keeping the army. Frederick could not have forged and tempered Prussia without the assistance of the Junkers, the landed class of East Germany. The Junkers were extremely hard-working and competent and therefore prosperous farmers. Few were aristocratic by birth; most were middle-class or upper middle-class. As they were dedicated to efficiency, Frederick made use of them and through him the Junkers gained monopolistic control of all civil and military office. The Junkers served Frederick so he served them; together, conscious of what they were doing, they served Prussia.

The Junkers had a more profound effect on the Prussian and later on the German Army than is generally realized. They were autocrats and despots and they exercised an irresistible over-lord–serf relationship with their employees and peasants in Prussian rural life. When the Junkers became Frederick's officers they carried this relationship into the army and it was to this beginning that the German Officers' Corps owed much of its tradition—at least until World War II.

Frederick did not contemplate uniting Germany with Prussia. Germany at this time was a mass of principalities—over three hundred of them. When he captured German territory Frederick treated it no differently from that of any other nation.

It is important to realize, however, that each of these three hundred principalities had an army of its own—large, small, efficiently led, poorly led, all colourfully uniformed. Some were the toys of the prince who owned them and could do nothing more martial than parade prettily for the entertainment of his guests; others were trained fighting men.

The Prince of Hesse-Cassel had an army of 16,000, disciplined on the Prussian plan. He enjoyed exercising his men, but not having a drill hall he often manœuvred up to three hundred of them in the dining-room of his palace.

The Prince of Hesse-Darmstadt spent almost all his time with his 5,000-man army, and so that he could drill them in any weather he built a hall capable of holding 1,500 men. He heated the hall by sixteen stoves and each day an order was posted stating at what temperature the hall should be.

An English visitor, John Moore, M.D., wrote: 'There is no regular fortification around this town, but a very high stone wall, which is not intended to prevent an enemy from entering ... but is designed to stop the garrison from deserting, to which some are exceedingly inclined, taking no delight in their sovereign's warlike amusements.'

Every detail of garrison duty was performed with a rigorousness normally found only in wartime. The Prince had a small cavalry force, big men magnificently accoutred.

In those days a competent foreign officer, not particularly keen on actually fighting, could easily get himself a job with a German prince. Many Englishmen could be found in German service.

Each principality, too, had its own orders and decorations and as they increased with the years there was eventually an extraordinary profusion. As we shall see, successive Prussian and German leaders played on the German thirst for martial adornment, a thirst which at times exceeded even that of the French.

CHAPTER II

Prussian Drill

Frederick wanted the most efficient army in the world, but his methods were vastly different from those of his father. He gave his soldiers tremendous *esprit de corps* and accommodated them with private citizens and not in barracks, so as to 'keep them human'.

Nevertheless, it would be wrong to give the impression that all soldiers were happy with their lot. Probably many would have deserted had they had the slightest opportunity. Frederick drew up elaborate rules to prevent desertion. Night marches were to be avoided and men detailed to forage or bathe had to be accompanied by officers so that they could not run away. Even pursuits of the enemy had to be strictly controlled 'lest in the confusion our own men escape'. Other armies could afford a percentage of deserters; Frederick's supply of men was limited.

He held numerous field days near Berlin, partly to keep his troops in form, but also to impress foreign visitors. John Moore, the English traveller, painted an intriguing word picture of Prussian military discipline. He wrote:

'The Prussian discipline on a general view is beautiful; in detail it is shocking. When the young rustic is brought to the regiment he is at first treated with gentleness; he is instructed only by words how to walk and how to hold up his head and to carry his firelock. He is not punished, though he should not succeed in his earliest attempts. They allow his natural awkwardness and timidity to wear off by degrees; they seem cautious of confounding him at the beginning or of driving him to despair and they take

9

care not to pour all the terrors of their discipline on his astonished senses at once. When he has been a little familiarized . . . he is taught the exercise of the firelock, first alone, afterwards with two or three companions. This is not entrusted to a corporal or sergeant; it is the duty of a subaltern. In the park at Berlin every morning may be seen the lieutenants of the different regiments exercising, with the greatest assiduity, sometimes a single man, at other times three or four together. And now, if the young recruit shows neglect or remissness his attention is roused by the officer's cane, which is applied with increasing energy, till he has acquired full command of his firelock.

'He is taught steadiness under arms and the immobility of a statue. He is informed that he is to move only at the word of command; that speaking, coughing, sneezing are all unpardonable crimes. When the lad is accomplished they tell him that now it is perfectly known what he can do and that the smallest deficiency will be punished.

'The officers are not subjected to corporal punishment, but they are obliged to bestow as unremitting attention on duty as the men. The captain knows that he will be blamed by his colonel and can expect no promotion if his company be not perfect; the colonel loses the King's favour if his regiment should fail in any particular; the General is answerable for the discipline of the brigade or garrison under his command. The King is not satisfied with the General's report on a subject but examines everything for himself, so that from his Majesty down to the common sentinel, every individual is alert. And as the King never relaxes, the faculties of every subordinate are kept in constant exertion. The consequence is that the Prussian Army is the best disciplined and the readiest for service at a minute's warning of any now in the world or perhaps that ever was in it.'

Frederick sought his officers far and wide and for their speciality. He paid them highly, the amount varying according to an officer's abilities and qualifications. Many officers received double that of their British counterparts. The pay of the common soldier was eight groschen or 1s. 4d. a week, out of which he had to spend threepence in washing and in materials for cleaning his arms.

His recruiting sergeants plied their trade as vigorously as had those of his father. Captured soldiers were nearly always forced to become Prussians and to be prepared to shoot down their fellow countrymen—though there was nothing new in this system. Some young foreigners were given officers' commissions but as soon as they had crossed the border they were reduced to the ranks. On one occasion, according to report, the authorities in Mecklenburg were locked up until all the militarily eligible young men had been rounded up.

One writer has said that Frederick ordered that soldiers dismissed from the service for incompetence or bad behaviour were to have the letter S branded on their hand and 'cut it deep', but I can find no verification of this and I doubt if it occurred.

The training of the Prussian Army was highly advanced, with war situations produced authentically and carried out with a vigorous realism that was much ahead of its time.

History has given too little importance to Frederick's cavalry and artillery. When Frederick became king the cavalry was composed of large men mounted on powerful horses and carefully trained to fire in line both on foot and on horseback. The force was of the heaviest type and incapable of rapid movement. In fact, the cavalry of all European states had degenerated into unwieldy masses of horsemen who, unable to move at speed, charged at a slow trot and fought only with pistol and carbine.

Frederick was quick to see the error of this system and following the example of Charles XII of Sweden he introduced reforms which made his cavalry the most efficient body of horsemen that had ever existed. Frederick was probably the first to pay close attention to the training of the individual cavalry soldier in horsemanship and swordsmanship.

His first change was to prohibit absolutely the use of firearms mounted and to rely upon the charge at full speed, sword in hand. He taught his horsemen, who were carefully handpicked, to disregard the fire of the enemy's squadrons and to charge home. He lightened the equipment and armament and trained them to move rapidly and in good order over every kind of ground. Even so, cavalry serving as flank guards, scouts or on outpost duty carried firearms and used them efficiently.

Guibert, a French observer, said, 'It is only in Prussia that the horsemen and their officers have that confidence, that boldness in managing their horses, that they seem to be part of them and recall the idea of the centaurs. It is only there that 10,000 horsemen can be seen making general charges for many hundreds of yards and halt in perfect order and at once commence a second movement in another direction.'

The great Marshal Saxe, the real victor of the Battle of Fontenoy, 1745, had already laid down that cavalry should be capable of charging at speed for 2,000 yards in good order, but in fact the cavalry of most countries could not meet this standard. Frederick wanted an even higher standard. Frederick's older generals opposed his innovations but he was ably supported and helped by Seidlitz and Ziethen. Von Seidlitz was one of the most brilliant cavalry officers in history and in his day he certainly had the reputation of being the best cavalry officer in Europe. He and Ziethen, another dashing cavalry leader, were probably the two officers on whom Frederick most heavily relied.

It is not surprising that the world was soon ringing with the fame of horsemen who were organized, trained and commanded by such brilliant and impetuous leaders.

Out of twenty-two great battles fought by Frederick his cavalry won at least fifteen of them. At no time in ancient or modern history have more brilliant deeds been performed by cavalry than were achieved by Frederick's horsemen in his later wars. The secret of their success lay in the constant training of the individual soldier, in constant manœuvring in masses, in reliance upon the sword and in the fiery energy as well as prudent judgment of the generals who commanded the cavalry.

In his Regulations for Cavalry, Frederick wrote, 'His Majesty will guarantee that the enemy will be beaten every time they are charged in the manner directed.' Should some soldiers be unconvinced of victory and in doubt about accompanying the charge, Frederick added: 'N.B. If it is found that any soldier is not doing his duty, or is wishing to fly, the first officer or sub-officer who perceives it will pass his sword through his body.'

Prohibiting cavalry from firing was to expose them at times to deadly fire from artillery and infantry without a chance to retaliate. To remedy this defect Frederick organized horse artillery which, by its rapidity, could follow all the movements of the cavalry and camp and fight with it. By its fire and by keeping the enemy's batteries at a distance it paved the way for the cavalry charge.

Some countries had no horse artillery even as late as 1750 and until the 1790s Prussia had the best horse artillery in Europe. The Russians employed such artillery from the beginning of the Seven Years War, even before Frederick saw its possibilities as cavalry support, but under Frederick horse artillery became a permanent and independent arm. This was one of the most striking results of the King's genius. He also ordered many howitzers for his army—great, booming pieces with which he lobbed shells on the Austrians when he discovered that they made a habit of sheltering their reserves behind hills.

Foreign observers remarked on the 'miserliness' which put Prussian soldiers into short coats, but Frederick knew what he was doing. Short coats were better than long ones to fight in. The coats, too, had leather elbows for extra strength.

A British traveller, J. Hanlay, wrote: 'A Prussian soldier is never seen in rags, but all appear as gentlemen in respect to the cleanliness of their persons. In winter they have breeches of woollen cloth, but in summer they wear breeches of white dimity or linen, which are very clean and light. The caps of the grenadiers and the soldiers' hats are small, but at the same time answer all the purposes of a uniform and covering and by this means their heads are kept cooler, which must be a considerable saving in marching and in action.'

It has been said that Frederick's system was based on fear. But the acts of Prussian soldiers were often heroic, individually and collectively, and heroism is not inspired by fear. Frederick himself shunned no danger or hardship, often spoke with veterans, and displayed no royal pomp in the field. He was a benevolent despot, something new in kingship. He saw everything as he travelled around his dominions and he settled every problem and dispute on the spot.

While he was shaping his soldiers and his army Frederick was also thinking deeply about strategy and tactics. He decided that he faced only one basic problem—how to take a superior enemy by surprise. It was axiomatic that any enemy of Prussia would have numerical superiority. He produced this answer: concentrate the inferior strength of my own forces at a particular point with the apparent intention of launching a main attack which will throw the enemy off balance. The only question now remaining is how to launch the genuine main attack successfully. Frederick achieved immortal fame as a general by finding a satisfactory answer to this fateful question. He revived the military art of classical antiquity. He dragged the secrets of Epaminondas, Alexander and Scipio from the darkness of history. In order to be able to employ them he needed an army which was drilled like a *corps de ballet*.

More than other generals he had to demand renunciation, intelligence, resolution and fearlessness of death. As a Prussian writer saw it: 'Frederick not only had to make his troops march in rhythm with the beat of their own hearts, he also had to act upon their hearts.' Frederick inspired the Prussians by his tolerance, his fanatical desire for justice and his personal bravery. That is why he was able to make of his soldiers an effective instrument of war.

The difficulty of Frederick's method, which was always aimed at launching an attack on the enemy's flank, was the skilful development of the column on the march to form the battle order. The slanting battle formation demanded of the officers and N.C.O.s a high degree of efficiency in giving orders, and of the men not only obedience but also an instinctive realization of the situation, the ability to feel what would happen the next minute.

Frederick's drill was intended, as he explained himself, to make the soldier in battle feel conscious of his heart as the result of the harmony between the pace he took and his heart-beat. His marching pace made him calm and drill had trained him to do what he ought to do.

The marching pace allowed officers and N.C.O.s to form up their fighting units and to move them precisely to the inch as they needed them. The muskets of those days permitted no precision; it was impossible to take particular aim. The men merely fired straight in front of them. By directing, moving and forming his men exactly as he required them, the N.C.O. or officer took aim for all. A man acting on his own initiative could throw the whole line into confusion.

The Germans did not invent the idea of marching in step; the idea probably first occurred to the Greeks. The Prussians developed the marching pace from marching in step. Marching in step was introduced into Prussia in the 1730s by an officer who had served with the Hessians, who had become acquainted with it in Sicily. The Prussian marching step differed from marching in step by reason of the fact that it did not take its time from the big drum but from the heart-beat of a healthy man. The human heart beats 72 times a minute. The Prussian infantryman took the same number of paces. The pace was carried out with knees stretched and the foot placed on the ground sharply and audibly.[1]

[1] Behind the apparently futile *Parademarsch*—the goose-step—later Germans saw a serious purpose. Half an hour of this exercise did as much for muscles of the legs and abdomen as a half-day route march.

Frederick realized that the tactics of his age were slow. He planned a system of war based on mobility and rapidity of fire; in short, he was following Gustavus Adolphus.

He regarded a Prussian battalion as a moving battery and he wanted its men so finely trained that their fire power would be threefold that of any other troops.[1] Nevertheless, he did not ignore the bayonet—always the weapon of offensive troops.

His system of manœuvres came to be called 'Prussian drill' and so much silly comment has been made about this drill that its importance has always been either underrated or overrated. In fact, it was simply the method by which Frederick taught his battalions how to respond quickly and decisively to orders.

Some writers have called Prussian drill brutal. It was certainly hard, but it was not brutal. It was hard because Frederick, unlike many rulers of his day, did not regard war merely as a rough game. He engaged in a war or battle with the object of winning it quickly. He disliked long wars because the civilian population suffered during them; also the longer a campaign went on the more soldiers tended to lose their will to fight. Therefore he trained his soldiers to fight with astonishing vigour.

Basically, Frederick's tactics were extremely simple. He saw that if his army was much more mobile than that of his enemy he had only to wait until the enemy had deployed into line of battle, then attack it violently on the flank.

For this flank attack he used only part of his force, for he believed—and he proved—that 30,000 men could defeat 70,000 in double quick time. The remainder of his army he held ready for an emergency or to move in when the rout started.

Probably, Frederick was the first great leader since the Byzantine generals to state that many military lessons could be learnt from books and to insist that his officers study their textbooks. In speaking of officers who relied on practical experience alone, he said caustically: 'The Prussian commissariat department has two mules which have served through twenty campaigns—but they are mules still.'

His textbook, *Military Instructions*, is often called a masterpiece. And so it is—a masterpiece of common sense, for few of his maxims were profound. Here are some of them:

[1] But, curiously, Prussia still used some old-fashioned muskets. She did not generally adopt the flintlock until 1808. (*Small Arms of the World*, Sixth Edition, 1960, by W. H. B. Smith.)

—The first object in the establishment of an army ought to be making provision for the belly, that being the basis and foundation of all operations. (The origin of the famous expression 'An army marches on its stomach'.)

—It is an invariable axiom of war to secure your own flanks and rear and endeavour to turn those of your enemy.

—The conquering wing of your cavalry must not allow the enemy's cavalry to rally, but pursue them in good order.

—To shed the blood of soldiers, when there is no occasion for it, is to lead them inhumanly to slaughter. (A lesson not taken to heart by the generals of the Great War.)

—Though our wounded are to be the first objects of our attention, we must not forget our duty to the enemy.

—In war the skin of a fox is at times as necessary as that of a lion, for cunning may succeed when force fails.

—Those battles are the best into which we force the enemy for it is an established maxim to oblige him to do that for which he has no sort of inclination, and as your interest and his are diametrically opposite, it cannot be supposed that you are both wishing for the same event.

Some of Frederick's maxims might appear cynical but if we remember the standard of education and the class distinctions of his era they make good sense. This one, for instance: 'All that can be done with the soldier is to give him *esprit de corps*—a higher opinion of his own regiment than of all the other troops in the country—and since his officers sometimes have to lead him into the greatest danger (and he cannot be influenced by a sense of honour) he must be more afraid of his own officers than of the dangers to which he is exposed.'

Or this: 'If my soldiers began to think, not one would remain in the ranks.'

Did he mean that all his men would want commissions or that they would all desert?

At times he was familiar with his common soldiers. Once a deserter was brought before him. 'Why did you leave me?' Frederick asked.

'Things are going very badly with us, Your Majesty,' said the soldier, fearing execution.

'Indeed they are,' Frederick said. 'But come, come, let us fight another battle today. If I am beaten we will desert together tomorrow.' Then he sent the man back to his regiment.

Frederick's preoccupation with the army and war and plans for Prussia's future did not prevent him from enjoying the fine arts. At Sans Souci, his country house at Potsdam, he gathered a group of poets, philosophers and wits whose company he enjoyed. But power politics soon took his attention. Count Kaunitz, Maria Theresa's Chancellor, was busy explaining to France that in the face of Prussia's aggression the old rivalry between Austria and France was outmoded. If France would help Austria to regain Silesia she could have the Austrian Netherlands. This coalition of 70,000,000 people could crush Prussia's 4,000,000. Maria Theresa and Kaunitz prepared their ground well, but before final agreement could be reached Prussia and England made an alliance in January 1756. In May France and Austria signed the Treaty of Versailles binding them to a defensive alliance in which they were supported by Russia, Sweden and Saxony. Frederick had brought Russia into the circle of his enemies by making witty and scurrilous remarks about the Tsarina Elizabeth.

In July Frederick detached 11,000 men to watch the Swedes, 26,000 to watch the Russians, 37,000 to guard Silesia. In August, with 70,000 men, he invaded Saxony without declaration of war. This step was described as defensive but it was the direct outcome of the decision of 1740. The chances of survival, let alone victory, seemed slight. England provided money, but her world-wide conflict with France prevented her from giving effective military support.

Frederick pretended to have documentary evidence that Austria was only waiting until her preparations were complete to launch the whole forces of the coalition against him. His one chance was to strike first and to deal Austria a blow which would at any rate cripple her offensive. At the end of August he suddenly marched his army into Dresden, Saxony. Here he found other documents which he claimed to prove the existence of a concerted plan to partition Prussia and he quickly published a careful selection of these documents. He had learned that he was to be attacked by six powers—Austria, France, Russia, Saxony, Sweden and the German States. It was a rare compliment and, in a way, it delighted Frederick for it meant that Prussia was now taken seriously. He blockaded Pirna and in October he fought the Austrians at Lobositz, and though Prussians and Austrians have claimed victory ever since it was really a drawn battle.

The campaign of 1757 opened at Prague, held by 70,000 Austrians under Prince Charles. Frederick had 120,000 men at this time, his army having been increased by the conquest of Saxony, but he had only 60,000 at Prague. He took Prague, but at great cost; 18,000 Prussians fell, including Marshal Schwerin, 'who alone was worth 10,000 men'. Frederick then marched on Kolin, held in strength by General von Daun. Frederick devastated his army by throwing battalion after battalion at the Austrian guns. He did not realize that he had been defeated until an officer, replying to the King's order for yet another charge, said: 'Does Your Majesty mean to storm the batteries alone?'

Scenting victory, the Allies now moved to squeeze Frederick within a ring of fire, using 400,000 men against him, and by the end of May the ring was tightening.

Frederick was undismayed and though he suffered losses and Prussia was reeling under the blows, he struck back, sending his cavalry to raid enemy camps and regrouping his scattered troops. Berlin, his capital, was occupied by the Austrian Count Hadik, who accepted a ransom of 300,000 thalers to depart.

The Russians devastated parts of Prussia, inflicting horrible barbarities on the civilian population. By October Frederick's position was so critical that even he began to believe that the war was lost. But throughout the war the world was amazed at Frederick's capacity continually to recover and rise up afresh. Wax figures of the monarch were exhibited in the towns and cities of Europe. In Lisbon a crowd was thronging around one of these statues when a young man pushed his way through them. With tears streaming down his face he cried out: 'Look at me, I too am a Prussian.'[1]

[1] The young man's name was Nettelbeck, a sailor and travelling craftsman. Much later, in 1807, when the French laid siege to Kolberg, Nettelbeck, now an old man, was the soul of the resistance against the surrender of the town. Until General Gneisenau was ordered to take over the defence of the place, Nettelbeck, a civilian and now a brewer, commanded the defence. Until 1945 every Prussian child learned the story of Nettelbeck at school and perhaps still does.

CHAPTER III

The Victories of Rossbach and Leuthen

On 4 November 1757 Frederick moved his camp to Rossbach. With him, as always, was von Seidlitz, the youngest and most recently appointed major-general in the army.

Seidlitz exercised his cavalry at full speed over very broken ground and men were often killed. Frederick once commented on the number of deaths. 'If you make a fuss about a few broken necks, your Majesty,' Seidlitz said, 'you will never have the bold horsemen you require for the field.' It was a significant statement in view of later German training.

He taught Prussian cavalry to rally to the front instead of the rear, in other words to rally after a charge while pursuing, which prevented a reckless, disorderly pursuit and enabled the commander to follow up victory with greater certainty. The usual task of hussars was to harass a retreating army in detached parties; Frederick's hussars charged in a large body like heavy cavalry.

Seidlitz had impressed Frederick since his days as a young officer. He could not conceive how an officer of cavalry could be made prisoner if his horse was not killed and he said as much to the King, when escorting him as captain of the guard. A few minutes later, when the party was in the middle of a bridge, the King stopped and said: 'You say, Seidlitz, that a cavalry officer ought never to be made prisoner. It is the idea of a brave man, but there are occasions when one could surrender without dishonour. Suppose, here and now, you were among enemies and unable to escape by force. What then?'

Seidlitz drove spurs into his horse and leapt over the bridge, falling twenty feet into the river. Unharmed, he returned to the King a few minutes later, saluted and said: 'Sire, my reply.'

Seidlitz displayed this sort of decision and daring on 5 November when the French and Austrians at Rossbach were foolish enough to offer their flank to the Prussians. Virtually the whole of the Prussian cavalry, in beautiful formation and moving at 'incredible speed', as a French officer described it, charged the enemy. Four times the Prussians cut their way through the French, who were under Soubise, and routed them.

Where the Allies were still in column the Prussian artillery destroyed them and then the systematic Prussian musketry smashed into those Allied infantry who held their ground. The retreat became a rout. The French and their allies lost 3,000 killed and wounded, 5,000 prisoners including eight generals and 300 officers, 67 cannon, many colours and most of their baggage. Those who survived became a deplorable rabble on the run. The French Army at this time was rotten with in-discipline, effeminacy and intrigue, but this does not discount Frederick's victory.

The Allied leaders showed no generalship at Rossbach. Had they held a line along the River Saale and remained on the defensive they must have won, for Frederick had not the strength to attack a static line. Inept at manœuvre, and believ-ing that superiority in numbers was sufficient to ensure victory, they offered battle—which was exactly what Frederick wanted them to do.

They made every major mistake it was possible to make. They sent out no scouts and had no vanguard; they advanced in full view of the enemy and across his flank at that; they did not attempt to evolve a system of co-operation among the three arms; they had no plan for rallying or reinforcing.

The immediate results of this remarkable Prussian victory were that Europe realized that the French armies[1] were pathetically weak and that Britain granted Frederick £1,200,000. Even so, Frederick's position was still critical and the situation in Silesia was dangerous.

In those days battles were not fought in winter. Armies retired to winter quarters and no military activity more serious than patrolling was carried on until the spring. But on 13 November Frederick marched from Leipzig with 13,000 men to Parchwitz. On 14 November the fortress of Schweidnitz

---

[1]Not until the efficiency of the ruthless Committee of Public Safety in the days of the French Revolution restored spirit, discipline and her natural fighting capacity to France did the legend of the invincibility of the Prussians fade temporarily from European literature.

surrendered to the Austrians and on 22 November General Bevern was beaten at Breslau. At Parchwitz, which he reached on 28 November, Frederick put General Ziethen in command of Bevern's beaten army and ordered a concentration on Parchwitz for 3 December. Frederick himself captured Neumarkt, where he learned that Prince Charles and Marshal Daun had advanced to Lissa. Their right rested on the village of Nippern and their left on that of Sagschütz.

Their army was impressively strong. It consisted of about 70,000 men (possibly as many as 80,000), including strong cavalry squadrons and supported by 210 guns. They held a front of five and a half miles, with the right protected by bogs and the left covered by abattis. The centre was at Leuthen.

Against this strong force in an equally strong position, Frederick had only 36,000 men, made up of 24,000 infantry and 12,000 cavalry. His artillery consisted of 167 guns, including 71 heavy pieces. The battlefield was an open plain over which Frederick had manœuvred in times of peace.

On 5 December, at five o'clock on a cold morning, Frederick led his army towards Leuthen. A few miles off he assembled his generals and briefed them for battle.

'I should think that I had done nothing if I left the Austrians in possession of Silesia,' he said. 'Let me tell you then, that I shall attack, against all the rules of the art, the army of Prince Charles, nearly thrice as strong as our own, wherever I find it. I must take this step, or all is lost. We must beat the enemy or all perish before his batteries. So I think, so will I act. Now go and repeat to the regiments what I have said to you.'

The last instruction is revealing for in that era and for long after the men in the ranks were never told what the commanding officer had in mind. Frederick believed, rightly, that if he took the men into his confidence they would fight better.

As usual his plan was uncomplicated. He would advance straight up the Breslau[1] road and feint at the Austrian right. Then he planned to march across Charles's front and attack his left to cut his communications. The vanguard moved off, with the men singing a hymn.

> Grant that I do whate'er I ought to do
> What for my station is by Thee decreed;
> And cheerfully and promptly do it too,
> And when I do it, grant that it succeed!

[1] Breslau is now in Poland and known as Wroclaw.

An officer asked Frederick if he should silence the men. The King said: 'No, with such men God will certainly give me victory today.'

First contact with the enemy was made at Borne, just as dawn was breaking. Through the mist a long line of cavalry stretched across the road. Frederick ordered a charge and the Austrians were attacked in front and on the flank. The force, found to be a detached one of five regiments under General Nostitz, was scattered and 800 taken prisoner. Nostitz was mortally wounded.

Frederick now waited for the mist to clear. When it did the whole Austrian Army was visible, regiment upon regiment, rank after rank—a formidable and impressive sight.

The taking of Borne gave Frederick not only a vantage point, but its height screened from view the advancing Prussian columns. At this point Frederick sent his cavalry against the Austrian right. They made such a display that Count Lucchessi, commanding the Austrian right, called frantically for support. In haste, Marshal Daun sent the reserve cavalry and even part of his cavalry from the left wing.

While this was happening the four Prussian columns were formed into two. At Borne they wheeled right under cover of high ground and marched south. The whole movement was carried out with the usual Prussian precision, with an advance guard under General Wedell. Then came, on the right wing, General Ziethen with forty-three squadrons and Prince Maurice of Dessau[1] with six battalions. The left wing consisted of the major infantry force under General Retzow, flanked by forty squadrons under General Driesen. Each body of cavalry was supported by ten squadrons of hussars, while in the rear was Prince Eugene of Württemberg with another twenty-five squadrons.

The Prussians seemed to be heading away and this pleased Prince Charles and Marshal Daun, who observed the movement from the mill at Frobelwitz. Daun said delightedly: 'The Prussians are off! Don't disturb them.'

But just after noon the columns wheeled again, formed line of battle and drove towards the Austrian left near the village of

[1] The son of Prince Leopold, nicknamed the 'Old Dessauer', the great drill-master of the Prussian Army. He succeeded during a retreat in marching his troops out of battle in full order and gaining the protection of a wood. They retired at marching pace and even the fire of their pursuers did not cause them to shoot aimlessly and without receiving orders. Prince Leopold is said to have invented the iron ramrod. Up to this time musket ramrods had been made of wood; if it broke the soldier could not fight.

Sagschütz. General Nadasti, the Austrian commander on the spot, saw the overwhelmingly superior force advancing towards him and ordered away rider after rider, asking Charles urgently for help. Help could not come in time.

At one o'clock, Wedell, supported by infantry and artillery, stormed the defences at Sagschütz. It now became clear that the Austrians had learned something of the spirit in which cavalry should be handled, for Nadasti dashed out with his cavalry and charged Ziethen's leading squadrons. The Prussian horsemen regrouped behind their six supporting infantry battalions then followed Ziethen in a counter-charge against Nadasti. It was difficult ground and the Prussians were skilled in riding over such terrain while the Austrians were not; they were broken and driven into Rathener Wood. In ninety minutes the entire Austrian wing was scattered, with Prussian hussars pursuing the flying Austrians. Then the Prussians began to roll up the enemy line like a carpet, with their heavy artillery enfilading the Austrian positions further along.

A fierce fight developed at Leuthen itself, where the Austrians fought bitterly and gallantly. Unfortunately for them, their generals had not learnt the lesson of the battle of Blenheim (1704)—that a village should not be overcrowded with troops. Leuthen was packed as tightly as Blenheim, with the troops in places from thirty to a hundred deep. Artillery case-shot played havoc in these rigid lines.

Frederick used some very heavy guns during the battle. With requisitioned farm horses he had brought up many of the heavy guns from the fortress of Glogau. This formidable artillery, as much as the redoubtable infantry and dashing cavalry, won the battle.

The Prussian Guards assaulted the Austrian positions and carried them. Possession of Leuthen did not help Frederick immediately, for the Austrians had formed another line at right angles to their first and had brought up artillery in support.

Frederick's infantry was held off until he sent for his heaviest guns and established them on high ground called the Butterberg, from where they drove the Austrians back.

Frederick was master of the battle throughout. He had riders bringing him information constantly and so was able to move infantry, guns and cavalry about the large battlefield as necessary. This was unusual for the period; normally once an army was committed the general in command could do little to influence events but had to depend on the initiative of his subordinate generals. Frederick gave his trusted leaders plenty of rein, but he rarely allowed overall control to pass from his hands.

During the battle Frederick personally distinguished himself by leading a small party to the rescue of a staff officer returning with a message. A group of Austrian horsemen had struck the officer from his horse and were about to kill him when Frederick, well ahead of his party, charged into the midst, slashing with his sabre. A magnificent horseman, he kept his animal protectively astride the fallen officer, while he engaged and killed two Austrians. He did not normally court death in this way, but as a general should he kept aloof from the scramble of conflict. Prussia could ill afford to lose him—and he knew it.

The battle raged on with little respite until four o'clock. Dusk was approaching. Count Lucchessi, a very brave cavalry leader, had assembled a large force of horse and saw his chance to use them when Prussian infantry under General Retzow was held up. Lucchessi made a flank attack, but he had not seen forty squadrons under General Driesen hidden behind the village of Radaxdorf.

Waiting for just such a moment as this, thirty of Driesen's squadrons charged Lucchessi frontally while five drove against his flank and the other five galloped round the Austrian rear.

These enterprising tactics overwhelmed Lucchessi who was killed as his troopers broke and scattered. After losing so much of their cavalry support the Austrian infantry was vulnerable. Driesen charged them in the rear, while General Wedell attacked their flank near Leuthen.

The anecdote about Frederick which the Prussians like best of all tells how Frederick rode frantically and anxiously about the battlefield after hearing that von Wedell, his favourite, had been killed. Frederick shouted his name continually. 'Wedell! Wedell!'

While the King was shouting, a corporal lying among a heap of dead and wounded sat up and, making a great effort, said: 'Your Majesty, we are all Wedells here.'[1]

Frederick stopped, gazed at the dying man, and said: 'You have taught me a good lesson and I thank you for it.'

Hopeless confusion followed as darkness fell and the Austrian

---

[1] Frederick preferred noblemen officers and though he used *bourgeois* officers when necessary he dismissed them the moment a campaign was over. In the Seven Years War no fewer than 4,000 Prussian officers died and the others wanted to retire, but Frederick forced them to serve on. 'It is more becoming for a nobleman to serve as an officer than to live in the country and raise chickens.'

force disintegrated, many of the troops bolting towards Lissa. Frederick, victorious but tired, also made for Lissa, riding through mobs of broken Austrians.

He rode into the grounds of a château and outside the building met about a dozen Austrian officers. 'Good evening, gentlemen,' Frederick said courteously, 'I dare say you did not expect me here. Can one get a night's lodging along with you?'

The Prussians lost about 6,000 men killed and wounded. The Austrians lost 10,000, plus 21,000 prisoners, 116 guns, 51 colours and 4,000 wagons. But this was only an instalment. Prussian troops took 2,000 more prisoners on 9 December and on the 19th Breslau surrendered 17,000 men and 81 guns to Frederick.

As a power Austria was virtually wiped out, while Prussia emerged as the most dangerous military power in Europe. Frederick had retaken the whole of Silesia except for a single fortress, Schweidnitz.

Few victories have been so enthusiastically acclaimed as Leuthen. Frederick's system and success astonished those who were accustomed to calculate effect by mere quantity. His tactics were to fascinate even Napoleon, who wrote: 'The battle of Leuthen is a masterpiece of movements, manœuvres and resolution. Alone it is sufficient to immortalize Frederick and place him in the rank of the greatest generals. All his manœuvres at this battle are in conformity with the principles of war. He made no flank march in sight of his enemy . . . He carried out things I never dared to do. He was above all great in the most critical moments . . . It was not the Prussian Army which for seven years defended Prussia against the three most powerful nations in Europe, but Frederick the Great.'

But Frederick had trained that army.

Frederick's biographer, General Tempelhoff, wrote: 'Ancient history scarcely furnishes a single instance, and modern times none, that can be compared either in execution or consequences, with the battle of Leuthen. It forms an epoch in military science and exhibits not only the theory, but also the practice of a system of which the King was the sole inventor.'

General J. F. C. Fuller, most discerning of military historians, believes that 'except for Alexander the Great and possibly Charles XII, Frederick was the most offensively minded of all the Great Captains.'

All this is very high praise.

The victory at Leuthen was largely due to the perfect co-operation of the three arms—infantry, artillery and cavalry—

but the confidence of the ordinary soldier in Frederick as a general was the most decisive factor.

Thinking over his victory, Frederick realized how important artillery was. He transferred all the 24-pounders he had captured in Austrian fortresses to his field army and with these guns defeated the Russians at Zorndorf in 1758. Even when the fortunes of war changed, Frederick remained true to his fundamental principle that the battle was won when the heavy artillery dominated the decisive heights and when the light artillery was made so mobile that it could be used on any part of the battlefield. Thus he became the real developer of field artillery. He reduced all the light guns to 3-pounders and attached them to the cavalry. He gave the field artillery medium howitzers so that it could cope not only with moving targets but also with fortified positions. As a result of this reform he was so strong that he was able to support the natural deterioration of his infantry during his long wars. He started with 1,000 guns and finished with 10,000.

The victory of Leuthen did not end the war; it went on for another five years and Frederick and Prussia suffered.

After the victory at Zorndorf Frederick was defeated at Hochkirch. He drove the Austrians from Saxony and Silesia but in August 1759 he was overwhelmingly beaten at Kunersdorf by the Russians, who also occupied Berlin.

Frederick was never able to act simply on the defensive because it was imperative to prevent Russians and Austrians from uniting in overwhelming force. He could never strike at either with much less than his whole strength; the necessary concentration against one always gave the other the opportunity of behaving aggressively. The King had to hurry from one point to another. To hold his own required a supreme combination of skill, of audacity verging upon recklessness and of indomitable resolution.

In 1760 he twice beat the Austrians—at Liegnitz and Torgau. Even so he was a bitter man at the end of 1760. 'I am no saint,' he wrote, 'and I own that I should die content if only I could first inflict on others a portion of the misery I endure.' He had, of course, brought it all on himself by his initial act of robbery in 1740.

Commenting on Frederick's campaign of 1760, the great Prussian military writer, Clausewitz,[1] said: '. . . a perfect masterpiece of strategic skill . . . Is there really anything to

[1] Clausewitz's contribution to German military history is discussed later.

drive us out of our wits with admiration . . . ? Are we to see profound wisdom? No, that we cannot, if we are to decide naturally and without affection. What we rather admire above all is the sagacity of the King in this respect, that while pursuing a great object with very limited means, he undertook nothing beyond his powers, and just enough to gain his object.'

The year 1761 was a poor one for Frederick, but in 1762 the Tsarina Elizabeth died. Her youthful successor, Peter, was an admirer of Frederick and Peter recalled his troops. The Seven Years War ended.

In any study of Frederick as a general it is important to remember that nearly always he was vastly inferior in numbers. At the defeat of Hochkirch he opposed 37,000 men to 90,000 and at Kunersdorf the Russians had 70,000 to Frederick's 26,000. He had only 30,000 when he beat the Austrians at Liegnitz; they had 90,000. In this he created a precedent. For the next 200 years Prussian and German troops were out-numbered almost everywhere they fought—with a few important exceptions.

Frederick spent the next twenty-three years in devoted work for his country, restoring it after the devastation by war. He encouraged schools, too, but the Prussian youth was sometimes educated by ex-sergeants, armed with rods, for Frederick saw teaching jobs as a way of rewarding veterans. It was also a way of encouraging the martial spirit.

Frederick believed that the *bourgeois* must be kept in place in order to heighten the officers' feeling of honour. If the officer enjoyed supreme prestige in peace, he would be all the readier to sacrifice himself in war—this was Frederick's view and it was a sound one for the Prussian mentality. 'On decisive days . . . one learns to love these men, seeing with what high-minded contempt of death, with what unshakeable strength of mind they oppose the enemy and force him from the field.'

But if Frederick could keep the *bourgeois* in order, he had no real control over his noble officers. He and others tried to subdue the officer-groups, but never with success. Frederick tried hard to stop duelling; he was against it because it deprived him of valuable men. In the end he had to condone it. More than that, he was forced to admit that an officer who declined a duel would not find a job anywhere in Europe. Eventually, the officers themselves set up a 'court of honour' to settle disputes, but even then many officers refused to accept the court's rulings.

Frederick had to prevent another coalition against him and in 1764 he made an eight-year alliance with Catherine the Great. Combining with Austria and Russia in the first partition of Poland in 1772, Frederick acquired West Prussia (without Danzig and Thorn), thus connecting East Prussia with Pomerania and Brandenburg. He attracted thousands of settlers by generous offers, he improved agriculture, reclaimed the swamps of the middle Oder, fostered elementary education, speeded up legal procedure and began the Prussian Landrecht, the first German code. Six years later he drew the sword for the last time to prevent the Emperor Joseph II from seizing Bavaria, but no pitched battle was fought.

Frederick died on 17 August 1786. In his will he wrote that it was man's destiny to work from his birth until his death for the weal of the community to which he belongs. He had fulfilled his destiny.

The battles of Rossbach and Leuthen were sufficient in themselves to save Prussia from extinction. Memories of many battles fade; those of Rossbach and Leuthen became brighter. Their importance can hardly be over emphasized, which is why I have discussed them in detail. From practically the day after they were fought they have dominated German history. They were the rocks on which German pride and sense of superiority were built, as were the ideas of 'Germany against the world'— 'one German is better than three Frenchmen'.

A German historian, writing in 1942 in the middle of Hitler's war, claimed that Leuthen was 'the model and ideal of all future battles of annihilation'. There is much truth in this, for all the architects of Prussian and German might who followed Frederick acknowledged that they were building on the foundations he had laid—especially the martial foundations.[1] However, Frederick's service was given not to Germany but to Prussia and it is a myth to suppose otherwise.

Leuthen was certainly Frederick's greatest and favourite battle and, with Rossbach, it had a far-reaching effect. It helped to create Germanic unity and it saturated the German soul with martial spirit. The world can largely blame Frederick for the militant, militaristic nation which, with its jackbooted legions, was to become the scourge of Europe.

[1] Many other armies copied parts of the Prussian system. The cavalry tactics and formations of most armies were based on the cavalry of Seidlitz and Ziethen.

CHAPTER IV

The Defeat at Valmy

Between the year of Frederick the Great's death, 1786, and the disastrous year of 1806 everything in Prussia looked back to Frederick; there was no forward thought or movement at all. In retrospect, it is difficult to understand how Frederick William, Frederick the Great's successor, and his generals could have so little realized that the character of war was changing rapidly. The lessons were there to be seen; Napoleon had won battle after battle and presumably the methods with which he had won them percolated through to the minds of the Prussian leaders.

A modern critic has said: 'Immersed in drill-ground tactics, Frederick lost all sense of practicability in battle. He achieved victories, but at the expense of martially emasculating the soldier. He did not encourage courage and thought and by introducing foreign customs he introduced as well the germs of decay. He over refined and mechanized tactics to the point where they were as fascinating as they were often useless.'

This attack is not justifiable in any way. He had introduced not the germs of decay but the germs of success; his successors allowed them to decay. His 'over refined and mechanized tactics' were essential for his period. They should have changed and developed but the Prussian Army had not realized that it could not live on past glories. The generals naïvely believed that Frederick the Great's victories at Leuthen and Rossbach had granted Prussia perpetual reputation as the leading military nation in Europe, if not in the world.

Gradually, almost from the day Frederick died, his army became a museum piece. Towards the end of his life perhaps he himself had sensed the decline but by then he had not the vigour to fight it. In the Prussian Army list of 1786 all fifty-two generals were nobles—and some of them were dull nobles at that.

These nobles resisted change, and refused to follow any example set by a foreign army, no matter how clearly profitable or sensible it might be. One Prussian wrote: 'The numerous nobility who serve as subalterns in our army and, in a way which all Europe recognizes, constitute the greatest strength and the greatest superiority of our army, would be humiliated, mortified and degraded below a status which birth and education granted them up to now, by measures which would make them the equals of common soldiers. This would make them vexed and dissatisfied with their estate. The well-to-do would leave the service, and those serving out of need would lose their self-confidence; the subalterns and officers generally would sink in the estimation of the common soldier, and this, the most beautiful ornament and the greatest superiority, would be lost.'

One of the 'degrading' measures suggested was that subalterns should give up their horses and march with their men. Another, that they should spend more time with their men. But the privilege system remained until the inevitable catastrophe occurred.

Naturally, some Prussians were far sighted and intelligent and wanted to move with the times. Early in the eighteenth century Marshal Saxe, a Saxon prince serving in the French Army, pleaded for universal military service. Saxe's vehement pleas, which received a lot of publicity, may have influenced the Prussian writer and bureaucrat Justus Möser, who in 1770 published a book about Germany's future. Möser said, in almost as many words, that all men should be made into soldiers to give them honour, pride and self-respect. The suggestion, as it related to pride at least, was a sound psychological one.

Möser wrote: 'The Nordic peoples connect honour mainly with weapons and in the long run despise those who are not entitled to carry and use them. And therefore there is no other way but to tie up again the sword with the handicrafts, if we wish to obtain the necessary honour for this estate ... A hundred years from now the national militia will everywhere be the main thing and will reaffirm liberty and property which would perish were our present constitution to be continued.'

A German prince, Count William of Schaumburg, teacher
of the great military reformer Scharnhorst, also advocated that
the whole nation should take part in a war; he introduced
conscription into his own territory. In theory conscription was
general in Prussia in 1792, but in practice the idea did not go
far, for King Frederick William II and his generals were uneasy
about having the populace in arms. They preferred to use
imported troops, especially Poles, to fight for Prussia under
Prussian leadership. The army at this time was 50 per cent.
foreign.

In 1792 the Prussian war machine was held up for the first
time—at what became known as the Cannonade of Valmy.
Germany has always played down this unusual battle and did
not accept it as a reverse. In 1942 a German, writing in the
Nazi propaganda magazine *Signal*, claimed that 'what took
place at Valmy has not been disclosed to this day', and 'that it
was an artillery duel without much effect on either side'.

He was being evasive. What took place is known in detail and
there were some important results. Prime among them was that
it drew a line between the type of warfare since 1648 and the
type it was to become in the future.

Valmy was a Prussian defeat and no amount of German
juggling with facts can disguise the truth—though it was a
defeat of Prussian leadership, not of Prussian troops. Yet,
paradoxically, the Prussians were commanded by the Duke of
Brunswick, a nephew of Frederick the Great and regarded
everywhere as the greatest soldier in Europe. His rival in the
field was General Charles Dumouriez, a political and military
adventurer lifted to high rank by the Revolution—but a
capable commander nevertheless.

Brunswick's reputation was founded largely on his successful
campaign in Holland in 1787, regarded as an example of perfect
generalship. This was true enough, for the Dutch had acted as
Brunswick expected them to behave and having the typical,
methodical Prussian mind he had been able to counter all their
moves. But Brunswick was handicapped by his monarch,
Frederick William II, who thought of himself as another
Frederick the Great—without the slightest justification. There
was no unity between Brunswick and the King, except that
Brunswick usually dutifully deferred to his monarch.

The Prussian Army at this time had strong contingents of
émigrés—monarchist Frenchmen who wanted to see the
revolutionaries crushed. Brunswick detested and distrusted

them and saw no soldierly qualities in them. Brunswick, too, was against the Prussian plan to invade any part of France but the final plan was to invade Lorraine with three armies, with a total force made up of Prussians, Hessians, Austrians and *émigrés*, a total number of about 80,000.

Among them was the poet Johann Goethe, who later had much to say about the campaign.

Brunswick had some initial victories, including the taking of Verdun. He planned then to take Sedan and go into winter quarters—it was now nearly October—around Montmédy and Mézières and so establish himself for the following spring.

But the King, the leading *émigrés* and several of Brunswick's own officers opposed the plan. They pointed out that the Frenchmen confronting them were not a normal army but an undisciplined, revolutionary rabble. Go into winter quarters when they could sweep into Champagne and destroy the French, who could not possibly stand up to the superior discipline of the Prussian Army! In any case, the *émigrés* pointed out, a decisive victory was needed to save Louis XVI and Marie Antoinette.

During the next several days the Prussians moved slowly and Brunswick acted ineptly and missed two chances to destroy large parts of the French Army. Dumouriez was acting with more skill and speed. Finally, the Prussian King countermanded an order of Brunswick's that might have saved the day and set in train the inevitable fiasco.

Incredibly, the Prussians, without making a single reconnaissance, without sending forward a single officer and without any plan for battle, moved towards the known French positions, where the great French soldier Kellermann was one of the senior commanders. Through no brilliance on the part of the Prussians the French were caught unprepared and forced on the defensive, but Dumouriez had no intention of abandoning the offensive altogether and ordered two audacious attacks on the Prussians—one on their rear and the other on their baggage train.

For some reason the Prussians expected to find the French in precipitate retreat but about noon on 19 September, as the morning fog cleared, they saw the French drawn up in line of battle. Kellermann, posted at a commanding point near a windmill, raised his hat, adorned with a tricolour plume, on his sword and shouted '*Vive la nation! Vive la France!*' And the men, taking up the cry, replied, '*Vive notre général!*'

The French had 52,000 men in the vicinity that day, but only 36,000 were present at Valmy. The Prussians had 34,000.

At this point the fifty-eight guns of the Prussian artillery commanded by the renowned General Tempelhoff were in position, or hurriedly getting into position, to face Kellermann's forty guns, under General d'Aboville, on Valmy Ridge. The distance between them was about 1,350 yards.

Goethe wrote: 'Now commenced the cannonade of which so much has been spoken, but the violence of which at the time it is impossible to describe . . . the whole battlefield trembled.' It probably did, for each side fired more than 20,000 shot. But 1,350 yards was a long range for cannon of 1792 and as the ground was sodden clay most of the shot buried itself.

Brunswick ordered an attack on the Valmy position. The Prussian infantry began to form into two lines, but the moment they advanced Kellermann's artillery played on them. Brunswick stopped the advance before it had gone two hundred paces.

At 2 p.m. a Prussian shell blew up three ammunition wagons behind Kellermann and both sides stopped firing. Two French regiments broke, but Kellermann rallied them, though he could not stop the artillery drivers, who were civilians, from running to the rear.

The Prussians again considered storming the ridge but the French artillery came into play again. Brunswick was impressed by the steadiness of the French infantry and noticed that the French cavalrymen stood to their horses. He well knew that once a Prussian infantry attack was under way the French cavalry would charge. He pondered the problem, then called a council of war at which, for the first time in months he acted as a real commander-in-chief. '*Hier schlagen wir nicht.*'[1]

The cannonade ceased. At 4 p.m. the Prussians moved to cut off the French retreat towards Paris, as driving rain drowned the battlefield. The French had lost about 300, the Prussians 185.

Goethe, as he left the field, said to his comrades: 'From today and at this spot there begins a new era and you can say that you were present. Thirty years will be required to make good this day and its consequences.'

A Prussian colonel, Massenbach, wrote: 'You will see how these little cocks will raise themselves on their spurs. They have undergone their baptism of fire. We have lost more than a battle. The 20 September has changed the course of history. It is the most important day of the century.'

[1] 'We do not fight here.'

It was certainly as important a day as any, for the French under Dumouriez and Kellermann had repulsed the most formidable army in Europe and had discredited the most famous commander. Brunswick never admitted it publicly but the French generals and their men, throughout the campaign, had been superior to him and to his slow-moving, slow-thinking, deliberate troops.

Generally the Prussians were fairly ready to learn a lesson, but Valmy taught them nothing. 'It was a mere artillery duel,' the aristocratic officers said, 'we couldn't bring those wretched French rebels to fight.'

So the Prussian war machine went its inevitable way to destruction. It was to be deferred fourteen years, but it had to come.

CHAPTER V

The Disasters at Jena and Auerstadt

One young officer entered the army that year of Valmy on whom the implications of the battle were probably lost. He was, after all, only twelve years of age. The son of a Prussian officer, his name was Karl von Clausewitz and he had been born at Burg on 1 June 1780. He was to see two years of campaigning against the French revolutionary armies before being commissioned at the age of fifteen.

Many young Prussian officers, while they boasted about Prussian supremacy, privately praised the French system, which used exclusively national armies—and very successfully. In 1798 some outspoken reformers demanded that 50 per cent. of the foreign privates be sent home and that the rest be nationalized. The reformers' frustration was justifiable. Apart from other considerations, the foreigners' morals were low and they infected the Prussians.

The reformers went further. They wanted the individual soldier to be given more initiative and freedom. They protested against the 'great restraint and those artificial movements which rob man, born after all as an individual, of independence, and which are not needed in actual war'.

But all the reformers' many proposals were turned down. The generals still thought in terms of the human machine. Count von der Goltz spoke for the Staff. 'Personal bravery of a single individual alone does not decide the day of battle, but bravery of the corps, and the latter rests on the good opinion and the confidence that each individual places in the corps to which he belongs. This confidence, however, is produced and promoted by that so-called pedantry. The exterior splendour, the regularity of movements, the adroitness and at the same time firmness of the mass—all this gives the individual soldier the safe and calming conviction that nothing can withstand his particular regiment.'

One of the most brilliant military writers of the time, Dietrich von Bülow (1757–1808), took issue with him. The battles of the future, he said, would be decided by *tirailleur* fighting. Discipline and courage were merely contributing factors; the mass and quantity of the combatants decided the issue. 'A general must praise the men in order to make them worthy of praise,' he said, echoing Napoleon, of whom he was a great admirer.

Some leaders did praise their men, but leaders and Government soon forgot them once they were too old or unfit for fighting. The only pension granted to the discharged veteran was a licence to beg publicly.

Another great reformer was Georg von Behrenhorst (1733–1814) who had been an aide of Frederick, but had broken with him. Behrenhorst wrote, in 1797: 'The art of war calls for a vaster amount of knowledge and more inborn talents than any of the other arts, in order to form a system of mechanics which does not, like the actual one, rest upon immutable laws, but upon the unknown and therefore indirectable indications of the soul, and works with levers and windlasses which have feeling and will.'

Behrenhorst wanted the soldier 'returned to the natural', encouraged to exploit his intelligence. As a start he suggested a reasonable hair-cut and a comfortable uniform. At this time the troops were compelled to wear long hair, which was powdered, greased and twisted into shape.[1]

This self-styled military pacifist saw further than his contemporaries. 'New inventions allow passing advantages, then they become general, and then the whole thing reduces itself to mere bare manslaughter, just as it was in the beginning. The art of fighting *en masse*, because it necessarily frustrates itself by its own development, cannot possibly belong to those steps of progress which mankind is destined to make.'

All the pleas and claims made no difference. The Prussian Army had been invincible under Frederick and he had manœuvred with mathematical precision. His system must still prevail. The diehards pointed out that at Crefeld in 1758 the first Prussian volley had laid low 75 per cent. of the enemy—it

[1] Contemporary British troops endured the same indignity.

had, too—and anybody who dared face the Prussian Army would find history repeating itself.

The Prussian leaders believed only in the spirit of machinery and the magic of the number 72—Frederick's famous marching pace. Spiritless drill prevailed on the Prussian parade ground. Instead of being ridiculed, a Prussian war theorist, who thought that by altering the prescribed paces per minute he was making an important suggestion for improvement, was gazed at in high esteem.

The Prussians were flattered, too, that the British had tended to copy Frederick's system. Reide, in his *Military Discipline* of 1795, noted: 'A very great change has taken place within the last four or five years in the discipline of the British Army which is now entirely modelled on that of the Prussian, as established by Frederick the Great. The utility of that monarch's tactics has long been known and in part adapted into our service.'

Not enough attention was paid to health. In Poland in 1794–5 a third of the Prussian Army died of illness, many more than of wounds. Some of the reformers believed that foreign troops employed in the Prussian Army died more readily than nationalist troops; they did not have the same will to live. History seems to bear out this contention.

Blücher—at sixty-four a man of enormous energy and a great cavalry leader—added his voice to those calling for a national army. 'It is not as difficult as one thinks,' he said. 'The foot-rule must be abandoned, no one must be exempt and it must become a shame not to have served excepting in case of infirmities . . . It is a conceit to suppose that an exercised soldier would forget so much in two years that he could not be used again after a week. The French have proved otherwise . . . our useless pedantries the soldier might very well forget altogether.'

It was sheer self interest that brought some officers in on the side of the reformers. Reform and then war was the best way to promotion, as even Clausewitz admitted.

He wrote to his fiancée:[1] 'My country needs the war and—let us admit openly—the war only can bring me to the happy goal. In whichever way I might like to connect my own life with the rest of the world, my way always takes me across a great battlefield; without my entering upon it no permanent happiness will come to me.' He was merely expressing the views of many.

[1] He was engaged to a countess but could not afford to marry her until 1810, when he had reached higher rank.

In April 1806 Scharnhorst pleaded for an increase of the Army and a regular militia. He wanted a special propaganda war newspaper to stimulate and arouse the nation and its soldiers. He spoke out against the prevalent idea that the talent of the general was the sole deciding factor. A resolute nation could win even under mediocre leaders—if the nation had strength of will and high character.

'When the necessity of a war is once recognized by a nation, nothing further is needed than the resolution of the leader to conquer or die,' he wrote.

Of the approximately 8,000 names of officers in the Army List for 1806 only 695 were not nobles.

But when Scharnhorst spoke in April 1806 it was too late.

The army was organized and trained to fight ranged battles on level ground—army against army. A carefully dressed line of men at forty or fifty paces from the enemy fired a volley, devastated their opponents and gave the waiting cavalry its opportunity to dash in and finish the slaughter. The Prussian soldier was taught nothing about skirmishing or mobility; he was not even encouraged to run; it was undignified. The Prussians in 1806 had very few light infantry regiments, yet these took the longest to train. By this year, too, Frederick's magnificent cavalry had been split up into separate commands without unity and without the dashing leaders of old. Even his theory about reserve artillery had been ignored and there was now no reserve artillery. And because the Prussians persisted in their vast supply trains, from which the fighting divisions were fed and supplied, rapidity of movement was impossible.

Yet, in this year, Prussia was stupid enough to challenge the French—the recent victors of Austerlitz, a success which by now had echoed throughout Europe as one of the most decisive and brilliant battles in history.

Frederick William III demanded that French troops cross the Rhine and leave German territory. One can admire the Prussians' confidence, but not their common sense. Napoleon had crushed Austria; he had driven the Russians back beyond the Vistula. On 9 August Prussia ordered mobilization and had an army of about 200,000, hopelessly divided among many commanders. Frederick William knew nothing of war, so he took Field-Marshal von Mollendorf with him as confidential adviser; the Field-Marshal was aged eighty-two. The King also took into the field his Military Cabinet, comprising the inspectors general and heads of departments. The confusion among these men and the actual commanders of corps was incredible.

Napoleon expected Frederick William to retire behind the Elbe and dispute its passage until the Russians could join him. He was surprised when he heard that the Prussians were concentrating west of the Elbe; this forward movement defeated the Prussians from the beginning, and so completely defeated them that the Prussian Army disintegrated.

The French advanced in three great columns into the rocky valleys that led from Franconia into Saxony—an army—when the cavalry and artillery of the Guard joined it—of 186,000 men, led by martial masters—men like Davout, Murat, Ney, Lannes, Augereau, Bernadotte and Lefebvre.

The basic Prussian plan was to cut off Napoleon from his base in the Main Valley, but when they heard that his advance was across their left and centre they changed plans and attempted a concentration around Weimar, a move which exposed their magazines, threw open their flank invitingly and necessitated marches by crossroads and byways in a country for which the Prussian staff had not one reliable map.

The very first action was ominous for the Prussians. In a short sharp fight with Marshal Murat they left 2,000 muskets, 500 prisoners and 300 killed and wounded. On 10 October the French captured a Prussian baggage train and a pontoon train.

That day, too, the Prussians lost a national hero—Prince Louis Ferdinand. Commanding the rearguard, Louis undertook to hold the little walled town of Saalfeld. Aged thirty-four, brave but insubordinate, he had eighteen guns, eighteen squadrons of hussars and eleven battalions of infantry. With this force he took on the veteran troops of Marshal Lannes.

Louis led several magnificent charges and slashed open a French quartermaster's face before the quartermaster ran him through. The Prussian defeat was a foregone conclusion and they lost heavily at Saalfeld.

After many skirmishes came the clash at Jena. Napoleon, who never made the mistake of underrating an enemy—even the Prussians of 1806—addressed Lannes's corps. 'Soldiers,' he said, 'the Prussian Army is turned as the Austrian was a year ago at Ulm. . . . Fear not its renowned cavalry; oppose to their charges firm squares and the bayonet.'

Some Prussian regiments and leaders were worthy and formidable opponents. The regiments led by Grawert, Zathow and Lanitz fought with the old Prussian obstinacy and the cavalry took some guns. But the only capable senior leader was Prince Frederick Louis of Hohenlohe who, although sixty years of age, was everywhere that day, leading cuirassiers, encouraging infantry, racing from one part of the field to the other.

Hohenlohe sent for reinforcements and General Rüchel arrived with 20,000 men, but they made a poor stand. Rüchel was seriously wounded; Hohenlohe's own regiment gave way and then General Hahn's grenadiers. Then, in a terrible charge, Murat and his cavalry arrived and swept through the Prussians in a whirlwind of slaughter. No battle can show carnage more merciless and horrible than that surge of the heavy horsemen among the flying Prussians after Jena. They spared nothing in their path and every one of those 15,000 long swords was red with blood from point to hilt. And all the while the French bandsmen played, while Prussians in their many colourful uniforms scrambled for brief safety.

But Jena, sanguinary though it was, was not the major battle of the campaign, even if it is the best remembered. Another action, fought near Auerstadt at the same time, broke up the main body of Prussians and covered Marshal Davout with glory.

Learning from some prisoners that the Prussian centre was before him, Davout ordered his troops to march at midnight and occupy the heights between the enemy and the river over which he must pass; then he went to Bernadotte to plan the assault. But because of an old quarrel between the two men, Bernadotte (who later became King of Sweden) chose to interpret certain orders of Napoleon's to his own liking and marched his corps of 20,000 men away from the scene.

This left Davout with 28,750 men to face at least 35,000 Prussians. He set about his task with characteristic attention to detail. Between the bridge at Koser and the village of Auerstadt, twelve miles due north of Jena, there is a natural hollow dissected by a rivulet through which the high road ran, then descended by a defile to the Saale River.

Davout marched to this position in the darkness of early morning and formed a division at the edge of the dip at six o'clock as Blücher's advance guard of cavalry reached the other ridge. The fog was so dense that the combatants could not see each other until their cavalry screen clashed. The Prussian staff held a conference at which the Duke of Brunswick advised caution, but he was overruled by the King and Marshal Mollendorf.

After the fog lifted Blücher four times charged the French flank, but the French squares stood firm. Blücher commented later about the gallantry of the French 25th Regiment, clad in white uniforms—a Napoleonic experiment later abandoned because the white only emphasized the blood from wounds.

Davout sent his cavalry after Blücher, then prepared his line to meet a furious Prussian attack. General Wartensleben led his division into a village where there was much bayonet fighting for an hour before the Prussians were pushed back. The King of Prussia had his horse killed under him, Mollendorf was knocked down and later captured and several Prussian leaders were killed and wounded.

At one time the French General Morand hastily ran his troops into squares as Prince William's 10,000 cavalrymen charged them. The numbers were there but not the spirit of the Seven Years War; the theoretically strong Prussian cavalry could make no impression on the French squares. On the contrary, the French volley fire created a rampart of corpses around them.

After six hours of ceaseless fighting on ridge and slope, in village and marsh, the Prussian reserve under General Kalckreuth was still intact and the King, backed by Blücher, wanted to make a final effort. But all the other Prussian leaders were against it. They wanted to retreat to Weimar, where they said Hohenlohe and Rüchel would join them; they knew nothing yet of the battle of Jena.

Kalckreuth did his best to protect the wreck of the Prussian Army as it set off to the rear, lashed by French artillery and harassed by cavalry. Davout took 115 guns and 3,000 prisoners, but not having numerical superiority could not bring about the chaos Murat had caused at Jena. He sent to Bernadotte for help, but received none.

The Prussians lost about 10,000 killed and wounded at Auerstadt. Then Hohenlohe's fugitives from Jena began to mingle with the retreating men from Auerstadt and the whole army broke and fled, the King himself escaping only because the valiant Blücher commanded the escort.

By this time there was no cohesion left. The great fighting machine of Prussia was systematically taken apart. The whole country was covered with fugitives, wagons, guns. General Dupont destroyed the forces of Prince Eugene of Württemberg at Halle on 17 October. Erfurt, Magdeburg, all the fortified places fell one after another into French hands and in twenty days from crossing the frontier Napoleon was in Berlin.

Among the many prisoners taken was von Clausewitz, aide to Prince August of Prussia. The prince and Clausewitz, among other officers, were kept in France until 1808.

Napoleon's bulletin announcing the double victory of 14 October shows him in an unsavoury light. He blended the two battles under the single name of Jena, merely saying of Davout: 'On the right the corps of Marshal Davout performed prodigies. . . .' And yet Napoleon himself had overthrown only the corps of Hohenlohe and Rüchel with the bulk of his Grand Army, while Davout with only three divisions, forty-four guns and three regiments of light cavalry had routed the Prussian centre. Still, in recompense, Davout was made Duke of Auerstadt.

Between Baeumburg and Merseburg, on the road to Halle, Napoleon sent General Savary into the stubblefields to look for a monument of former French defeat. Savary signalled to him and Napoleon rode over the field to gaze upon a little stone pillar with an almost indecipherable inscription commemorating Frederick's victory of Rossbach in 1757. Jubilantly, Napoleon had it loaded upon a wagon and taken to France. Later the sword and orders of Frederick the Great were taken from his coffin lid and taken to France.

Later Prussians, seeking a reason for the annihilating defeat at Jena and Auerstadt—a military collapse without parallel in European history—said that 'the rulers of the Prussians had lost touch with the ideals and will of the people'. There was much truth in this.

It was not the Prussian soldier who failed—for he was just as brave as he had always been. It was the country's rulers who were no longer in harmony with the people. It was the Prussian reform from above and application of conscription which first led to the national awakening of the Germans and gave the Prussians the strength and dynamic force to rise against Napoleon.

CHAPTER VI

Scharnhorst, Gneisenau, Clausewitz— the Great Reformers

The Armies of 1813, 1870, 1914 and 1939 and of today were the offsprings of the remaking of Prussia after the disasters of Jena and Auerstadt.

Not merely victorious, but angry as well, Napoleon ended medieval Germany by reducing its three hundred states to thirty. He did not intend to give German nationalism a mighty push forward, but this is what happened. German militarism owes a never acknowledged debt to Napoleon.

For a long time two Germanies had existed—the Germany of the two real powers, Prussia and Austria, and the Germany of the princes; hundreds of them, some petty, some great, some despotic, a few enlightened. All were egotistical and feudal. Napoleon, by giving Germany a new political, legal and educational code, freed Germany from the confusion and tyrannies of centuries.

Within Napoleonic Germany—the former Germany of the princes—there was little resentment against French rule; most people were better off than ever they had been before. The Austrians and Prussians showed resentment, but Austrian resentment was comparatively mild, because her defeat had not been overwhelming. In Prussia the resentment was deep and profound. Her existence was precarious and her distress bitter. Only the intercedence of Tsar Alexander I with Napoleon prevented the French Emperor from stamping Prussia out of existence.

Even so, with the approach of a surgeon to diseased tissue, he cut away so much of Prussia that he reduced its population from ten million to five million and imposed a crippling indemnity.

The Prussians were sour, but they knuckled under, believing in the day when they would get their revenge.

They set about planning it at once, in typical Germanic style, guided by some masterly minds which we shall shortly study. The Prussians, in fact, had been too soundly trounced. Had they merely been tactically defeated they might never have become so determined to become so militaristic. But every Prussian man and most Prussian women said to themselves: 'How could this happen to *us*—the people of Frederick the Great?' They were as bewildered as they were bitter.

It is still too little known how intimately German philosophy was connected with the revolt of the German peoples against Napoleon. It was not a revolt of mass against mass, but of a nation against mass. The revolt of the German people against Napoleon was the effect of its national spirit. A people is something different from a mass, because the conformity of the individuals in the nation is not the consequence of chance and general spiritual reactions but of racial and geographical features common to them.

The military eulogists of the Revolution and the worshippers of Napoleon were wrong when they thought that the French victory had thrown the military principles of Frederick the Great on to the scrap heap.

Prussia's position in Europe was that of a terrier surrounded by bulldogs. In comparison with the bulldogs all round him the terrier in the middle was only a poor dog and the Prussians realized it. If Prussia was to engage at all in a military conflict with her enemies she was obliged at the outset to use methods different from those employed by the mighty and rich. She had to wage war offensively, flexibly and economically. Prussia could not operate by ruthlessly throwing in masses of troops. She could win victories and successes by taking the enemy by surprise.

Frederick William III, more mortified than any of his subjects, called on Gerhard Johann David von Scharnhorst to reorganize the Prussian Army.

The creator of the new German military idea was the pupil of a most exceptional man, Count William of Schaumburg-Lippe, with the odd rank of Field-Marshal of Portugal. He was a contemporary and comrade in arms of Frederick the Great, and ruled over a small piece of land in Westphalia, a considerable part of which consisted of the so-called Steinhuder Lake, a large piece of water, five miles long and three miles wide. At that time the German princes were sovereign lords and the inhabitants of their territories were their property. Many German princes sold their subjects to England as soldiers. Count William could not do this even if he wanted to; he had too few subjects. Being filled with a passionate love of soldiering he entered the service of Frederick the Great. He acquitted himself well there and eventually took his leave. The English had made him Field-Marshal of Portugal, but the role of British mercenary did not suit him, so he returned to his own country, a thin, courteous gentleman with a somewhat strained and melancholy face and a great star on his coat.

This thoughtful man astounded his countrymen by a fantastic undertaking. He had an artificial island built in the Steinhuder Lake and constructed a fortress on it, which he called 'Wilhelmstein'. In this fortress he drilled his subjects and thought so much about the art of war that he formed a small military school there. This first military academy of modern times never took more than twelve pupils, who were admitted without regard to birth or means. The Prince himself examined every candidate as to his suitability. In contrast to other military schools, the boys there were not only initiated into the secrets of one kind of fighting, but into military matters and theory in general. In the year 1773 the son of the Westphalian peasant farmer Scharnhorst was taken into the school on the Wilhelmstein. The enthusiasm with which this shy farmer's boy followed the instruction pleased the Prince. He made the seventeen-year-old lad his favourite pupil. The pupil developed as remarkably as the master. After the death of his Prince, Scharnhorst went into Hanoverian service as an ensign and became a most remarkable artillery captain, who, on returning from his first war, made the admission: 'I have learnt nothing in this war. As a matter of fact no one who has systematically studied military science can learn much in war.' In these cool and remarkable words, which might have originated from an opponent of war, can be seen the future adversary of the Corsican.

Scharnhorst was fanatically systematic, a lover of thought, a quiet organizer, in short a master of all the things that Napoleon despised more and more as his victories became greater.

Scharnhorst owed his great career solely to his own efforts. His exceptional intellectual powers, the greatness of his character which combined strong passions with acute sensitiveness, the tireless energy with which he fought his way upwards are now legendary. He found his origins—as the son of a small peasant landowner in Hanover—a handicap. The reputation he acquired as a military writer and teacher and the proof he gave of his ability during the 1793-4 campaigns in Flanders could not overcome his initial social disability. 'The silliest ass gets on as well as the most intelligent,' he wrote about the Prussian Army of those days.

But Frederick William III made repeated offers to him to join the Prussian Army, which he did in 1801 with the rank of lieutenant-colonel and a patent of nobility; that meant he became a 'von'. He had a rather unmilitary appearance and did not at once go down with the Prussian officers, one of whom said, 'I know not a single non-commissioned officer in the force who is not Scharnhorst's superior in military matters'. He certainly was not popular, yet somebody—the King perhaps—realized that here was a man on whom Prussia could build anew.

Clausewitz, the most devoted and intimate of his pupils, said that Scharnhorst found it difficult to express himself articulately in speech and in writing.

But Scharnhorst was astute enough to form a Military Society, which gave him a platform from which to expound his beliefs. He knew how to beat Napoleon, but the Prussian mind was inelastic and Scharnhorst must have often been frustrated and exasperated. He was entrusted with the reorganization of the military school at Berlin, which he greatly expanded and where strategy proper was taught. While his suggestions for reform failed to win approval he was training and inspiring younger officers—men like Grolman, Boyen, Tiedemann and Rühle—and especially Clausewitz, his most promising pupil.

Had Scharnhorst been in command during the campaign which culminated with Jena and Auerstadt he probably would have won it. A week before the battles he wrote to his daughter: 'What ought to be done I know only too well; what is going to be done, only the gods know.' He was present at Jena, but had insufficient authority to make any difference to the outcome.

Not that the King, despite the many signs of his favour, yet gave Scharnhorst an entirely free hand to reform the Prussian Army. Stupidly, he packed 'Scharnhorst's commission' with a majority of nonentities and opponents of Scharnhorst's policy. At the beginning Scharnhorst could count on only one supporter —General Gneisenau.

Nevertheless Scharnhorst applied these powers thoroughly. He dismissed 150 generals who had not 'preserved themselves and their troops from shame'. Many were punished and seven were executed. Many great names of noble families figure in this list. One, an ancestor of Field-Marshal Hindenburg, had surrendered a fortress without a fight. Of the 143 generals in service in 1803 only eight remained in 1812 and of these only two, one of them Blücher, held a command in 1813–15. All the Prussian regiments that had surrendered in the Franco-Prussian war of 1806 were disbanded.[1] A commission of inquiry examined every officer concerning his conduct.

Scharnhorst and Gneisenau saw after the defeat of 1806 that military leadership could not remain the privilege of the nobility, but that fresh blood was necessary to stimulate the army. They created a genuine national army in the face of great opposition. They told Frederick William III that commissions should be available for the sons of the middle classes and for any common soldier who had shown his worth in the face of the enemy.

Germany's military power and her subsequent unification began with the abolition of flogging in the army. In 1807 it was declared that honour was the foundation of discipline and with this declaration of human dignity began the new glory of the Prussian Army.

Most people speak of Prussian militarism as blind people do of colours. The first Prussian military power, which lasted from the Great Elector to Frederick the Great and collapsed in 1806, was only the private power of princes. From 1806 until 1813 it was transitional and from 1813 onwards it was the power of the people.

The difference is fundamental. When general military service was introduced in Prussia it became impossible to buy an officer's commission and regiments could no longer be granted. The managements of companies by captains and of regiments by colonels immediately ceased.

Until then things had been no different in Prussia from what they had been in other countries. Deserving soldiers or princes were granted regiments with the additional object of helping them financially. The commander of a regiment was granted a certain sum of money by the monarch for clothing, feeding and paying his troops. The more economically he spent this money

---

[1] The new regiments were first given numbers and at the end of the last century were called after the dead heroes of the Prussian-German Army. From the regiments of the land army, this practice extended as far as small units in the navy and air force.

the more his own finances improved. This system continued downwards. The various company officers, the captains, were given lump sums with which to feed and pay their men. Because it was the system in Prussia to grant a patent of nobility to men who had rendered great service to their country, the impression grew up abroad that only the nobility had any say in military matters.

Great moral and spiritual effort was needed to abolish this pernicious system. But Scharnhorst and Gneisenau were men in the mould of Frederick the Great. They realized that Prussia had to be reforged and to do this they had to militarize the Prussian people. They first of all inspired the schoolteachers of the country; the schoolteachers from primary school to university went to work with a will on the minds and emotions of the children and young people. They were infected with nationalism, filled with militaristic fervour and a belief in 'Prussia's destiny'.

At this point nationalistic enthusiasm in Germany took interest in Prussia and by a sort of cross-pollination the two peoples began to draw closer together, although German aims were rather less realistic and more romantic than those of the Prussians.

Many German nationalists had no real interest in Prussia; they saw her merely as the tool by which Germany could be released from French rule. Some influential thinkers were already advocating that the Germans were clearly the best people to govern France and the rest of Europe, though they were cautious enough to point out that such domination would be under Prussian leadership.

So serious did this idea become that much of Germany was swept by a 'be-strong campaign', with the country's youth embarking on physical fitness programmes in readiness for *Der Tag*.

Through indiscretions on the part of the great statesman, Baron vom Stein, Napoleon found out about Scharnhorst's reforms. These indiscretions irritated Napoleon. He fixed Prussia's army at 42,000 effectives—about a third of its normal strength—rigidly determined the proportions of the various arms and prohibited any form of national militia. Scharnhorst and Gneisenau could not develop a large, powerful professional army so they got around the problem by organizing general military service on a short-term basis. This created an invisible army of trained men.

Between 1808 and 1813 a reserve of 36,000 trained men was built up, behind the officially allowed 42,000.

Simultaneously, many men were banded into the Landsturm, a sort of Home Guard. This force was poorly trained and equipped and discipline was lax, but in theory they were expected to rise to great heights of martial valour and competence. In 1813, at the time of testing, the Landsturm was an abject failure and after a few years was abandoned.

Without Gneisenau, Scharnhorst would have been discouraged. Gneisenau was a great, impressive, martial man—every inch a warrior. A man of action, energy and enthusiasm, he had served with a Prussian contingent in the war of American Independence. Back in Prussia he found himself posted to a provincial regiment in a small Silesian garrison—a disappointment, for he wanted to serve on the Staff. After Jena, with so many officers failing and falling, Gneisenau so stood out as steady and competent that he was given greater responsibility. In the following spring he was sent to take over one of the few points which still held out behind Napoleon's lines—the little fortress of Kolberg on the sea coast of Pomerania. His brilliant defence of the place until the armistice won him unique popularity throughout the country.

Scharnhorst himself, Gneisenau, Clausewitz, Grolman and Boyen—both majors—were the inner circle of the reformers and like all reformers their way was hard. A German historian (Herbert Rosinski) said that 'perhaps never in the whole history of mankind have the concrete issues of the day been approached and attacked with such deep feeling for the great problems of humanity involved in their solution'. The intensity of their zeal was only equalled by the feeling against them of the hordes of diehards.

Scharnhorst believed that the French had survived from and triumphed against the attacks launched against them because 'they were able to conduct the war with the resources of the whole nation and in the last resort to sacrifice literally everything to the continuation of the struggle'.

But in France the reform had come from below. In Prussia it had to come from above and the reformers' task was much more formidable and complex.

Scharnhorst and his group demanded the abolishment of the cruel system of corporal punishment which had permeated the Prussian Army. They saw that no man's honour and sense of national feeling could be appealed to as long as he could be flogged. After a tough struggle the 'inner circle' won a complete victory on this point. But it was the only complete one they made.

One cardinal principle of the new Prussian system was localization. Each army corps was a little army complete in infantry, cavalry and artillery, recruited and permanently stationed in a particular province. Each regiment was raised in and permanently connected with a town or group of villages. Not that this adaptation of the old tribal system to modern war was anything new, but the Prussians intensified it. It made mobilization a simple business in the case of reservists.

The reformers faced tremendous opposition from the 'Old Prussians'. One of them, Field-Marshal von Kalckreuth, complained in 1808 that the new kind of dispersed fighting might be good for the French, 'a vivacious race', but that it dishonoured the Germans, 'peoples with a countenance'. The German national character would be dishonoured and disfigured if their system of line and platoon fire was taken away from them.

But gradually Scharnhorst and his group triumphed. Scharnhorst insisted that a claim to an officer's commission in peacetime must be based on knowledge and education, in wartime on special bravery, activity and good judgement.

The officers' 'courts of honour' he was unable to change and perhaps he did not really want to change them. Three-quarters of the officers of a regiment met as a court of honour to hear cases of 'dishonourable conduct'. A majority verdict was necessary for a finding of guilty, although an officer was entitled to have his case investigated by another regiment. It was probably as good a system as any, but a popular officer had the advantage over an unpopular one.

In 1809, for the professional training of the future officers, three military schools for ensigns were created, at Berlin, Königsberg and Breslau, and for staff work and higher facets of war the Military School for Officers—the famous War Academy —was developed in 1810.

Clausewitz was one of the first professors of the Kriegs-akademie, whose teaching staff was made up not only of soldiers but of civilian experts. Karl Ritter, one of the founders of modern scientific geography, was a professor there for thirty-nine years and organized the efficient map department of the General Staff.

It was no mere significance that in this year the Prussian order, the *Pour le Mérite*, was made an award for military merit against an enemy in the field. In fact the order was the highest reward for individual gallantry in action.[1] Scharnhorst believed in military awards.

Beyond doubt, the most drastic, far-reaching, controversial and unpopular edict was that comfort in war had to end. This policy foreshadowed the German Army of the future, but it furiously angered Prussian officers at the time. Even in Napoleon's armies officers were accustomed to a fair degree of comfort, including the time spent on active service.

Subalterns lost their riding and pack horses, as a step towards the revolutionary theory that officers should set an example to their men. The number of horses in a regiment of infantry was reduced to one-sixth. Even the bread-wagon was eliminated; from now on the army would requisition what it wanted, in the French style. Tents went out and greatcoats came in; soldiers were expected to be hardy enough to sleep in the open. Officers were told that they had to be as physically fit as the men and they were not to take luxuries into the field. That the reformers were able to get away with all this is as much an indication of changing military thought as it is a tribute to their determination. Recruiting abroad was ended and foreigners in the army were used only as long as they lasted.

The reformers performed another major service to military efficiency. They restored the artillery and engineers to their rightful place of honour, wiping out the insult that in the Seven Years War they had merely tried to surpass each other in mistakes, though Frederick himself had never said this. Scharnhorst and his colleagues were not interested in inter-service rivalries. They wanted to win any war in which Prussia might engage.

Scharnhorst set about reforming the artillery. He did away with the last remaining differences between garrison and field artillery—in future there was only field artillery—and he dismissed from the artillery every man who was not a soldier. The drivers in the field artillery, for example, were still private employees.

Scharnhorst also eliminated the scientific part of the secrecy in artillery. 'With the single exception of theology,' he said, 'there is no study which is so full of prejudices as artillery.' He

[1] The order was founded by Frederick I, when he was Prince Frederick, about 1667, as the Order of Generosity. It became the Order of Merit in 1740 and Frederick the Great granted it for civil and military distinction. It was not awarded after the defeat of Germany in 1918.

founded schools for training artillery N.C.O.s and ensigns and created the first artillery testing board. Every technical innovation had to be submitted to this board so that no general could disregard it merely because it was new or inconvenient to him. The revolutionary change brought about by Scharnhorst was that he initiated the men in the ranks into the technical and mathematical knowledge which until that time had been the secret possession of the guilds and of the high commanders of artillery. Seven years after the introduction of this reform Napoleon was beaten.

Perhaps Scharnhorst's greatest deed was that he relieved the subordinate commanders of their fear of assuming the responsibility of taking action. Their training in physics and mathematics now made them masters of their guns.

In 1942 a German writer (in *Signal*) said that Frederick's and Scharnhorst's ideas have continued to live until our own day, and that no fundamental change has taken place in the sphere of artillery tactics since Frederick the Great. The principles have only been developed down to the last detail.

Despite the hard-won successes of Scharnhorst and his reformers in one thing they failed completely—conscription. In vain they pointed out that war demanded preparation before hostilities began. In vain they stressed that France, alone in Europe, had introduced conscription, and, alone in Europe, was successful everywhere. The powerful nobility dug in their heels about conscription. They called it, among other things, 'the tomb of civilization'—whatever that meant.

The reformers tried to push the King into joining Austria in her revolt against Napoleon in 1809, but failed. In 1809, Grolman, after joining the Austrians, went on to the Peninsula to join Wellington's Army fighting against the French; Gneisenau, eased out of his post by Napoleon's influence, was sent on a diplomatic mission to London. In 1811 Scharnhorst, forestalling a French demand for his dismissal, asked Frederick William to relieve him of his post as head of the General Department of War.

Officially Scharnhorst went, but Napoleon did not find out what the theorist of battle had done. Behind Napoleon's back he had built up a new secret army, and had created an institution, which, enormously enlarged, carried on the military school of Steinhuder Lake in the Prussian Army. The new thing was called the great General Staff. The name was to be found elsewhere, but the thing itself was not. In most other countries the 'general staff' was merely the association of individual army leaders plus some additional senior officers too old for field commands. In contrast to this the Prussian creation was an independent organization with two great tasks—the preparation for war and the training of a suitable younger generation of officers for the future General Staff.

In the academy and in the General Staff the officers once more learned Frederick's idea of destruction. Prussia was small and could only resist strong enemies when it thought and lived in the idea of destruction.

Officers were told—as Hitler was to tell them much later—that the history of the art of war proved that only those army leaders who had trained and intelligent troops at their disposal, troops, that is, whose training and good sense enabled them to distrust instinct on the field of battle, had been able to apply the idea of destruction. Instinct drove people together on a battlefield into one great mass, but logic kept them apart and made them obey the commands of the leaders.

Scharnhorst created a new type of soldier. Up till then the Prussian Army had been a mercenary one. The enthusiasm and vigour of the French soldiers played havoc with the tactics of all the mercenary armies. The mercenaries fought in long, thin lines and only fired when ordered. These thin phalanxes were suddenly broken through by the deeply echeloned columns of the French and then the columns were surrounded by swarms of riflemen who waged war entirely on their own lines, throwing themselves on the ground and often firing on their own initiative. A mercenary army was not equal to this new war spirit. This was why Scharnhorst abolished mercenary armies and wanted to introduce general conscription. Only a free man had the inclination to fight the oppressor with enthusiasm. Scharnhorst was largely responsible for associated social and political reforms; feudal rights were abolished and the right of the parishes to self-government and free ownership of land by farmers was introduced.

New rights brought new duties with them: every Prussian had to go to the elementary school. In a short time illiteracy had been eradicated and this helped Scharnhorst with his creation of the new soldier.

In 1811, the patriots' hopes were high when a clash between Napoleon and Alexander of Russia was imminent. Despite pleas from his impassioned officers, Frederick weakly placed half his small force at Napoleon's command for the March to

Moscow. And well they fought for him, too. But a number of officers, refusing service under French colours, joined the Russian Army. Clausewitz was one of them.

Scharnhorst understood and sympathized with his friends' motives, but could not follow them. He retired to Silesia, after telling the King that he could call on him at any time. And the time came. In the spring of 1813 he met the King at Breslau, was reappointed head of the Military Department and organized the Prussian revolt against Napoleon.

This was a great effort and possibly one that only the Prussians could have accomplished. The standing army was mobilized and by bringing in reservists was raised to about 100,000. Then, under the famous Landwehr edict of 9 February 1813 the whole untrained manpower of the country was mobilized. Money, arms and equipment were lacking but somehow Scharnhorst had the men trained and the Prussians began the spring campaign with 135,000 men.

The officers of the regular army did their best to discredit the Landwehr units and they went out of their way to make it difficult for them to get good quarters and supplies. They were so damaging the reputation of the infant force that later the Cabinet issued a statement to the effect that the regulars and the Landwehr were equally brave and of equal birth. Blücher later praised the Landwehr as equals of the regular regiments—'once they had tasted plenty of powder'.

In fact, the Landwehr had no great military value—much less than the British Territorials—but it did provide an emergency force and it did enhance Prussia's reputation abroad. What enhanced it much more was the victory she was soon to have at Leipzig.

CHAPTER VII

'A Halo Around the Profession of Arms'

Prussia's opportunity to regain her military prestige came about almost accidentally, although German historians have done their best—they were especially active during Hitler's régime—to show that there was a deliberate military campaign to re-establish the country.

War was forced on Frederick William by one of his own generals, von Yorck, representing a powerful clique of professional officers who were solely concerned with re-establishing their military reputations, so painfully damaged in the débâcle of 1806. The modern parallel is the case of the French generals of the O.A.S. in Algeria.

On 30 December 1812, General von Yorck—commanding 30,000 Prussians with Napoleon's Army retreating from Moscow—concluded with the Russians the Convention of Tauroggen, according to which his troops were declared neutral. Yorck's defection was the signal for a great popular rising in Prussia which, on 26 February, induced Frederick William to make an offensive alliance with Russia. On 13 March the treaty was published and on the 17th Prussia declared war on France.

Significantly, three days before the publication of the treaty the King introduced the award of the Iron Cross. It is difficult to say now whose idea this was, but it seems probable to me that Scharnhorst recommended it.

The founding decree of the Iron Cross stated: 'In the present great catastrophe in which everything is at stake for the Nation, the vigorous spirit which elevates the nation so high deserves to be honoured and perpetuated by quite peculiar monuments.

That the perseverance by which the Nation endured the irresistible evils of an iron age did not shrink to timidity is proved by the high courage which now animates every breast and which could survive only because it was based on religion and true loyalty to King and Country.'

The cross was to reward those, either military or civil, who distinguished themselves in the coming conflict; rank was to have nothing to do with its award. It was to be worn by soldiers with a black ribbon with two white stripes near the edge and by civilians with a white ribbon with black borders. There were then three grades of award.

Iron as the material for the award appealed to the Prussians more than gold or silver ever could. German women of the Napoleonic wars gave in their gold jewellery and replaced it with delicately made ornaments of iron.

The Battle of Leipzig, which followed the declaration of war, has been represented as a national German uprising against Napoleon, but it was nothing of the kind. The German people as a race were not emotionally involved and, in fact, only about 3,000 German troops were physically involved. Significantly, the French were never troubled by guerrillas in Germany, as they had been in Spain and Russia.

The Prussian people wildly supported the proclamation. The King ordered a *levée en masse*. Every man not in the regular army or Landwehr was to help the army by guerrilla warfare. They were ordered to burn French food stocks, destroy enemy bridges and boats, murder stragglers. In the Russian fashion, they were to destroy their own homes and food supplies rather than allow the French to use them.

Probably the Prussians believed that the French retreat from Moscow had wrecked the French Army. It was damaged, but not wrecked; of the 600,000 men who entered Russia only 200,000 were French. Napoleon now aimed to raise an army of 656,000 men. He never did reach this figure but by the middle of April, when ready to take the field, he had 226,000 officers and men and 457 guns. This was a magnificent performance in a short time, though he was short of cavalry. But the face of war was changing fast; armies had grown so much in size that no single commander could direct all troop movements. A battle was now too complex and widespread even for Napoleon's genius.

Before, too, he had always acted on the offensive—violently so. Now he was forced on the defensive. Opposed to the new

French Army were 110,000 Russians and 80,000 Prussians. About 30,000 of the Russians were cavalry and Cossacks, undisciplined but savage.

The most appalling mistake, as the Prussian die-hards saw it, was the decision to give the Prussian high command to Blücher. On the surface, they were justifiably irritated. Blücher was nearly seventy; he was a psychopath, an irresponsible talker and gambler. He suffered from fits of melancholia and he had crazy notions. Perhaps the oddest was that because of his sins he was pregnant with an elephant produced by a French soldier. (He told Wellington about this belief.) It was Scharnhorst who persuaded the King to give Blücher the supreme command, 'because here is a man who is all-soldier'. At least he looked the part and, despite his age, he was energetic and could appear quite dashing.

The selection of Blücher was a symbol—a symbol of the unconventional which was to dominate German arms. From now on, with increasing impetus, the Germans deviated from the pattern, the conventional and the accepted. Gneisenau wrote in 1813: 'War is always and everywhere a state of contingency.' He and the others were prepared to meet contingency by expedient.

Soon after the campaign began—the Prussians called it the War of Liberation—Schwarzenberg, the Austrian and Allied Supreme Commander of the Coalition Forces, complained about the Germans: 'They trample with their feet on all rules of war.'

This was not so. The Prussians had merely created some new rules. Scharnhorst had said: 'The theory of war is knowledge of all the circumstances, especially of the arms, the country and the means of transport.'

The Prussian leaders, Gneisenau in particular, wanted complete separation of Prussian troops from other armies; that is, they wanted no joint-commands. When this point came up at the time of the Inter-Allied War Plan of Trachenberg, Gneisenau said: 'They (Prussian troops) would have to share the blame of defeat with other troops, but the Prussian name would never be mentioned in case of a victory. The national honour would be mortified.' Sayings like this were widely published and had the inevitable effect of boosting Prussian pride.

The first actions began in May 1813 but there was an armistice between 1 June and 16 August, ostensibly in order to enable peace terms to be discussed at Prague. It seems probable, however, that Napoleon merely wanted to strengthen his forces before the great battles he knew had to come. After many bloody actions the Battle of Leipzig took place between 16 and 19 October. In these three days the allies lost 54,000 killed and wounded and the French about twice this number, including desertions. But they had fought hard. On 18 October the French fired 95,000 cannon shots and during the three days more than 200,000, using nearly all their reserves.

The French Army was broken. Six French generals were killed, 12 wounded and 36 captured. The allies took 28 flags and eagles, 325 guns, 900 ammunition wagons and 40,000 muskets. Napoleon might have been able to make some valid excuses for defeat, but nobody would have listened, least of all the Prussians. They were jubilant and probably few spared a thought for General Scharnhorst who was mortally wounded in the closing stages of the battle.[1] He was fifty-seven.

The Prussian Army had regained its old confidence; and this confidence infected the whole nation. Their catch cry could well have been, 'We are a martial nation again!' A Prussian feudal army had been vanquished at Jena; a Prussian national army had triumphed at Leipzig.

Scharnhorst was dead, but Gneisenau lived on to be the chief director of Prussian field strategy during these campaigns and during that of Waterloo, even though Blücher was the Prussian commander in the field. Clausewitz served on the staff of an army corps during this campaign.

After Napoleon's downfall it was Gneisenau who carried on and perpetuated Scharnhorst's work of reorganization, while Clausewitz gave the Prussian Army, in his writings, a practical theory of war on which it acted for the next century. No military theorist has been so deified as has Clausewitz—and far beyond the borders of his own country.

After the first defeat of the French in 1814 the allies met at the Congress of Vienna and here something happened that was to have a profound influence on subsequent German militarism. A ruler had to be found for the lands on the left bank of the Rhine—and they were given to Prussia. Neither Frederick William III nor the population of these lands wanted this union. They had no spiritual affiliation whatever and in any case, the area was not even joined geographically to Prussia.

[1] Clausewitz said of Leipzig: 'One cannot see all this without incessantly thinking of Scharnhorst.'

Still, Prussia, weakest of the allies, reluctantly took over Rhenish Prussia, acquiring three million Germans instead of the three million Poles she had hoped to recover. Rhenish Prussia was to become the most productive industrial area in the world, but nobody knew about that in 1815.

Another important consequence of the Congress was the foundation of the Confederation of Germany, which had an almost instantaneous and electrifying effect on German nationalism. Secret societies sprang up by the dozen, the 'be-strong' groups became stronger, other groups began to wear uniforms, verbal and physical violence erupted all over the country; Jews were reviled and assaulted; books were burned. But all these manifestations of unrest came to very little.

Germany at this time was no competitor in world trade. She owned no big factories, produced little coal, had no efficient machinery. She was an agricultural country and her people, generally, were no more than comfortably off. This was largely because confederation was merely a word; Germany was no more confederated than the pieces of a watch awaiting assembly. There was no federal army and many federal forts had no garrisons; some of them crumbled into ruin. Nevertheless, the German princes maintained their own armies, dressed them flamboyantly and distributed the most remarkable decorations for bravery to officers who had never been in action. Many, if not most, of the princes were insane, the result of ceaseless inbreeding.

The Prussian Army consolidated on Scharnhorst-Gneisenau lines, imbued its soldiers with the theory of invincibility and read Clausewitz with avidity. Clausewitz's philosophical writings on war overcame the prejudice of the intellectuals in Germany against war, who had held that war was an affair for rough people. Clausewitz had died of cholera in 1831 but by now Prussian officers swore by Clausewitz's work. It was a point of honour among them to insist that he was the best and most knowledgeable writer on war; no officer would have dared to differ from an opinion expressed by Clausewitz. Indeed, why should they? Everything he said made good sense.

Several military writers and leaders had enlightened political ideas about military reforms as well as purely practical plans for military improvements. Unfortunately, their attempts to bring about political reformation were rarely successful and their principles were forgotten, especially if their propounders fell from grace, but their purely military work lived on. This

even happened to Clausewitz. Military-political moderation
and tolerance did not get a chance to flourish.

Clausewitz was certainly definite and his disciples seized on
his bolder statements. Clausewitz ranked the military profession supreme over all. It was, he said, an intellectually determined activity of men. His description of an army imbued with
soldierly spirit is especially illuminating for in it we see the
German Army of the future.

'An army which retains its accustomed order under the most
devastating fire, which is never overcome by fear and fights for
every foot of ground, which even in the chaos of defeat does not
lose its discipline or the respect for and confidence in its leaders,
an army which regards every effort as a means towards victory
and not as a curse on its banners, which is reminded of all these
duties and virtues by the short catechism of one single conception—the honour of its weapons—such an army is imbued
with the soldierly spirit.'

Clausewitz's notes—for that is all they were—were published
in 1832, the year after his death. Some of these notes had been
delivered as lectures or had been separately published before
this, but the publication of them in book form—a 1,000-page
tome under the title *On War*—crystallized his whole martial
philosophy. As a philosophy on war it remains unrivalled.

An English traveller in Berlin in the year in which Clausewitz's book appeared painted a vivid word picture of the
capital in an article in the publication *La Belle Assemblée*, little
realizing how much he saw was due to Clausewitz:

'How martial is the aspect of the Prussian capital. On
approaching Berlin none of the vulgar features of the other
large cities offend the traveller's eye; no range of mean-
looking suburbs; no lines of carts, lumbering omnibuses . . .
All is noble, beautiful, and grand.

'We entered Berlin from the Carlottenburg Road, and
as we approached the magnificent Brandenburger Road,
some battalions of the Grenadiers of the Guard and two
regiments of Lancers were defiling in column beneath its
stately arches. The measured tread of infantry, their proud
and gallant bearing, the waving pennons of the Uhlans,
the loud breathings of their brazen bands, the architectural
magnificence of the Gate itself, with its chariot of victory
rearing aloft in lordly pride the Black Eagle of Prussia,
produced a beautiful effect.

'As our britscha rolled down the Unter den Linden some of the most picturesque features of Prussian life burst upon our view. Groups of military of every arm, the tall Grenadier of the Guard, the graceful Uhlan, the heavy Cuirassier, the splendid Hussar, were seen, twitching their moustaches, and lounging with a listless *air de garnison*: others standing with folded arms, turning their proud eyes on the fair occupants of the line of open carriages that crowded the centre of the drive. Many a nod of recognition was exchanged; many a bright eye, with sidelong glance, looked furtively on the handsome figures of their country-men, who, for martial grace and military carriage, surpass the soldiers of every other country.

'After all, there is a halo around the profession of arms that appeals to the imagination of the most phlegmatic; but to the fair there is magic in the glitter of an epaulette, music in the jangle of a spur . . . To the soldier, Potsdam, the *berceau* of a new war-system, is as interesting a source of association as the abode of Copernicus to the astronomer. It is still what it was in the days of Frederick, a vast barrack yard—on every side of which you behold recruits in the various stages of military education.'

Thousands of German officers of all ranks appear almost to have made decisions, paramount and petty, with a copy of Clausewitz's book in their hands. It was largely his teaching which led Prussia and Germany, as a unity, into preparation for unconditional and absolute war, and the determination to put this preparation into effect. A brief study of some of his sayings makes this clear.

Whole generations of Prussian, German and Austrian soldiers were brought up on his book and as we shall see there were times when Clausewitz's ideas were used by other nations against the Germans, and times when these nations, by over-rigid adherence to his teachings, defeated themselves. Clausewitz said:

'War belongs to the province of social life. State policy is the womb in which war is developed, in which its outlines lie hidden in a rudimentary state, like the qualities of living creatures in their germs. . . .

'War is the province of physical exertions and suffering. A certain strength of body and mind is required, which produces indifference to them. With these qualifications, under the guidance of simply a sound understanding, a man is at once a proper instrument of war. If we go further in the demands which war makes on its votaries, then we find the powers of the understanding predominating. War is the province of uncertainty; three-fourths of those things upon which action in war must be calculated are hidden more or less in the clouds of great uncertainty. Here, then, above all a fine and penetrating mind is called for. An average intellect may, at one time, perhaps hit upon this truth by accident; an extraordinary courage at another may compensate for the want of this tact; but in the majority of cases the average result will always bring to light the deficient understanding. . . .

'As long as his men, full of good courage, fight with zeal and spirit, it is seldom necessary for the Chief to show great energy or purpose in the pursuit of his object. But as soon as difficulties arise—and that must always be when great results are at stake—then things no longer move on of themselves like a well-oiled machine. The machine itself then begins to offer resistance, and to overcome this the commander must have great force of will. . . .

'The military virtue of an army is one of the most important moral powers in war and where it is wanting we either see its place supplied by one of the others, such as the great superiority of generalship, or popular enthusiasm or we find the results not commensurate with the efforts made. . . . The astonishing successes of generals and their greatness in situations of extreme difficulty were only possible with armies possessing this virtue. This spirit can be generated from only two sources and only by these two conjointly. The first is a succession of campaigns and great victories; the other is an activity of the army carried sometimes to its highest pitch. Only by these does the soldier learn to know his powers. The more a general is in the habit of demanding from his troops, the surer he will be that his demands will be answered. The soldier is as proud of overcoming toil as he is of surmounting danger. . . .

'We do not ask, how much does the resistance which the whole nation in arms is capable of making cost that nation? But we ask, what is the effect which such a resistance can produce?

'We never find that a state joining in the cause of another

state takes it up with the same earnestness as its own. An auxiliary army of moderate strength is sent; if it is not successful, then the ally looks upon the affair as in a manner ended, and tries to get out of it on the cheapest possible terms. . . .

'War is nothing but a continuation of political intercourse, with a mixture of other means. . . . Is not war merely another kind of writing and language for political thoughts? It has certainly a grammar of its own, but its logic is not peculiar to itself. . . . In one word, the Art of War in its highest point of view is policy, but, no doubt, a policy which fights battles instead of writing notes. According to this view, to leave a great military enterprise, or the plan for one to a purely military judgement and decision is a distinction which cannot be allowed, and is even prejudicial. . . .

'Even the final decision of a whole war is not always to be regarded as absolute. *The conquered state often sees in it only a passing evil, which may be repaired in after times by means of political combinations.*[1] How much this must modify the degree of tension and the vigour of the efforts made is evident in itself. . . .

'There is no human affair which stands so constantly and so generally in close connection with chance as war. But together with chance, the accidental, and along with it good luck, occupy a great place in war. If we take a look at the subjective nature of war . . . it will appear to us still more like a game. Primarily the element in which the operations of war are carried on is danger but which of all the moral qualities is first in danger? Courage. Now certainly courage is quite compatible with prudent calculation, but still they are things of quite a different kind, essentially different qualities of the mind . . . From the outset there is a play of possibilities, probabilities good and bad luck, which spreads about with all the coarse and fine threads of its web, and makes war of all branches of human activity the most like a gambling game. . . . The passions which break forth in war must already have a latent existence in the peoples.'

Clausewitz never dissembled. 'We do not like to hear of generals who are victorious without the shedding of blood,' he

[1] Author's italics.

wrote. 'If bloody battling is a dreadful spectacle, that should merely be the reason to appreciate war more and not to allow our swords to grow blunt by and by, through humanitarianism, until somebody steps in with a sharp sword and cuts our arms off our body . . . The political object, as the original motive of war, should be the standard for determining both the aim of the military force and also the amount of effect to be made . . . The waste of our own military forces must always be greater the more our aim is directed upon the destruction of the enemy's power. . . .

'Superiority in numbers becomes every day more decisive. . . . The principle of assembling the greatest possible numbers may therefore be regarded as more important than ever.'

The influence most men have dies with them; this is especially so of soldiers. In fact, their influence often dies as they retire, though some of more recent years have refused to lie down. This is not true of Clausewitz; his influence increased after his death and it remains today a potent force.

CHAPTER VIII

Blood and Iron

The battle of Nisib on 23 June 1839 took place on the border of Syria and Kurdistan, and major conflict though it was at the time it is now forgotten. However, it is important in any study of the German soldier because it was here that Helmuth von Moltke—the future Field-Marshal of the German Empire—took part in his first battle. Prussian officers of those days were encouraged to seek temporary service in foreign armies, merely to gain experience.

Born at Parchim in Mecklenburg in 1800, the son of a German officer in the Danish Army, von Moltke was educated at the military school of Copenhagen and was commissioned into the Danish Army. But in 1822 he transferred to Prussia and a year later he went to the Kriegsakademie, where Clausewitz was then Director. Clausewitz made Moltke into a specialist in terrain. In 1834, as a captain on the general staff, he was attached to the staff of the newly organized Turkish Army, then preparing for an inevitable war against the Ottoman Empire. Moltke, a genius in warfare, did the work of a general for the Turks but their leadership was so inept they could not hope to win. At one stage of the battle of Nisib, Moltke tried to reason with some stupid staff officers to extricate 30,000 soldiers from a trap in which they had placed them. Not so long after, he was to direct with all but absolute command a million soldiers, and all Europe looking on at the brilliant strategy by which he was sealing the fate of France.

As it was, the overwhelming Egyptian advance against the Turks nearly finished Moltke. He and the only other two Prussian officers with the Turks had to ride practically non stop for nine hours to escape. He said years later that he had learned a lot during his years with the Turks.

In 1840, following a scare that France was on the warpath again, the Germans realized that only the Prussian Army along the Rhine was between them and the unpredictable French. This realization drew Prussia and Germany closer than they had been for twenty-seven years, but the union was brief. Germany stagnated, the two Germanic powers, Austria and Hungary, had had varying fortunes, while Prussia recovered only slowly from her calamities of 1806, but gradually over the next forty years caught up on Austria's great lead.

Prussia's administration increased in efficiency and her people became more Germanic in outlook and even in character. This change reached its climax in 1848 when the idea of Prussian leadership of Germany was put forward as a definite and practical scheme, though it was largely a selfish one, with Prussia and not Germany as the main beneficiary.

Amid the erratic noble families of the time the House of Hohenzollern stood out as abnormally sane, but even it had its misfortune in Frederick William IV, who was eccentric and eventually went mad. But it was this Prussian ruler who so deeply involved Prussia in German affairs that she could never hope to extricate herself. Still, what happened would have come about sooner or later.

Frederick William IV was, in fact, the prototype of Hitler. He had the same trick of rousing oratory, the same passionate turn of phrase, the same grandiose visions of supremacy. In 1848 his mouthings were repeated by intellectuals and pseudo intellectuals who worked the Germans into a fine if confused fervour. They wanted a People's Republic, which appealed to the masses of peasants, most of whom were oppressed by money-lenders.

In March 1848 there was a serious riot in Berlin. The army was quickly on the scene and was competently repressing the large-scale insurrection when Frederick William, who hated the army as much as the martial traditions of his family, made a pact with the citizens to withdraw the troops if they removed the barricades. This was agreed to. Frederick William's action in stopping his army from acting gave the burghers the impression that they had won their revolution. The idea was false. The army had not been defeated and now it was angry because of its humiliation.

An intense social conflict was going on in Germany at this

time, but this social upheaval did not have the far-reaching effects of Germany's reactions to foreign war. The Prussians and Austrians were having wars against the Poles, the Danes and the Hungarians, and the radical Germans supported them. The more moderate Germans were talked down.

The German liberals, and there were many of them in the mid-nineteenth century, surrendered to the Prussian Army and, in ultimate consequence, to the evil geniuses of Bismarck and Hitler.

One cause of this surrender was Germany's claim to possess the northern duchies of Schleswig and Holstein, at that time (1848) under Danish rule. There was some justice in the German claim, as Holstein was inhabited entirely by Germans and Schleswig had a large German population. The Germans, as usual, were disinclined to political manœuvres; they wanted the two states and they wanted them fast. Denmark was no great power, but she was too strong for Germany, which had no national army. Germany appealed to the Prussian Army, which made good progress against the Danes until Britain and Russia took a hand; then Prussia backed down, much to Germany's annoyance. Serious riots followed as people demonstrated against Prussia. Matters got so badly out of hand that the National Assembly, to its great embarrassment, was forced to ask the King of Prussia for troops to restore order. This request was a significant one, with far-reaching effects. It was the beginning of a road from which there was no turning back. Towards the end of 1848 the National Assembly was actually protected at its meetings by Prussian soldiers.

Prussia was not only protecting Germany, but dominating her and, logically, was also serving the cause of German nationalism. Not that the Prussian generals had any sympathy for nationalism; in fact they favoured disunion. They saw German confusion merely as a cover for land-stealing—and the Prussians were inveterate and skilful land-stealers.

In 1849 the National Assembly offered Frederick William the crown of national Germany. The King would have accepted it had it been offered by the German princes, but the princes, selfish and insular, would not voluntarily make themselves subservient to Frederick. In any case, being offered a crown by commoners smacked too much of democracy—and democracy was a stranger to Prussian minds.

With the liberals and moderates discouraged and disbanded the radicals took control of popular feelings and stirred up further uprisings in their demand for a new, national Germany.

Again the Prussian Army put down all disturbances. It was at this time that many of the better German families—worried by militarism—mass-emigrated to the United States. Their sober stability would be missed in the years to come.

With Austria distracted by foreign wars, Prussian domination in Germany grew. Army forces were moved about the country to help any prince unable to handle trouble on his own. By mid-1849 the army was an inevitable fact of life for Germany.

Frederick William, still hungering for a German crown, employed an adviser named Radowitz, a somewhat sinister character who formulated the Erfurt Union—a coalition of princes organized for defence under Prussia's protection. The princes were lukewarm about the whole idea, but they were manœuvred into acceptance. Then when they saw that Austria would protect them they began to break away from the Erfurt Union. There might have been war, but the Prussian generals were convinced that their army was inferior to the Austrian Army, so they did not try conclusions.

Russia, which did not want any German unification—perhaps Tsar Nicholas had a shrewd idea of what it would one day mean—supported Austria, and Prussia was left high and dry. This was the end of the Erfurt Union and a setback for Prussian power.

The Prussian Constitution of 1850 nominally gave the Diet control over military budgets and the war ministry, but as always the army managed to circumvent this order. The North German Constitution of 1867 compelled the other states to model their armies on standards of Prussian efficiency and to put them under the command of the King of Prussia as President of the Confederation.

In 1871 when this constitution was transformed into one for the new German Empire, with the King of Prussia as Kaiser, the leadership of the Prussian military leaders was confirmed.

But Prussians have always learnt from errors and the first thing the generals did after 1850 was to reorganize the army for more rapid, incisive movement. Prussia was on the verge of great advances in many ways. The Ruhr—part of Rhenish Prussia—began to surge ahead with an industrial programme modelled on the British system. Almost overnight Prussia became an industrial power and with the face of war changing so rapidly this was important. Railways were snaking over the country and the Prussian generals were not slow to see the military possibilities of the new form of transport.

In fact, no railways were built until first approved by the Prussian General Staff as having strategic value.[1]

In 1852 a service term of two and a half years was introduced for all infantry and in 1856 the term was extended to three years. War Minister von Roon and the High Command believed that three years was necessary to produce the 'true soldier spirit'. This spirit, Roon said, was not produced by mere patriotism and enthusiasm but by unwavering discipline for war, which 'suited the character of the people'. The whole weight of Prussian military opinion was against revolutionary, volunteer armies of the Napoleonic era.

In 1859 the Prussians staged a full-scale mobilization in which they made full use of the railways. The experience gained on this occasion gave Prussia a flying start in her campaigns of 1866 and 1870.

During the 1850s Otto von Bismarck loomed on the Prussian scene—and almost at once he loomed large. He was to have the most profound influence on Germany and Europe. A harsh, violent and self-willed man, deep, devious and ruthless, he was clearly not always sane. But his insanity was of the kind that appealed to the Prussian mentality.

A true Prussian and a Junker by inclination, he hated the Germans and he detested democracy, but paradoxically he created national Germany and gave the Germans most of the things they hungered for. Oddly enough, in some ways he himself was very German, particularly as he, like most Germans, admired force and authority. It was Bismarck who so moulded Germany as to make her the diseased apple in the middle of the European basket. The issue which was to bring Bismarck to power in a few years' time was not the survival of Prussia in Germany, but the survival in Prussia of the military monarchy and the military caste, which he fought to maintain.

It is significant and important that in every stage of German history the army has triumphed over the civilian government. The army always had its way. Reforms that came about were enforced by soldiers, not civilians. This tradition of military dominance does much to explain the 'civilian vacillation' and 'government weakness', so criticized by foreigners.

By 1860 it had been decided by the General Staff that the

[1] In contrast, the dim-witted Austrian generals opposed the building of railways as 'they interfered with our strategic plans'. They allowed the railways of Northern Italy to be sold to a French company at the same time that they were planning to fight the French in Northern Italy.

Landwehr militia would not again be used in combat but for secondary tasks, such as the occupation of enemy territory and as fortress garrisons. Men in the Landwehr aged thirty-six and over were thrown out and the maximum age for the regular field soldier was reduced from thirty-three to twenty-eight. The High Command reasoned that at twenty-eight a man started thinking for himself and this was dangerous to the principle of mass obedience. Over twenty-eight, too, a man began to think politically; the High Command did not want soldiers with political thoughts. Landwehr officers were discarded because they often disagreed with the military bureaucracy and were somewhat liberal in thought.

But from 1862 onwards there was some broadening and young men from any of the 'better classes' were welcome, unless they came from the capitalistic class, which the generals distrusted.

By the army reorganization of 1860–1 all power over the army was concentrated in the crown, which really meant that the army controlled itself, for the King was acutely influenced by senior officers. The 1860 clean-up was an intense weeding-out process, too. Fewer than 1,000 non-noble officers among the 3,000 of the infantry remained and of these other 2,000 most had passed through the cadets' institution, which meant that they were the sons of poor nobility. The officers of guard cavalry were 100 per cent. noble, while officership of other cavalry regiments was 95 per cent. noble. At this time Prussia had a population of 18,000,000 including 68,000 nobles, so their power in the army was disproportionate.

Frederick William IV, who had gone mad in 1858 and died in 1861, was succeeded by his brother William, a hard-headed man who was by upbringing and taste a soldier.

He was eager to wipe out the failure of 1850 and generally to improve the standard of the army. One of his immediate aims was for more conscripts, to keep pace with Prussia's growing population.

Roon was also imbued with the desire for revolutionary changes. A rather obtuse man, he planned to do away with the military reserve and to have only the one, regular army. He had no faith in volunteer armies, and especially did he distrust middle-class reserve. Fortunately for Prussian officers he did not have long enough to complete his changes.

Parliamentary dispute over the army brought about such an acute political crisis that William saw abdication as the only way out. At this point Roon persuaded William to try Bismarck as a last resort. On 8 October 1862 Bismarck became Prime Minister. Roon little knew the power he had unleashed.

Bismarck told Prussia and the world: 'The great questions of the day will not be settled by resolutions and majority votes . . . but by blood and iron.' It was a phrase the Germanic peoples would hear many times.

Bismarck had many aims, but one he did not have was unification of all Germans in one great national state, for he believed that such a state would swallow up Prussia and eventually control it. It would also want to protect German communities in east and south-east Europe and this would lead to conflict with Russia. Bismarck wanted Prussian friendship with Russia so as to keep Poland subdued and the great Junker estates intact.

CHAPTER IX

Moltke Introduces Technical Warfare

Bismarck was soon busy. In 1864 Schleswig-Holstein, the cradle of the Anglo-Saxon race, was the beautiful province which formed the bone of bloody contention between the Prussians and Danes. This was just a year after the English Prince of Wales had married a Danish princess.

The cause of the quarrel was extremely complicated and is beyond the scope of this book. But in November 1863 Bismarck determined that the difficulty would be settled with 'blood and iron'.

Briefly, the King of Denmark, Christian IX, wanted to rule over the Elbe duchies—as Schleswig-Holstein was called—in a way, according to Berlin, 'unfavourable to the rights and aspirations of their German population'. The Germanic Diet, or Council of German Sovereigns at Frankfurt, decreed 'execution' on the King of Denmark, who had a seat on the Diet on behalf of the duchies, and selected two of its members, Hanover and Saxony, to enforce the decision.

But not content with this, Austria and Prussia, the leading members of the Diet, also decided to take the field, as executive bailiffs—and this they did, early in 1864, with a force of 45,000 men. The Prussians were led by Prince Frederick Charles, the 'Red Prince', so called from the scarlet uniform of his favourite regiment, the Zieten Hussars. Commander of the combined force was Field-Marshal von Wrangel—a grim old *beau sabreur* who looked and acted like a survival of the Seven Years War.

The Danes had a force of only 36,000.

On 1 February von Wrangel gave the order. '*In Gottes Namen drauf!*'[1] and the Austro-Prussian Army swept over the Eider in a

[1] 'In God's name, forward!'

blinding snowstorm. Much of the disputed territory was quickly overrun, but the Danes clung grimly to their well-fortified redoubts at Düppel, a formidable line of defence.

The Red Prince was one of the best and bravest soldiers produced by the Hohenzollerns since the time of Frederick the Great. Strongly built, broad-shouldered, bull-necked, rough in manner and speech—he inspired the affection and courage of the Prussian soldier.

While heavy guns and other siege equipment were brought up, the Prince set some of his regiments to poke out the forward Danes with the bayonet. The Danes here had numerical superiority—26,000 against 22,000. But while the Danes were armed with the old smoothbore muzzle-loading musket the Prussians had the new needlegun, a parent of all modern breechloading and repeating rifles.

In one encounter a party of Danes threw down their weapons and held up their arms in surrender, but as the Prussians came on the Danes grabbed their muskets, fired a volley and charged with the bayonet. The Prussians, at twenty-five paces, shot them down to a man. This incident caused great bitterness among the Prussians, but later they put up a cross with the inscription 'Here lie twenty-five brave Danes, who died the hero's death'. In fact, the Prussians and Germans have always honoured brave foes.

Despite the weather and the difficulty of trench life, the young Prussian soldiers kept up their spirits. They mounted a water-pipe on a couple of cart wheels to make it look like a cannon and drew the fire of the Danes; they made sentries out of clay and they were cheered by frequent visits from the 'Red Prince'.

The Prussians were astonished at the presence on both sides of the line of English tourists—Kriegsbummler, the Prussians called them—who streamed over the battlefield in quest of sensation and adventure. They exposed themselves on parapet and skyline with what the Danes regarded as great bravery and the Prussians as damned stupidity. But neither side ordered the English civilians away.

By 17 April the Prussians had methodically dug several approach trenches towards the redoubts and had ninety-four heavy guns in position. The method of attack would have been a lesson for any foreign officer present, for by now the Prussian soldier had learned to be thorough. The attacking force was split into six columns. Each column comprised:

A company of infantry with orders to take extended front

about 150 paces from its particular redoubt and to open fire.

Pioneers and engineers with spades, axes, ladders, all storming gear, including blasting powder.

The storming party itself, a hundred paces to the rear.

Reserve-artillerymen, a further 150 paces back, to take over and fire the captured Danish guns.

At 4 a.m. on 18 April the Prussian artillery opened up and for six hours fired 11,500 shot and shell into the redoubt. A break of a few minutes followed, during which the Prussian padres—who were always at the front with their men—gave them some final words of religious encouragement and even shouted the order to advance. '*Nun, Kinder, in Gottes Namen!*' Then the Prussian charge went in, to the music of four bands.

At one point the Prussians could not force their way through the Danish palisades and were slaughtered where they stood until a pioneer named Klinke, shouting, 'Better one of us than ten!' rushed forward with a bag of blasting powder with which he blew the palisades and himself to pieces. The Prussians built a monument to him at the exact spot; and it stood there until the 1940s. They also built a Victory Column in Berlin on which they showed in lifelike bas-relief the figure of a Danish hero, Lieutenant Anker, most heroic Dane of the battle.

The battle was short, sharp and decisive and within fifteen minutes it was over. The Prussian success was hailed throughout Europe as a 'glorious victory', but to win it they had lost 16 officers and 213 men killed and 54 officers and 1,118 men wounded. Among the officers mortally wounded was General von Raven, who, as he was carried to the rear, said: 'It is high time that a Prussian General again showed how to die for his King.'

The King himself, with Bismarck, hurried to Düppel and reviewed his troops, clad exactly as they had been the day of the fight. Two weeks later picked men of the Düppel stormers escorted into Berlin the 118 Danish guns and forty colours captured. This parade made a tremendous impression on the Prussian public and, significantly, many young men rushed to enlist in the army.

This, the first of the three hammer blows that the Prussians were to strike within seven years, made a ringing sound throughout Europe and disturbed the rest of many a European statesman.

If the redoubts of Düppel hinted at the frightening efficiency of the Prussians, the great battle of Königgrätz (or Sadowa as the Austrians called it) showed it off completely.

Bismarck wanted a good pretext for going to war with Austria, simply to decide which of the two was to be the leading power among the German-speaking peoples. He found it over the captured duchies of Schleswig-Holstein, for both Austria and Prussia had different plans in mind for them. It is likely that Bismarck, a farsighted politician, had this in mind as early as 1859.

Bismarck consulted Moltke, who promised him victory—but only in a short war. Moltke had his short war; technically it lasted seven weeks, but hostilities were limited to three weeks, and the actual fighting to seven days and to one decisive battle.

Moltke was that rare combination—a realist-visionary. He saw that the new inventions would allow a war to be opened quickly and concluded quickly. He founded a Railway Department in the General Staff. In 1866 he had a Railway Corps, the first in Europe. Such troops had been successful in the American Civil War, just finished, at which Moltke had had hand-picked observers. Moltke also ordered ready-made mobilization plans, kept up to date day by day, so that the army could go into action within hours.

He showed how it was now possible for a commander-in-chief to remain many miles behind the lines yet intimately control complex troop movements by telegraph. At any moment a divisional general could contact the C.-in-C. because the C.-in-C. was always in the one spot. No longer was there a frantic search by gallopers to find the man in charge. Moltke was one of the first generals to run battles from a large map. At the same time Moltke gave his subordinate commanders a great deal of individual initiative.

Some of the German states sided with Austria, some with Prussia. Prussia soon defeated those who had chosen to fight her and was then free to tackle Austria. Unfortunately for the Austrians, Moltke directed the Prussian operations. The great battle thinker, 'the silent one in seven languages', as the Prussian General Staff called him, had many maxims, but perhaps the most important was—'March separately, strike together'.

Late in June 1866 he sent three main armies into Bohemia, on the upper Elbe, where the Austrians were concentrating. Totalling 220,000, they were led, respectively, by the Red Prince, the Crown Prince, who was Queen Victoria's son-in-law, and General von Bittenfeld. These three armies left from separate points and marched towards different points. Moltke sat among his maps in the offices of the General Staff, with his hand on the telegraph wire.

When the troops were marching up, the King of Prussia began to doubt whether a victory could really be won if an army were divided into so many parts, and these parts were transported along many routes to the battlefield. How could one be certain that this disjointed and complicated machinery would join itself up again when it got there? The King sent Bismarck to Moltke to inquire about the state of the operations. Bismarck came back and merely said: 'It is all right.'

The Austrians tried hard to block all three armies, but the destructive needlegun, the long lance of the plunging Uhlans and the slashing sabre of the cuirassiers cleared the way through a series of preliminary triumphs. The Austrians, though strong in cavalry, still had muzzle-loading firearms.

By 29 June all the Austrians with their Saxon allies and Hungarians—about 215,000 of them—had retired under the shelter of the guns of the fortress town of Königgrätz, on the left bank of the Upper Elbe. This united force was commanded by General Benedek.

On 30 June King William, then aged seventy, Moltke, Bismarck, and von Roon left Berlin by train for the scene of war.

The Austrians had chosen their position well. Along their front ran the boggy Bistritz brook, its banks dotted with farmsteads, villages and clumps of wood, fine cover for infantry. Behind the infantry was ground rising to a ridge, from which the Austrian batteries commanded the field. The Austrians had transformed the whole field into a natural fortress. The battle took place on 3 July along a front of five miles. In the centre the Prussians pushed battery after battery into action and kept up heavy fire, but the Austrians had ranged the ground better and their fire was more effective.

Columns of Prussian infantry moved forward to storm the villages of Sadowa, Dohalitz, Dohalicka and Benatek, where desperate hand-to-hand fighting occurred for the first time. But the mêlée here was nothing to the furious fight in Sadowa Wood. The Austrians clung to their positions under shells and bullets, but by eleven o'clock they had been bayoneted out.

King William wanted to storm frontally some entrenched Austrian batteries on Lissa Heights, but Moltke abruptly countermanded the royal order. A frontal charge against guns was not heroism to Moltke, but military stupidity. Bismarck was another Prussian who did not want to see his own soldiers wasted. He believed in weight against an enemy position, but he was against mass charges. Also, he did not want fighting troops taken out of the line to guard prisoners. A few years later he was to make it clear that he considered the army was taking too many prisoners.

Bismarck, a nicotine addict, was fond of telling a story about himself at the battle of Königgrätz. 'I had only one cigar remaining in my pocket, which I treasured carefully towards the end of the battle as a miser guards his hoard. I painted in glowing colours in my mind the happy hour when I should enjoy it after the victory. But I miscalculated my chances. A poor dragoon lay helpless, with both arms crushed, murmuring for something to refresh him. I felt in my pockets and found I had only gold. But stay—I still had my treasured cigar. I lit it for him and placed it between his teeth. You should have seen the poor fellow's grateful smile. I never enjoyed a cigar so much as that one which I never smoked.' Somehow, I just do not believe this story.

After hideous bloodshed and frightful scenes, the Crown Prince turned the Austrian right flank according to Moltke's plan. By four in the afternoon the Prussian line of attack resembled a huge semi-circle hemming in the masses of battered and broken Austrian troops. The nature of the ground had prevented much use of cavalry but on the line of retreat to Königgrätz several lance and sabre conflicts occurred. An Austrian cuirassier brigade, led by an Englishman named Beales, charged Prussian dragoons from the flank, but were in turn charged by Prussian Uhlans and were forced back.

The Austrians were in full flight towards the fortress, pursued by cavalry, volleyed at by infantry, showered with shells. Throughout the battle the King stayed exposed to shell and bullet, despite efforts by his staff to get him to safety. The Crown Prince rode up to meet his father and kissed his hand; the old man embraced him and handed him the *Pour le Mérite*.

By superior arms, superior numbers and superior strategy Prussia, at the cost of 10,000 casualties, had won a resounding victory. Austria lost 40,000 men, including 18,000 prisoners and 174 guns.

It had taken Frederick the Great seven years to humble Austria; it had taken Moltke seven days to achieve the same result. There was yet no such word, but 'blitzkrieg' could have been applied to Königgrätz. The legend of invincibility was building.

The infantry alone virtually decided this German fraternal war. Moltke said: 'The infantry has in every respect accomplished great deeds, in marching as well as in fighting . . . It met the attacks of the Austrian battalions with annihilating salvoes and countered the effect of enemy batteries by sending its snipers forward as far as the range of their own rifles, shooting down the gun crews and horses and capturing the guns. It is to such an extent conscious of its superiority over cavalry that in many cases it did not consider it worth while to form squares or clusters.'

Austria lost no territory to Prussia, but she withdrew from German affairs. Prussia annexed all German states north of the Main except Saxony and they were forced into a North German Confederation, controlled by Prussia.

Later in 1866 parliamentary developments established Prussia and her satellite German states as a blatant military monarchy. Clever middle-class men, finding no scope in politics, went into business. Restless, ambitious and able, they were also true patriots—they wanted to make their country great. Soon German industry became the most efficient in the world, with the emphasis on goods which would make her powerful rather than merely prosperous. Even at that early date they were experimenting with ersatz substitutes so as to lessen the country's dependence on raw materials from overseas. The nightmare of German industrialists was the knowledge that Britain controlled the seas.

Prussia was getting ready to take on France, but Bismarck's preparations were not complete. Amusedly, he even allowed France to protect the German states south of the Main, knowing that the protection afforded by Napoleon III was not worth much.

Moltke carried on the work of perfecting the military machine. With the help of the railway and the telegraph he managed armies of a size hitherto unknown.

Unlike most other German generals Moltke was not martially vain. Not for him the conceit that one German soldier was worth three of any other race. He shared with Bismarck and Roon the theory that one man equalled one man who merely cancelled each other out. Therefore to win a battle a general needed a majority and the bigger the majority the better. This was at a time when the French still believed that quality outweighed quantity; one Frenchman was at least as good as one and a half Germans, ergo, a small French army could defeat a big German army.

It was von Moltke, who with his narrow pale face most resembled Frederick the Great, who became the great representative of the German school. The will of Napoleon was in him united with the mind of Scharnhorst and Clausewitz. He combined vast knowledge with great will power. His pupil, Count Schlieffen, said in his memory: 'This man of action, when he was called to do immortal deeds, was sixty-five years old. He came from the writing-desk, from the loneliness of the study. He was a man of the map and the compasses and the pen. He could not boast, as Napoleon had, of having for nineteen years made a military promenade through Europe, but within six weeks he succeeded in encircling three proud armies. He did not conquer, he destroyed!'

Without being so well acquainted with the battle of Cannae (216 B.C.) as his pupil Schlieffen, Moltke, through his critical study of the Napoleonic campaigns, had arrived at Hannibalic, or, to be accurate, Greek ideas. Napoleon had often had failures through not succeeding in bringing enough troops on to the battlefield at the decisive moment. He marched his troops along a military road till a short way before the objective and only separated them to get every army group into its position.

Moltke, at his writing-desk, calculated the distance that a marching army corps took up on a road, and arrived at the surprising figure of $4\frac{1}{2}$ to 5 miles. If one wanted to march a second army corps along the same road and from the same place, the second corps could not start till the next day. It needed the rest of the time to let the first corps pass and then to get started itself. From these desk calculations Moltke drew the conclusion that every army corps needed its own road. That is to say, the armies march separately and only join forces on the battlefield to strike the great blow. Translated into Hannibal's way of thinking: 'It is important to know in advance how I am going to place my army. If I know that, I can arrange the march. All my available forces must be on the scene of action in time, the rest is determined by courage and luck!'

To translate such a seemingly simple idea into deeds, he needed an exact knowledge of every detail of troop movement and every apparently unessential thing. The troops had to know every movement necessary for the manœuvre, and Moltke needed to know to the second how much time the individual needed. An enormous amount of calculation was necessary to collate and work out all these thousands of small facts. Moltke achieved this preliminary work with compasses and pencil.

War has two aspects—a decipherable one, that of the intelligence, and an impenetrable one, that of the soul. Prince Frederick Charles of Prussia said: 'The soul has qualities by which battles may be won or lost.'[1]

The epoch-making importance of Moltke is to be found in the fact that he had clearly recognized these two aspects of war and acted accordingly. Everything that can be done by intelligence in the case of war should, according to Moltke's doctrine, be done before the battle. With Moltke begins the modern era, the era of gigantic armies, the age of 'technical' warfare. Napoleon III was still of the opinion that it was not necessary to make any dispositions before the commencement of the fighting. Moltke, on the other hand, once the fighting had begun, merely played the part of an observer on the battlefield. During the battle of Sedan, Moltke did not issue one single order to the troops engaged in the fighting. This is probably the greatest triumph ever celebrated by intelligence on the battlefield. He considered that the task of the Commander-in-Chief of an army had been carried out when the plan for the disposition of the troops had been decided even down to what might seem to be the most trivial details.

Moltke placed everything else in the hands of his officers, but in order to be able to do this, he considered the spiritual and moral preparation of the soldier in peacetime as of the highest importance.

The famous 'Secret Instructions for Higher Officers', which Moltke issued in 1869, were considered by foreign military attachés, who had got to know of the existence of these instructions, to be a clever recipe for the art of war, a collection of ruses and tricks. When these 'Secret Instructions' were published a few decades later, the military experts of foreign powers were astounded to find that the gist consisted of such sentences as: 'In peacetime the moral element comes into play only

---

[1] The leading teacher of military history in Moltke's time, Major Max Jähns, claimed that all the intellectual progress of tribal societies had been the result of war. He wrote: 'These steps have been the more manifold and quick, the more various and the more difficult has been the struggle of peoples for survival.' Goethe had said that army conditions reflected the state of society generally.

seldom, in wartime it is the primary condition of all success and forms the true value of an army. In war the qualities of character are of more importance than those of intelligence. In the activities of warfare what one does is often less important than how one does it. Determination and the resolute execution of a simple sort lead most surely to the goal. War places higher demands upon the officer who must obtain the confidence of the soldier by his personal conduct. It is expected of him that he should retain his calm and assurance even in the most difficult situations and that he should be seen in the forefront where the danger is greatest. The strength of an army lies in the platoon commander at the front, in the captain on whom all eyes are fixed.'

CHAPTER X

German Method versus French Élan—
The War of 1870–1

'Few nations have had so bad a neighbour as Germany has had in France.' So says no less an historian than General Fuller. He is right. France's complaints that Germany has always been the aggressor are false and have been fostered in the last half century as an excuse for French defeats.

Between 1675 and 1813 France invaded Prussia or Germany no fewer than fourteen times. Mostly she was victorious, but when she chose to attack Prussia in 1870 she made a disastrous mistake. Certainly Prussia was intent on uniting all Germany under her leadership and neither the King of Prussia, Bismarck nor Moltke were afraid of war, but Prussia did not seek it. Lieutenant-Colonel Baron Stoffel, French Military Attaché in Berlin, wrote to his Government on 12 August 1869: 'Prussia has no intention of attacking France; she does not seek war, and will do all she can to avoid it. But Prussia is farsighted enough to see that the war she does not wish will assuredly break out, and she is, therefore, doing all she can to avoid being surprised when the fatal accident occurs.' In fact, the Prussian General Staff had worked out a war plan in 1867 and had carefully kept it up to date ever since.

Careful registers were kept of the men in every town and district. A man could not move to another town or even change residence in the same town without at once notifying the police. When he turned twenty, every young man was required to report to the recruiting depot, or be classed as a deserter even before he was enlisted. If fit and intelligent he was at once enlisted, otherwise he was registered and sent away on the understanding that his body belonged to the army for the next thirty years.

When France declared war on 19 July 1870 every Frenchman was wild with confidence. The French certainly had many advantages. They had the revolutionary Chassepot breech-loading rifle with twice the range of the Prussian Dreyse needle-rifle; they had the *mitrailleuse*, a machine-gun of twenty-five barrels, axis grouped, which was sighted to 1,200 metres and could fire 125 rounds a minute. France had more men, more money and greater industrial output. Her army was one of veterans, who had fought in the Crimea, Italy and Algeria. Napoleon III was to command in person the armies in the field and would win back the old Rhine frontier, and his marshals were men like MacMahon, Bazaine and Canrobert.

But Prussia won because she intended to win, because the Prussian General Staff planned to win. Never had there been a General Staff like this. War had become the national industry of Prussia and its officers were war-businessmen. They brought to their trade a unique degree of efficiency. They used railways for war in a way the French had never dreamed of.

The Prussian soldier of 1870 had extraordinary endurance. He could march further, exist on poorer food and stand the test of battle better than French or Austrian troops. Many Prussians were citizen soldiers, with greater initiative than their professional opponents. They have been likened to the Crusaders, but this is absurd beyond the point that the Prussians and Germans fought with all the fervour of the Crusaders. But the Crusaders had a high and mighty cause; the Germans fought only for the sake of conquest and for the sake of fighting.

The old way of warfare was gone. The hallowed old combination of 'brilliant', usually intuitive, leadership, high morale and 'magnificent' cavalry charges was no match against a finely organized mass army, superior in number and directed not intuitively but with cold-blooded competence.

It has been said that the Prussian Army brought to France a 'martial barbarity' the French had never seen before.[1] This is a misleading term. The Prussians were not barbarous as the Russians were barbarous. Following Clausewitz, they merely fought without reserve. War was a game, as Clausewitz had said, but it was a bloody game for grown men.

---

[1] In 1870 Paris newspapers praised native troops for their bestialities. The *Indépendance Algérienne* wrote: 'Have no pity. Have no sentiments of humanity. Kill, plunder and burn!'

Perhaps, too, the Prussians enjoyed war for its own sake. According to Bismarck, when Moltke saw that war was inevitable in 1870 he became quite young and fresh again. 'He had got his war, his trade.'[1]

Far from being barbarous, the German High Command laid down definite rules about the treatment of the civil population. The people were not to be regarded as enemies and were to be free to continue their normal life. The High Command gave wide publicity to the severe punishments that would be inflicted on any soldier who harmed, robbed or even insulted an enemy civilian. But it also made clear that the inhabitants were expected to act peaceably and 'to abstain from every injury to the occupying troops'. Proclamations were made frequently to the troops.

An Army Order of 8 August 1870, on crossing the frontier, read:

> 'Soldiers! The pursuit of the enemy who has been thrust back after bloody struggles has already led a great part of our army across the frontier. Several corps will today and tomorrow set foot upon French soil. I expect that the discipline by which you have hitherto distinguished yourselves will be particularly observed on the enemy's territory. We wage no war against the peaceable inhabitants of the country; it is rather the duty of every honour-loving soldier to protect private property and not to allow the good name of our army to be soiled by a single example of bad discipline. I count upon the good spirit which animates the army, but at the same time I also count upon the sternness and circumspection of all leaders.
>
> Wilhelm'

Not all the soldiers were honour-loving, but the Germans pointed out that 'arbitrary destructions and ravages of the buildings' to which the French were so prone did not take place on the German side—except where they were due to the behaviour of the inhabitants in leaving their dwellings.

---

[1] Nietzsche (1844–1900), most famous of Germany's military-minded civilians, often praised war. He was fond of talking about 'the good war which sanctifies any cause', and he preached the principle of education through danger, which he believed brought lessons home more firmly than any other education.

The German historian Bluntschli wrote: 'If the soldier finds the doors of his quarters shut, and the food intentionally concealed or buried, then necessity compels him to burst open the doors and to track the stores, and he then, in righteous indignation, destroys a mirror, and with the broken furniture heats the stove.'

The French in return were not so charitable towards enemy civilians. On the outbreak of the war the French Press warned the Grand Duchy of Baden that 'even its women would not be protected'. The French Army and civilian officials encouraged civilians in all sorts of barbarities practised against the Germans.

The Prussian Army punished severely any soldier caught looting or robbing. Even two years after the Franco-Prussian (or Franco-German war) soldiers found with French private property were punished. However, this may not have been inspired by honest principle. The moment a soldier is allowed to pillage his discipline collapses and the German High Command would never tolerate that.

The Germans during the wars of 1870 punished severely any attack by their own men on envoys coming to the German lines under a white flag. The usual punishment was summary execution, but this happened rarely. The French claimed that only twice were their white flags violated. In contrast, Bismarck, in a dispatch on 9 January 1871, reported that twenty-one German envoys were shot by French soldiers while engaged on their mission.

There had been a time when an officer who gave his parole would have died before breaking it. In 1870–1 no fewer than 145 French officers, including three generals, broke their parole.

To check the prevalent escaping of French officers, General von Falckenstein commanded that for every escape ten officers, whose names were drawn from a hat, should be sent to a Prussian fortress. They lost all privileges of rank. The measure was condemned, but it was not contrary to international law.

Again, the Red Cross was frequently abused on the French side. The London *Times* reported instances of this and international observers reported breaches of the rights of the Red Cross.

No war has been fought without 'atrocities' and doubtless Germans were guilty of some in 1870–1, but the French were guilty of a great many more, especially when they realized they were losing. Then they became spiteful and malicious and frequently maltreated their own civilians.

Moltke reckoned correctly that the French would not be able to bring more than 250,000 men against his 381,000 and that, because of their railway communications, they would be compelled to assemble their forces about Metz and Strasbourg—which meant that they were separated by the Vosges Mountains. He assembled his three armies behind the fortresses of the middle Rhine and planned to split the French Army.

The two main French armies remained separate in Alsace and Lorraine and allowed themselves to be beaten separately. Moltke practised great enveloping manœuvres because of his numerical strength, and he succeeded in bottling up the larger parts of the French armies in Metz and Sedan.

The French people were impatient for action and a division drove in the Prussian detachment at Saarbrücken; this was represented as a great victory, but it was not. The German tide of invasion was soon pouring towards the frontier. On 6 August there were two French defeats—General Frossard beaten at Forbach and Marshal MacMahon and his fine Algerian regiments at Wörth. 'All may yet be regained,' Napoleon said in a telegram—an admission that much had already been lost.

On 12 August Napoleon, though he remained with the army, got cold feet and handed over supreme command to Marshal MacMahon. But the Prussians had one victory after another—Rezonville, Gravelotte, Spicheren, Beaumont.

Not that the Prussians had the war all their own way; they lost many men in frontal attacks until they introduced the system of running and falling—a dash forward and lying down to take cover and to fire.

Their leadership was not perfect. It certainly was generally good and retrospectively it has seemed superb because the French was so hopelessly inept. Sometimes on the battlefield soldier-courage and the innate quality of the men enabled them to fight well. But with the coming of the breech-loading rifle the French doctrine had changed; it decreed that the way to win battles was to sit tight on a good position, preferably on high ground, and destroy the enemy by rapid fire. The French military schools taught that the defensive was now the superior method.

The German doctrine was that only attack could give real results. It might be more costly, but the cost had to be paid. To attack was to assert from the outset the sense of power and the determination to win.

For hours on the day of the battle of Rezonville on 16 August the French had in their hands the opportunity for a great victory—if only they would attack. They let the Prussians attack and the Prussians won.

It was during this battle that the famous Todesritt—the Deathride—of the 16th Lancers and 7th Magdeburg Cuirassiers took place. This became to the German Army what the Charge of the Light Brigade is to the British.

The German general, Alvensleben, had to keep the French right occupied a little longer to give infantry time to arrive. He ordered General von Bredow to charge the French batteries on the right and their infantry supports. 'The fate of the army depends on gaining some breathing time,' he said.

The two regiments numbered little more than 600 sabres. The cuirassiers were the first into the line of French guns. They came charging through the dense smoke, surprising the gunners; von Schmettow, colonel of the regiment, cut down the battery commander. Every officer and man was ridden over or sabred, except one private who ran towards von Schmettow shouting that he surrendered. The colonel spared his life and let him go. As the cuirassiers dashed on towards the French infantry this solitary gunner, crouching beside one of the guns, watched the charge rolling away into the smoke of the rifle fire. The lancers had charged through another battery and followed up the cuirassiers; together they went through the line of infantry, which broke. Now the survivors of the charge were in turn charged by two French cavalry brigades, one led by Prince Murat, grandson of Napoleon's cavalry marshal.

Lieutenant Campbell of Craignish, a young Scottish officer serving with the cuirassiers, cut down the standard bearer of one of the French regiments and captured the eagle, but was wounded and lost it. Heavily outnumbered, the German horsemen kept together and fought their way out. Then they rode back through a storm of fire—rifles, machine-guns, cannon. Two-thirds of the officers and men strewed the 3,000 yards of ground over which they had charged. Only 104 cuirassiers and 90 lancers answered roll-call. It was a spectacular and historic charge.

At Mars-la-Tour—a place that was to become famous in 1914–18—the Prussians came up against a storm of fire such as they had never before experienced. It was an awful revelation of the power of the modern rifle, even when used in the wild, semi-disciplined way in which the French employed it. Of a total of ninety-five officers and 4,400 men who went into the fight, seventy-four officers and 2,415 did not return—mown down in half an hour. One of the best military historians of the day, Captain Fritz Hoenig, who took part in the battle said, 'I am not ashamed of owning that the French fire affected my nerves for months after. Troops that have survived an ordeal of this kind are demoralized for a considerable time. . . .' But rapid fire in itself never won a battle and despite their losses the Prussians triumphed.

Finally came the climax. On 1 September the fortress town of Sedan fell and Napoleon surrendered.

Moltke had waited for his victory with the calm of a mathematician. In his novel *The Collapse*, Emile Zola described how the French negotiators, who had arranged the armistice at Sedan, returned to their quarters. One of them said bitterly of Moltke that he did not look like a soldier but a chemist.

The official German historian said: 'This victory . . . crowns the united efforts of the German leaders and their men with a success almost unprecedented in history.'

This was no exaggeration. The French lost 3,000 killed, 14,000 wounded and 21,000 prisoners. A further 83,000 prisoners at the capitulation and 3,000 disarmed in Belgium made a total of 124,000. About 420 guns and *mitrailleuses*, 139 garrison guns, 1,072 carriages and 6,000 good horses were also captured.

Throughout the many battles of the war German artillery played a great part. Efficient breech-loaders served by competent crews, they played havoc with French defences. The guns were never short of ammunition; Moltke's plans had seen to that. Prussia had the best army service corps in the world. And every shell burst, unlike many of the French ones which simply buried themselves. A French officer taken prisoner at Sedan ascribed the German success to 'five kilometres of artillery'.

At this time there was no better example of an army at such a distance from home being so largely fed and supplied from its own stores.

When German staff officers rode through areas and towns and fortifications devastated by artillery the lesson was not lost on them. 'We want more and better guns,' they said thoughtfully. 'If the artillery preparation is heavy enough the infantry can simply take over after it.'

The Germans also shelled Dijon, Chateaudun and Bazeilles —but with some justification. The French called the attack on

Chateaudun 'barbarous', but a French writer, Monod, stated that 'the inhabitants of Chateaudun, regularly organized as part of the National Guard, aided by franctireurs of Paris, did not defend themselves by preparing ambushes, but by fighting as soldiers. Chateaudun is bombarded; nothing could be more legitimate, since the inhabitants have made a fortress of it.'

German newspapers had complained loudly about the French shelling of Saarbrücken and Kehl, but the German High Command openly admitted that the attacks were legitimate, as German troops were in the towns.

By the end of September Paris was surrounded, and while Metz, Belfort, Strasbourg, Toul, Verdun and Mézières held out, the Defence Nationale raised new armies. Then one by one the fortresses fell, except Belfort, and on 17 December the bombardment of Paris began. On 21 January 1871 the city capitulated.

But eleven days before, an even more important event had occurred. In the Hall of Mirrors in the Palace of Versailles William I of Prussia was proclaimed Emperor of Germany. From now on, for all practical purposes, Prussia and Germany were one country politically, intellectually and emotionally.[1]

Not that William I received the crown gladly; he tried to avoid it and he refused to speak to Bismarck the day he was forced to accept it.

Bismarck was merciless. France was forced to surrender Alsace and Lorraine and to pay an enormous indemnity. It was Bismarck, riding the crest of victory, who induced the German princes to offer the Imperial crown to William I.

In a brief nine years Prussia, once the weakest of powers, had become the master state of Europe. Only Bismarck knew how fortunate Prussia had been. Had the European nations combined, they could have destroyed her before she achieved the astonishing victory over the French.

From the point of view of a military study the war had been won by Prussian regular officers, officers from Moltke down to the most junior officer—all skilled, unemotional and incisive, imbued with an almost sacred spirit of destruction.

The German common soldier emerged from the war with a tremendous reputation. Various writers of several nationalities

---

[1] The military capacity of the Prussians increased the more they developed as a nation until finally, with all Germans, they formed an empire. Prussian qualities proved to be German and the farther the Germans advanced along the road the more certainly their impurities fell from them. (*Signal Magazine*, May 1942.)

—men who had been observers during the war—referred to his physical hardness, his initiative, his loyalty and discipline. Especially to his discipline.

There were differences between German and Prussian soldiers—as indeed there were soldierly differences among the Saxons, the Bavarians, the Hanoverians and the others. But from henceforth to the world they were all Germans.

In addition to his love for lager the German soldier liked tobacco almost as much as the Tommy did. Many a German writer has seriously suggested that the German victory over the French was due chiefly to the fact that the Germans had plenty of tobacco, while the French had practically none. In a charge before Saarbrücken, German hussars rode into action smoking cigars and they went right on smoking, even at the height of the action. The Uhlan generally preferred a large German pipe capable of holding an ounce of tobacco at a fill.

Snuff-taking was prevalent. It became popular owing to Moltke's addiction to it. During the week of Sedan he consumed over a pound of it. Most N.C.O.s and privates carried a snuff-box and they took a pinch of it when there was neither time nor opportunity for a smoke. The habit persisted until 1914.

The Franco-Prussian War should have shown the trend of future wars to leaders of armies and leaders of nations. It was inevitable that the French would copy the Prussian prototype,[1] but nobody wondered what would happen if in the future two mass armies of equal strength met. Had anyone given this possibility sufficient thought the 1914–18 impasse might well have been prevented.

[1] Before 1871 was over a French parliamentarian demanded that the French Army model itself on the Prussian. 'The victory of Germany has been the victory of science and reason. Prussia is our best model. We need a military law closely copying the Prussian system.'

CHAPTER XI

German Army System 1870–1914

The war of 1870–1 made Germany the strongest power in Europe and determined to grow even stronger. The Germans, with their agile brains and capable fingers, with their ability to impose and accept discipline, and their growing pride were launched on a campaign for domination.

The government of Germany after 1871 developed quickly into a form of dictatorship—the King of Prussia being the dictator. Under him the General Staff handled military matters and the Chancellor civil ones. The Chief of the General Staff was really answerable to nobody and this gave the army great vanity and arrogance. In fact, though no war[1] occurred for more than forty years this was the golden age of the German Army.

The army worked out fantastically elaborate schemes for upholding and cultivating honour, for in this army rather more than in any other the officers were determined to place themselves apart from the other classes. 'Honour' was the stratagem by which they believed they could achieve this, and they gained honour by enthusiastic blood-letting.

Duels between officers had always occurred frequently—some contemporary German historians say the average was one a week—and they were practised when other nations had given them up. It became so serious that the King himself signed regulations to curb it. The regulations were reasonable, but they had little effect, for they did not make the officers change their opinions about duels. Both the victor and the vanquished gained status through a duel. In some ways,

[1] There were some foreign campaigns.

provided the vanquished was not too badly hurt, he came out of the fray in a better light than the victor. A visible bullet wound—officers fought only pistol duels—was not considered disfiguring but a masculine ornamentation and it fascinated women. University students who had acquired sabre scars shamelessly traded on them if they joined the army.

Officers were, in effect, above the civil law. An offence such as assaulting a civilian or damaging private property in a drunken rage was tried by the so-called court of honour, which was lenient about such aberrations.

The courts were much more strict about cases of 'abnormal behaviour', the charge levelled against any officer with independent thoughts or outspoken opinions. By getting rid of such dangerous characters the Officers' Corps kept its corporate intelligence to a satisfactorily stultified level. This was damaging to army efficiency.

Despite the great efforts of the reformers of the previous seventy years it was not possible for an able man in the ranks to reach higher than non-commissioned rank. Merit had nothing to do with advancement and a junior officer without social standing and without connections remained a junior officer.

In the 1870s and 1880s the educational standard of officer entrants dropped alarmingly. Right down to 1914 educational weaknesses in a candidate were overlooked if he had 'character', which in effect meant that if he was the dull or lazy son of a wealthy man, noble or otherwise. A study of applications shows that in many cases character of a candidate was only briefly described and in some cases the space allowed for a description was not even completed. But great importance was placed on the father's profession and his wealth. Once again, class was paramount.

A report by a military inspector in 1883 was unusually outspoken. The inspector had studied the cases of the worst 120 pupils in war schools and observed that 'an unpleasantly large proportion of them carry names which for generations have traditionally belonged to the officers' corps'.

An officer hardly dared show himself in the streets except in uniform and never without his sword, whether wearing dress or undress uniform.[1]

In its efforts to imbue its young soldiers with manliness the

[1] This persisted until the occupation after World War I, was revived during Hitler's mis-reign and vanished again during the second occupation.

German Army has long gone to almost unbelievable extremes. An Englishman who was sent to a German military college at the age of twelve some time in the 1890s has left a vivid account of his arrival.

'I was met at the gates of the barracks by one of the senior cadets, who roughly demanded my name. I introduced myself with as respectful a bow as I could accomplish, whereupon . . . he struck me across the face with a dog-chain. This was not because I was English, but because I was a newcomer ready to be broken in.

'The corporal of my room was one of those characterless men, very common in Prussian service, who can maintain discipline only by force.[1] He was the most finished bully I have ever met. One of his favourite pastimes was to order a recruit to hold three large German dictionaries under each arm, then stand on tip-toe, bend his knees, and remain for ten or fifteen minutes in this position. When he fell he was kicked or thrashed with a foil.'

In a German military college at this time reveille sounded at 6 a.m. and after preparing for the day, the boys had breakfast of weak coffee and black bread at seven o'clock. Classes began soon after this, with a short break at 10.30 a.m. then instruction until noon. From noon until 1 p.m. they drilled. At two o'clock they marched to dinner and at three they began an afternoon of fencing, gymnastics, swimming and dancing. At 8 p.m. they had supper of bread and cheese and twice a week a thin lager.

Any morals the boys took with them to college were soon lost. They strove to copy the dissipations and immoralities of their senior officers. Therefore to return to college blind drunk was as fine an achievement as winning the Iron Cross. The hero of the school was he who could claim the most intimate knowledge of women. Homosexuality was allegedly commonplace and was sometimes condoned by authority.

Still, methods and manners differed from college to college, depending on whether it was for Prussians, Bavarians, Hanoverians and so on.

Training lasted five years, ending in a relatively easy examination. A boy's father or guardian would then offer him to the regiment of his choice and the regiment, being satisfied, would accept the boy as an ensign—a rank corresponding to

[1] For many years the non-com problem in the German Army was acute. Commanding officers had to put up with what they could get and be grateful.

British sergeant's rank. After a year in the ranks the boy entered a probationary stage, throughout which he was under the charge of an officer.

He now dined in the officers' mess, where his manners were as carefully watched and reported on as his ability in manœuvres. He was expected to drink and to be able to hold his liquor. Heavy drinking was common until the General Staff began a temperance movement about 1910. It was only partly successful and even today most German officers are hard drinkers.

The cadet would fight a duel or two, though not too seriously, get into debt and into trouble with women and he would strut about the garrison towns in spectacular uniforms.

After another two years the cadet sat for another examination, this time to qualify for a commission. If he passed, the cadet would return to his regiment with the rank of sergeant major. His name was then brought before the officers of the regiment as a candidate for a permanent commission. Acceptance was by vote, which was then forwarded to Army Headquarters.

Snobbery was rife at this time—as it had been for a century—and a young man without the prefix von had little chance of gaining full commissioned rank, in a regiment whose members were vons; many of them, probably, would be Barons or Counts. There were other ways of gaining a commission, but once possessed it did not carry the same status as that gained in the recognized manner.

Many messes made a point of getting a newly joined officer blind drunk. Each officer would insist on drinking a toast with the newcomer; then he would be required to offer a toast to them, in turn from the senior to the most junior officer present.

The officers who eventually reached the General Staff and senior field positions were trained in the Kriegsakademie, the German counterpart of the British Staff College. The training was intense and non-stop and so arduous that there was a not altogether facetious belief in the army that a man who had been through the Kriegsakademie never looked happy again. The key requirements were concentration and constructiveness.

Nevertheless, selection for the Kriegsakademie was sought after. A posting to a garrison on the Polish frontier was long considered a form of punishment, while a posting to the colonies was a hell on earth to be avoided at any cost.

Unlike English officers' messes, the German mess did not bar conversation about ladies and their moral standards, a fruitful source of duels since the woman being discussed by one officer was often enough somebody else's mistress.

In sport the British and German officer had much in common. For the Englishman there was polo, tennis, riding; for the German, hunting, riding, shooting—and, of course, his eternal woman-chasing. The difference was that a British officer was expected to participate in sports; for the German they were largely optional.

German officers were expected to attend all garrison social functions as a matter of duty. They were even expected to take part in every dance and any junior officer who dared to 'sit one out' would be ordered to the centre of the ballroom and lectured by his C.O., who would point out that the officer was not there for his own amusement.

One tradition was that an officer did not write his memoirs. General von Alvensleben formulated the rule that 'a Prussian general dies but he does not leave any memoirs'. This became firm tradition.

In 1887–8 Moltke did indeed write his account of the Franco-Prussian War, but there was no personal vanity about this literary effort. He told his nephew that memoirs only served to gratify the writer's vanity. His only purpose was to give a concise account of the war, although he did indeed give some personal opinions. Many officers felt that even Moltke was guilty of breaking an unwritten law when he wrote the book.

Before 1914 the Prussian army leaders not only punished but persecuted officers who wrote critically of the army. Irregular opinions were taken as proof of disloyalty and on some occasions, as treason. There was the infamous case of Captain Hoenig, crippled in the Franco-Prussian War, who became a competent writer on military history. He seriously criticized the General Staff, one of whose members, General von Bernhardi, challenged him to a duel. Hoenig, who was not only crippled but half-blind as well, declined. But the Staff had its revenge. A 'court of honour', which included officers with whom Hoenig had served, deprived him of the right—almost sacred to any German officer—to wear the uniform. The court had dishonoured itself, not Hoenig, but how many Germans realized this?

The Germans devoted a lot of thought and literature to war after 1871, for when the German contemplated war he had to assume, in accordance with the geographical position of his country, that he would perhaps have to fight on several fronts. From the very nature of things, therefore, every military consideration of the Germans had to aim at the annihilation of the enemy's army. Annihilation was possible, however, as the examples of Epaminondas and Hannibal, Frederick the Great, Napoleon and Moltke proved, only when the attacker initiated a mobile battle with the object of falling upon the enemy's flank or of encircling and destroying piecemeal.

In 1893 General Graf von Haeseler is said to have addressed his troops in Lorraine with these words: 'Our civilization must build its temple on mountains of corpses, an ocean of tears and the groans of innumerable dying men. It cannot be otherwise.'[1]

The infantry tactics which developed from Moltke's period were a mixture of most adaptable speed and concentrated strength. The column had to be able to extend into a long line of riflemen or to move back into a powerful formation full of driving force as circumstances required.

This meant that the infantryman had to practise continually at moving at the double. The Prussian infantry, on the pattern of which all the infantry forces in the world were very soon trained, now practised two paces—Frederick's old marching pace and the double at 112 paces. Various battle formations were now carried out at the double. The battalion consisted of four companies. When deploying for battle the two flank companies advanced first and formed lines of skirmishers. The others brought up the rear as reserves at intervals of 150 yards.

The Prussian drill was the super-personal element which held together the persons engaged in the fighting. Drill, the continued practice of which was decried as soul-destroying, provided the guarantee that the individual made the right decision even in the most terrible, nerve-wrecking and soul-shattering moments of battle. It protected the soldier in battle because it prevented him from doing the wrong thing . . . Robots are no good in battle, but a man must learn to act contrary to that natural instinct of panic. The ordinary German soldier had the reason for drill carefully explained to him and he understood these reasons. It is a pity that other nations did not take so much trouble to explain its necessity.

After 1871 the French discovered Clausewitz and, as they

[1] According to the French Compte de Pange, resident in Lorraine.

thought, they put his doctrines to work for them. In 1908 Foch preached Clausewitz at the French Staff College, a stupid thing to do because Clausewitz's thoughts were more philosophical than practical and they had been tempered by the age in which he lived. A philosophy can be transplanted to another age, but not a method.

Clausewitz was working for the Germans, not the French. The Germans understood his philosophy. Devotion to his theories stifled independent French thought. Foch and his colleagues, accepting new weapons but not studying them, believed that they would give practical momentum to offence. The Germans already knew, from their observers in the American Civil War, that heavy artillery aided defence rather than attack.

Liddell Hart cites the French staff officer, Colonel de Grandmaison as saying that 'the French Army knows no other law but the offensive. All attacks are to be pushed to the extreme... charge the enemy with the bayonet to destroy him . . . This result can only be obtained at the price of bloody sacrifice'.

Many men did see that the next war would be a static one. As early as 1902 the Swiss *Military Review* published an article by Emile Mayer, in which he said: 'The next war will put face to face two human walls, almost in contact, only separated by the depth of danger, and this double wall will remain almost inert, in spite of the will of either party to advance. Unable to succeed in front, one of these lines will try to outswing the other. The latter, in turn, will prolong its front, and it will be a competition to see who will be able to reach farthest. There will be no reason for the war to stop. Exterior circumstances will bring the end of the purely defensive war of the future.'

Between 1871 and 1914 the German Army increased in size as it did in independence. The Prussian War Office was the 'impartial' ministry of war for the whole German Confederation.[1]

Nowhere else in Europe was the army so completely insulated from political interference, although, paradoxically it guaranteed political power for the class from which the officers came. Nowhere in Europe was the army more integrated and unified, nowhere was the civilian populace so successfully militarized. The civilians gave the German Army the support that most other armies dreamed about.

[1] By some anomaly three south German states retained war ministers of their own until 1919.

By the year 1898, when Bismarck died, whoever led Germany had almost ceased to count. Somebody could be relied upon to give the necessary leadership, the forging had already been completed.

One of Bismarck's last utterances was: 'We Germans fear God and nothing else in the world.' From here it was only a short step to the point where even God ceased to count.

Prussian patriotism has always been different from that of any other nation. It is compelled patriotism, and pre-1914 it was a rowdy jingoism appealing to basic lusts. At one time German boys living near the French border were encouraged to stand right on the border and see how far they could spit into France. School books preached racial hatred and ridicule. In pre-1914 textbooks there were passages laughing at England attempting to be a world power without national service. They were especially rich in stories about the weak, cowardly and treacherous French.

With admirable practical psychology—which Hitler was to take to the ultimate—the Kaiser introduced a great range of badges for proficiency. They included badges for marksmanship, riding, signalling, gunnery and so on.

But the German soldier has often been the victim of eccentric schemes dreamed up by civilian experts who happened to have the ear of somebody on the General Staff. In the early 1900s some professor urged a sugar diet and before long many senior officers were supporting the idea. It gathered so much momentum that it was almost the secret weapon by which the German Army would sweep Europe before it. The soldier was given sugar when he was tired, depressed, bad-tempered, ill, hungry and thirsty. Even when he felt like a lot of beer he was given sugar. Finally expense put an end to the scheme.

There was never any cameraderie between officers of high and low rank or between N.C.O.s and men. The gulf was deep and beyond bridging and remains so today, though not to the same autocratic extent. The only occasion on which officers and men had any association was the Emperor's birthday,[1] but the comradeship was by order.

The German system of courts martial was unusual and quite different from that of the British Army. The accused soldier was brought before a military auditor, a kind of lawyer, of which there is a regular staff attached to each corps. If he proposed a court martial the prisoner was tried by several

[1] And later on Hitler's birthday.

officers, three sergeants and three privates. The privates did not sit if the prisoner was a sergeant. The trial was conducted by the auditor, really a counterpart to the British Judge Advocate.

When the question—Guilty or Not Guilty?—was put, the most junior private answered first and so on, in progression.

The German Army on the march in the days before mechanization was a tremendous spectacle. Swarms of cavalry roved far and wide ahead of the main body, which was led along the roads by other cavalry formations. Then came the guns and the horse artillery, followed by long columns of infantry. Then more artillery, and still more. Each column had its supply wagons, followed in turn by reserves, more infantry, more artillery, heavy siege guns and more supplies. The whole mass moved with machine-like precision and regularity.[1]

The German Army took its manœuvres very seriously and usually invited foreign observers to watch the complicated convolutions of several corps at work in the field. They were mainly intended as a test for officers, all of whom assumed a rank one grade higher than usual. A platoon commander would control a company, a captain a battalion and a colonel a brigade.

But German efficiency did not always triumph. At the manœuvres in 1898 a colonel was tried as a brigade commander, but under the critical and intolerant eye of the Emperor he hurried his orders and failed to allow plenty of time for the great body of cavalry to carry out its movements. Sabres drawn and lances down, they charged full tilt into another cavalry formation. Several men were killed, dozens were thrown and riderless horses compounded the disaster which was soon clouded by dust. The incident was kept from the public and the colonel was kicked out of the army.

In 1900 the German Army sent a brigade to China at the time of the Boxer Rising. The Kaiser addressed the brigade in 'beautiful Imperial words', as the *Frankfurter Zeitung* expressed it. What he said was: 'Make for yourselves reputations like the Huns of Attila. Spare none!'

The brigade did as their Kaiser had ordered. They fired on unarmed Chinese at close range and plundered at every opportunity. For amusement they would stroll along the banks of the Pei-Ho and pot-shot at junks in mid-stream. They

[1] It was this rigidity which held up the German advance at Liège in 1914, for this battle was more of a German reverse than a Belgian victory.

strutted in the streets and made themselves unpopular with their allies.

Probably the General Staff hoped for war, even if only to justify its preparations. The German Army has always possessed the most perfect machinery in the world for swift and efficient mobilization of its forces, for the simple reason that everything is in perpetual preparation for war. No declaration of hostilities could ever take the General Staff by surprise.

From the 1860s all orders and instructions were in force and constantly being amended. Should mobilization be decided upon, the commanding officer of a unit would receive a one-word telegram—Kriegs-Mobil. It was enough to set the machinery in motion. Each unit fell in at once, was marched to the stores where every man had a little compartment of his own, already packed with a new set of equipment, right down to boots. The only equipment not renewed was the saddles of the cavalry. Recruits were handed over to the reserve battalion or squadron.

The preparations were so thorough that an army of 300,000 men could be in the field twenty-four hours after the sending of the Kriegs-Mobil telegrams. A carefully trained staff super-intended railway mobilization. All plans were modified every year to ensure secrecy and only the colonels and adjutants of regiments were admitted to the secrets.

The word had almost magical properties, as the following incident shows. In 1898 some irresponsible Frenchman called the Kaiser a liar. Berlin flashed Kriegs-Mobil to its commanders. Within a few minutes the leading cavalry squadrons were entraining; within two hours they were on the French frontier. On the train the officers were issued with French ordnance maps, on which were marked, in red ink, certain bridges, railway junctions and other key positions that had to be destroyed. Luckily for the French the scare was short-lived. The advance units received orders countermanding the advance and the men were back in garrison in time for dinner.

Germany's intention to dominate Europe was made evident by her plans for a grand fleet, which reached fruition in 1900. Supposedly the fleet was for defence, but Germany's limited coastlines needed coast artillery, not ships, and her colonies were not worth defending. In any case, German warships were built for speed and had only a short cruising range. Naturally enough, Britain looked on the massive German fleet as a direct threat—which it was. But it was also a symbol of Germany's hunger for greatness—greatness in the British fashion.[1] The General Staff, through jealousy, opposed the building of a large navy, but weight of public opinion, backing the naval experts—Tirpitz was one of them—brought it into being.

In the early years of the century there were complaints about perversion and homosexuality in the army. Army records are vague about it, but in 1907, following publicity about army brutality and perversion, many senior officers as well as non-coms were thrown out of the army.

Berlin Police Commissioner von Tresckow was explicit enough in a diary entry on 3 July 1907: 'The Commanders of the Berlin and Potsdam Guard regiments come to me almost every day to ask my advice as to what they can do to combat the pederasty which has become prevalent among the soldiers of their regiments . . . complaints had been made against the unabashed conduct of the soldiers especially in the Zelte neighbourhood and other parts of the Tiergarten. In these places the soldiers behaved like prostitutes. They directly offered themselves to the homosexuals, who mostly belonged to the cultured classes. . . . My men reported that the goings-on were absolutely scandalous.'

Many years later several important Germans were involved in homosexual scandals and, as we shall see, perversion was rife among leading Nazis, but there is no evidence to support any allegation that perversion was anything more than a minor irritation in the army. Perversion was much more pronounced in the French, Austrian, Turkish and Spanish Armies at various times. German officers and men never seem to have found it too difficult to get their own or foreign women to co-operate willingly.

Homosexual or not, some German troops, especially officers, could be very overbearing. This was starkly seen in the Saverne (Zabern) incident of 1913. Saverne was one of the few districts of Alsace loyal to Germany, but loyalty did not buy moderation from the officers of the garrison. Arrogant, overbearing members

[1] The Germans had not only a political but a spiritual dislike of being surrounded by 'great' powers. They had an inferiority complex, which showed itself in the arrogance of the troops and the hero worship the civilian populace gave to them. A great power had colonies, therefore Germany must have colonies, even if they were useless. By 1914 she had acquired some big territories—with just 5,000 Germans among the lot. What they cost in taxation only the Treasury knew, but nobody complained, least of all the troops.

of a regiment thoroughly soaked in the Prussian tradition, they provoked quarrels with the townspeople.

A German officer drew his sword and wounded a French Alsatian youth because the young man had laughed at him in the street. Eventually the commanding officer arrested and gaoled some civilians. This high-handed action brought a vote of condemnation against the government in the Reichstag—but nothing else happened. The army acquitted the C.O., thus condoning army bullying. It was part of the creed that the army could do no wrong.

The Prussian garrison was replaced by Saxon infantry, less aggressive men than the Prussians, but by now it was almost too late; to the French all troops from across the Rhine were arrogant Germans.

The rise in population kept pace with mounting German nationalism. By 1910 the population was 65,000,000—a great reserve of man-power. Armaments shot up. In the 1880s Britain, France and Russia spent much more on armaments than Germany did. In 1913 Germany was spending nearly as much as Britain and France together.

Not every observer was hypnotized by the German Army. After the manœuvres of 1911 the military correspondent of *The Times* wrote:

'There is insufficient test of the initiative of commanders of any units, large or small. There is nothing in the higher leading at manœuvres of a distinguished character, and mistakes are committed which tend to shake the confidence of foreign spectators in the reputation of the command.

'The Infantry lack dash, display no knowledge of the ground, are extremely slow in their movements, offer vulnerable targets at medium ranges, ignore the service of security, perform the approach marches in old-time manner, are not trained to understand the connection between fire and movement and seem totally unaware of the effect of modern fire. The Cavalry drill well and show some beautifully trained horses, while the Cavalry of the Guard is well handled. But the Army was in many ways exceedingly old-fashioned, the scouting is bad and mistakes are made of which our Yeomanry would be ashamed.

'The Artillery with its out-of-date material and slow and ineffective methods . . . appeared so inferior that it can have no pretensions to measure itself against the

French on anything approaching level terms. Finally dirigibles and aeroplanes present the fourth arm in a relatively unfavourable light.'

The *Times* man did not mince words. He said that the German Army, apart from its numbers, confidence in itself and high state of organization, did not show any signs of superiority over the best foreign armies and in some ways did not rise above second-rate. The army had trained itself stale and should be disbanded for a year to give everybody a rest. He even went so far as to say that the military spirit of the country was slowly but surely evaporating under the passion for making money.

Nevertheless, in 1914 the recruit was supposed to know almost as much as his superiors in military matters and technicalities. Among other things, he had to know the history of the Prussian Royal family and the history of the war of 1870. He had to memorize the stations of all the army corps of the German Army and the garrisons, divisions and brigades of his own corps and the names of the generals commanding them. He had to be able to take a carbine to pieces and put it together again. Within a few months he was expected to know everything there was to know of the theory of soldiering. But before long many cherished theories would be exploded.

CHAPTER XII

Handbook of War

Long before the Great War of 1914 the German General Staff issued to most of its officers a copy of the *Kriegsbrauch im Landkriege*—the handbook of war. This was something akin to the British officers' Field Service Pocket Book, except that it did not go into so much detail about actual military matters. The German War Book was a combination of philosophy and advice; it was intended as a guide to officers as to what was permissible and what was not. As the book was in such wide use there can be no doubt that the staffs of every army in Europe—and probably many other officers as well—had copies of it. Its contents were frank and left nobody in doubt as to how Germany would wage war in the future.

In 1915 the book was published in English, with sneering, almost vitriolic notes appended by the English editor, J. H. Morgan, Professor of Constitutional Law at University College, London.

In human terms his attitude to the War Book was understandable, for at that time everything German had a nasty smell and during war it was as legitimate to abuse and vilify the enemy as to shoot at him. But a jurist of Morgan's ability might have been more objective.

He observes that 'the German staff are nothing if not casuists. In their brutality they are the true descendants of Clausewitz, the father of Prussian military tradition'.

Since brutality is inevitable in war, the Germans were brutal, but brutality cannot be appended to the average German soldier[1] any more than irresponsibility can be appended to the

[1] I except the Nazi punitive units of World War II.

Australian or cowardice to the Italian, as national militaristic traits.

The German soldier was no hypocrite. Major-General von Ditfurth, writing in 1915, was quite frank about the German attitude—as frank, say, as General Sherman was about the reasons for his devastation of Georgia during the American Civil War.

The German General said: 'No object whatever is served by taking any notice of the accusations of barbarity levelled against Germany by our foreign critics. Frankly, we are and must be barbarians, if by this we understand those who wage war relentlessly and to the uttermost degree. . . . Every act of whatever nature committed by our troops for the purpose of discouraging, defeating and destroying our enemies is a brave act and a good deed and is fully justified . . . Our troops must achieve victory. What else matters?'

Professor Morgan quotes from Clausewitz: 'Laws of war are self-imposed restrictions, almost imperceptible and hardly worth mentioning, termed "usages of war". Now philanthropists may easily imagine that there is a skilful method of disarming and overcoming an enemy without causing great bloodshed, and that is the proper tendency of the art of war. However plausible this may appear, still it is an error which must be extirpated, for in such dangerous things as war the errors which proceed from the spirit of benevolence are the worst . . . To introduce into the philosophy of war itself a principle of moderation would be an absurdity. . . . War is an act of violence which in its application knows no bounds.'

Even so, the General Staff had long before laid down strict rules for the treatment of prisoners-of-war, stating, for instance, that 'the camps in which prisoners-of-war are quartered must be healthy, clean and decent as possible; they should not be prisons or convict establishments. . . . Prisoners can be put to moderate labour proportionately to their position in life; work is a safeguard against excesses. The tasks should not be harmful to health or in any way dishonourable. Prisoners should be killed only in the case of extreme necessity. Only the duty of self-preservation and the security of one's own state can justify it.'[1]

[1] Napoleon killed 2,000 Arabs in Jaffa in 1799. Other prisoners were shot out of hand in the rising of La Vendée, 1790–3; in the Carlist War of 1834–41; in the French campaign in Mexico and the American Civil War. Other shootings of prisoners occurred later, as we shall see.

Morgan comments: 'The only difference between Clausewitz and his lineal successors is not that they are less brutal but that they are more disingenuous.'

Elsewhere Morgan accuses the Germans of 'frightfulness', 'terrorism', 'ruining the soul of a nation', 'smashing a people's spiritual resources', 'notorious malpractices'. 'Can it be,' he asks, 'that this people which is always making an ostentatious parade of its culture is still red in tooth and claw?'

He paints a picture of Belgium's suffering as a result of the German war doctrine. 'In sorrow and in anguish, in anguish and in darkness, Belgium is weeping for her children and will not be comforted because they are not. The invader has spared neither age nor sex, neither rank nor function, and every insult that malice could invent or insolence inspire has been heaped upon her bowed head. The hearths are cold, the altars desecrated, the field untilled, the granaries empty. . . . The very stones in her cities cry out. Never since the captivity of Babylon has there been so tragic an expatriation. . . .'

Much of this was poetic extravagance. Belgium suffered as any overrun country suffers, but many of the stories of German outrage were sheer propagandist fiction which in itself is justified in total war. Belgian civilians also brought some of their sufferings on their own heads by sniping at German soldiers or by cutting their throats in the darkness of a side street. Did they expect no retaliation?

Many German field officers were distressed that some Town Majors—who in their restricted orbit had the authority of a dictator—made all civilian inhabitants, including women, salute all officers. It was this sort of idiocy rather than blatant atrocities that made the Germans unpopular.

Most of the civilized world points the finger at Germany as the inventors of atrocity, although it is as old as man itself and has been, at sometime or another, practised by every army in the world. There was a great outcry about German atrocities in 1914, but Englishmen and Frenchmen and Americans had advocated atrocious acts long before the war. Major-General Charles Ross in *Representative Government and War* was frank about it. 'War is a relapse to barbarism. There is no disloyalty in war save that which forbears to spare; no morality, save that which ends quickly. Love and sentiment are out of place in the struggle for existence. . . . The exercise of barbaric qualities governs the day. Atrocities are the last recourse of strategy in its efforts to force an enemy to its knees.'

The High Command expressed its views quite frankly in the War Book:

'Now although according to modern conception of war it is primarily concerned with the persons belonging to the opposing armies, yet no citizen or inhabitant of a State occupied by a hostile army can altogether escape the burdens, restrictions, sacrifices and inconveniences which are the natural consequence of a State of War. A war conducted with energy cannot be directed merely against the combatants of the Enemy State and the positions they occupy, but it will and must seek to destroy the total intellectual and material resources of the latter.

'Consequently the argument of war permits every belligerent state to have recourse to all means which enable it to attain the object of war. Still, practice has taught the advisability of allowing one's own interest the introduction of a limitation in the use of certain methods of war and a total renunciation of others. . . .

'In the modern uses of war one can no longer regard merely the traditional inheritance of the ancient etiquette of the profession of arms, and the professional outlook accompanying it, but there is also the deposit of the currents of thought which agitate our time. But since the tendency of thought of the last century was dominated essentially by humanitarian considerations, which not infrequently degenerated into sentimentality and flabby emotion, there have been attempts to influence the development of the usages of war in a way which was in fundamental contradiction with the nature of war and its object. Attempts of this kind will also not be wanting in the future, the more so as these agitations have found a kind of moral recognition in some provisions of the Geneva Convention and the Brussels and Hague Conferences. . . . By steeping himself in military history an officer will be able to guard himself against excessive humanitarian notions. It will teach him that certain severities are indispensable in war, that the only true humanity very often lies in a ruthless application of them.'

The High Command held that all methods of war were permissible 'without which the object of the war cannot be obtained'. But what was reprehensible included every act of violence and destruction which was not demanded by the object of war.

The Germans conceded that certain rules did apply. All these were banned: poison and the spreading of infectious diseases, assassination, proscription and outlawry of the opponent, the use of arms which caused needless suffering (soft-nosed bullets, glass), the killing of wounded or prisoners no longer capable of offering resistance.[1]

Closely connected with the unlawful instruments of war, the War Book stated, was the employment of uncivilized and barbarous peoples in European wars.

> '. . . the practice stands in express contradiction to the modern movement for humanizing the conduct of war and for alleviating its attendant sufferings. If troops are employed in war who are without knowledge of civilized warfare and by whom cruelties and inhumanities are committed . . . the transference of African and Mohammedan Turcos to a European seat of war in 1870 was a retrogression from civilized to barbarous warfare, since these troops had no conception of European-Christian culture, of respect for property and for the honour of women.'[2]

The War Book continued:

> 'Since town and fortifications belong together and form an insuperable unity and can seldom in a military sense and never in an economic and political sense be separated, the bombardment will not limit itself to the actual fortification, but it will and must extend over the whole town; the reason for this lies in the fact that a restriction of the bombardment to the fortification is impracticable; it would jeopardize the success of the operation and would

[1] Other nations, in the past, had not been so humane. The Spanish poisoned French water and food in the wars against Napoleon. The Allies declared Napoleon an outlaw in 1815. The Turks killed wounded soldiers in the Russo-Turkish War.

[2] The Germans felt bitterly about French native troops pushed into the fighting in 1914 and 1915. Private Peter Woolfe of Mainz wrote to his parents: 'The French have sunk so low as to use niggers against us. They are heathens and quite revolting and cruel. We fight fiercely against them because we know we can expect no mercy from these savages. You can smell them in the night.'

quite unjustifiably protect the defenders who are not necessarily quartered in the works. This does not preclude the exemption of certain . . . buildings such as churches,[1] schools, museums, so far as this is possible. But of course it is assumed that buildings seeking this protection will be distinguishable and that they are not put to defensive uses. Should this happen then every humanitarian consideration must give way.'

The War Book was unequivocal about what constituted dishonourable behaviour that would not be tolerated by the High Command.

'Such forms of artifice are under all circumstances irreconcilable with honourable fighting, especially those which take the form of faithlessness, fraud and breach of one's word. Among these are a breach of safe-conduct; of a free retirement; or of an armistice, in order to gain advantage over the enemy; feigned surrender in order to kill the enemy who then approach unsuspiciously; misuse of a flag of truce or of the Red Cross in order to secure one's approach . . . incitement to crime, such as murder of the enemy's leaders, incendiarism, robbery and the like.'

But the Germans held legitimate the use of the enemy's uniforms and the use of enemy and neutral flags and marks, but conceded that the Hague Conference had forbidden the use of enemy uniforms.

The War Book condemned the looting of museums and libraries, as well as private property such as money, watches, rings, trinkets or any *objet d'art*.[2]

It was commonly supposed that the German Army disliked the presence of newspaper reporters with the forces. This is

---

[1] In 1870 the Germans shelled Strasbourg Cathedral. The French had used the tower as an artillery observation post.

[2] In seizing paintings, rare manuscripts and ornaments the Nazis of 1939–45 were merely reverting to the right of the victor to any booty he could lay his hands on. This right had not been long dead. Every army in history had plundered, for loot was one of the benefits of war. In 1862 the British Army took from the palace at Peking a fabulous fortune in works of art. Napoleon presented stolen treasures to his friends and some of his marshals, Masséna in particular, loved looting as much as they loved fighting.

wrong. The War Book advised that reporters were indispensable.

> 'The army derives great advantages from this intellectual intercourse; it has to thank the stimulus of the Press for an unbroken chain of benefits. The importance . . . and on the other hand the dangers and disadvantages which may arise from its misuse, make it obviously necessary that the military authorities should control the whole of the Press when in the field.'

Military writers of all nations condemned the extraction of information from civilians about their own army, its strength and its operations. The Germans, however, said that the practice could 'not be entirely dispensed with'. Compulsion would be applied with regret, the War Book said, but the necessities of war would frequently make it necessary.

The Germans have long made use of enemy civilians for defence work, and they have never made a secret of it. In the war of 1870 they paid French workers well, so there was no need for compulsion. However, on one occasion workers detailed for repairs to a bridge declined to do the work. After other means of persuasion had proved useless, the German Civil Commissioner concerned, Count Renard, threatened to shoot some of the workers. The Frenchmen went to work.

French jurists protested bitterly about the threat, but the German High Command claimed that Renard had acted within the laws of war. *The main thing was*, the German War Book declared, *that it attained its object*, without its being necessary to practise it—a significant point of view.

One of Frederick William's 'Giant Grenadiers', also known as the 'Potsdam Blues' and the 'Lange Kerls', 'Tall Fellows'. *Ullstein Verlag*

General Friedrich Wilhelm von Seidlitz, 'best cavalry officer in Europe', and superb in battle.
Ullstein Verlag

Frederick the Great watches Seidlitz smash the French Army at Rossbach, 5 November 1757.
Ullstein Verlag

German soldiers of the eighteenth century at drill in the barracks ground. At left are two instruments of punishment: the wooden horse on to which a defaulter was strapped with weights on his legs, and 'the pole'. A defaulter stood with his bare heels on the spikes and with his wrists through the rings.
Ullstein Verlag

Prussian infantry overwhelming the Austrians at the Battle of Königgrätz, 3 July 1866. *Ullstein Verlag*

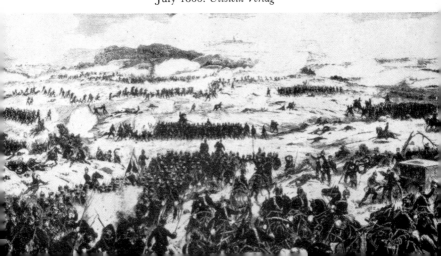

Prussian grenadiers storm the church at Leuthen, on 5 December 1757, an
action that helped to win the battle. *Ullstein Verlag*

An assault of August 1870, made by fusiliers this time, against the French,
who were holding St Marie-aux Chenes. *Ullstein Verlag*

Lichterfelde Cadet School, from which so many officers had come, was at its peak in 1912. Here a cadet goes over the bayonets in an athletics demonstration. *Ullstein Verlag*

Eight years later under the terms of the Versailles Peace Treaty, Lichterfelde was closed down. The commandant, 1, and Ludendorff, 2, take the final salute. *Ullstein Verlag*

German armoured might and menace, 1917 and 1944 (*below*). *Ullstein Verlag*

A cavalry machine-gun unit moves up to the Western Front, 1918 and (*below*) a heavy machine-gun crew in action against the Russians in June 1942.
Ullstein Verlag

A bomb-thrower in a trench at Arras, 1914, before steel helmets came into common use. *Ullstein Verlag*

The Artillery Memorial at Cologne, depicting the gallant German officer who served and defended his gun against British tanks at Cambrai, November 1917, until killed at his post. *Ullstein Verlag*

The Germans, too, were human. Here they rest in a trench in the summer of 1917. *Imperial War Museum*

Two others wash and shave in a water-filled shellhole near Amiens in May 1918. *Imperial War Museum*

The victor of the East African campaigns of 1914–1918, Paul von Lettow-Vorbeck, with his men, returns to a hero's welcome in Berlin, March 1919. *Ullstein Verlag*

Otto ('Scarface') Skorzeny, one of the most colourful German soldiers of World War II, at a Berlin rally in 1943. *Ullstein Verlag*

Jackboots. *Bibliothek für Zeitgeschichte*

Leaders of the new German Army:

(*left*) The legendary Erwin Rommel. *Imperial War Museum*

(*bottom left*) Hans von Seeckt, the Scharnhorst of the twentieth century. *Ullstein Verlag*

(*bottom right*) Gerd von Rundstedt. *Ullstein Verlag*

(*right*) Panzer leader (note the Death's Head insignia) Sepp Dietrich. *Ullstein Verlag*

(*bottom left*) Battle of the Bulge commander, Walter Model. *Ullstein Verlag*

(*bottom right*) The calmly competent Joachim Peiper. *Ullstein Verlag*

'Give me a child until he is seven years old . . .' and at sixteen, taken prisoner in battle, he will become a scared little boy who will break down and weep. *Imperial War Museum*

GIVE ME A CHILD UNTIL HE IS SEVEN YEARS OLD . . .

Hans-Georg Henke, now the administrator of a hospital in the German Democratic Republic. *Imperial War Museum*

General Paulus and General von Seydlitz during the bloody shambles of the Battle of Stalingrad. *Ullstein Verlag*

The fiercesome *nebelwerfer* . . .' a blood-curdling, vicious swish'. *Ullstein Verlag*

Cheerful in victory. The tough storm troopers who captured the 'impregnable' fortress of Eben Email, 1940. *Ullstein Verlag*

Depressed in defeat. The not-so-tough captives of 1945. *Planet News*

CHAPTER XIII

'To Seek the Death of Heroes'

The complex political reasons for the outbreak of the Great War are beyond the scope of this book, although I doubt if Germany was any more an aggressor than several other countries.

It did break out, it lasted more than four years and it involved the German soldier in fighting on several fronts and against troops of a score of nationalities and it laid the groundwork for the following war.

So much has been written about the various great battles—the Marne and Tannenberg, Mons and Ypres, Verdun and Amiens, the Lys and the Aisne—that I do not intend to deal with them here, except where some incident connected with them reveals something of the German soldier.

What is important is that while the German Army was formidable it had assumed even more formidable proportions in foreign minds. In 1914 an Englishman, author of *The German Army from Within*, wrote: 'The German Army is universally recognized as the most marvellous machine ever constructed by the mind and the sinew of man.'

Marvellous it was, but it was rotten at the top. Its commander-in-chief in all but name was General Count von Moltke, nephew of the great Moltke, and he was as incompetent as his uncle had been efficient. He owed his appointment solely to his name, for the Kaiser thought that it would instil fear into Germany's opponents.

Perhaps fortunately for Germany the military hierarchy of France, headed by Joffre, was also living in a dream, fully convinced that entrenched battles could not occur between

France and Germany, despite all evidence from other parts of the world—in the Russian-Japanese War, for instance—that trenches were inevitable. 'A battle cannot be lost physically,' Foch said, 'therefore it can only be lost morally. . . . A battle won is a battle in which one will not confess oneself beaten.' Morale, the French General Staff believed, was the infallible answer to the rifle bullet. This was criminal negligence.

Count von Schlieffen, Chief of the German General Staff 1891–1905, realized with Napoleon that 'it is with artillery that war is made' and he increased the number of German heavy guns to make the attack superior to the defence. But he did not realize that a whole new organization should be built around the guns.

The Germans believed in the general and his plan; the French believed in the initiative of their private soldiers.

The Germans planned to open an attack with a dense firing line, after which they would advance until the enemy's fire became 'unreasonable'. Then they would crawl as close as 400 yards from the enemy, fire, move forward again, and finally charge with the bayonet at 100 yards.

The French had a more naïve theory. They would move forward under controlled fire to 400 yards. Accurately aimed fire from the enemy would be impossible at this range, so they could then advance and carry the objectives with the bayonet.

Both French and Germans had many observers present in the Manchurian War and while both sides learned lessons, the Germans learned more. However, neither side saw that with fire power increasing so tremendously armies would have to dig in—unless, of course, a battle could be won in the first shock.

In 1914 the General had planned a battle of annihilation, the so-called Schlieffen Plan, aimed at bringing about a second and gigantic Battle of Leuthen with the intention of out-flanking the French Army from the German right wing and of attacking it from the rear. The German soldier had been trained for the battle of annihilation, and that he was able to hold out in trench warfare against the tremendous numerical superiority of the enemy, he owed to his better training.

Much nonsense has been written about drill. Drill as a means to an end is indispensable to every army, a fact the Germans realized as much as the British. It cannot be replaced entirely by individual training or by sporting instinct. A man, unless his inherent worth is beyond all doubt, must have obedience drilled into him, so that his natural instincts can be curbed by the spiritual compulsion of his commander even in the most awful moments. The Germans achieved this in high degree.

The General Staff had precise plans for a short war. France would be knocked out in six weeks, Russia in six months. Not that the Russians deserved six months, but there was a lot of ground to cover. England was discounted. She had no Continental army, would not be able to get a foothold and would simply be ordered to stay out of Europe. All Germans believed that the General Staff's time estimates were reasonable.

The year before, the General Staff calculated that in case of a European war Germany could at once put into the field 1,544,652 men as against 1,449,000 in France[1] and 127,000 in Britain.

Free and easy Britons could not imagine the intensity and completeness of the German military drive. Before the Great War German military maps of France showed new roads which had not even appeared on French official maps.

Peace strength of the German Army before 1914 was 36,300 officers and 754,600 men. This could be doubled by calling up reservists. By the end of August 1914 Germany had probably 4,000,000 men under arms.

The regulars were well-set and sturdy men and they travelled heavy—carrying from 90 lb. to 112 lb. when on the march, a frightening weight.

A lieutenant received only £60 per year, rising after several years to £85 and later to £120. A captain was paid from £180 to £250. On the outbreak of the Great War the ordinary German soldier was paid 1½d. a day.

The German infantry regiment in 1914 had almost the strength of a British brigade. It comprised three battalions, each of four companies, in turn divided into three platoons, or *Züge*. The strength of the company on a war footing was 250, but in peacetime it was cut to 180. On mobilization a draft of seventy reservists would bring it to full strength. A fully mobilized battalion consisted of twenty-six officers and 1,031 men, under command of a major. The three battalions united in the regiment were commanded by a colonel.

When war was declared the Kaiser said: 'A dark day has

[1] On the eve of the war coloured troops in the French service amounted to about nine per cent. During the war France drew from her empire 544,890 soldiers.

broken over Germany. Envious persons are everywhere compelling us to defence. The sword is being forced in our hand. I hope that . . . we shall, with God's help, wield the sword in such a way that we can sheath it again with honour.'

So the Germans marched to war. One soldier, Ernst Jünger, noted that 'we set out in a rain of flowers to seek the death of heroes. The war was our dream of greatness, power and glory. It was a man's work, a duel in fields whose flowers would be stained with blood. There was no lovelier death in the world . . . anything rather than stay at home, anything to make one with the rest. . . .'

To the German the horror was part of the irresistible attraction that drew him into the war; we have the word of many individual Germans for this. There was nothing abnormal about this; a long period of law and order produces a craving for the abnormal. Stories stimulate this craving but do not satisfy it. What is it like to have dead and mutilated men lying about? What would a battlefield look like?

They found out, but they never expected to see dead men left month after month to the scourge of wind and weather; they did not really expect to see a man blown into so many pieces that there was not enough of him to scrape together; they did not expect a shell burst to disinter corpses; they did not expect the spring thaw to reveal other dead soldiers in the mud; they did not expect to find corpses fixed like planks into the walls of trenches to strengthen the defences. They looked at the dead with their dislocated limbs, distorted faces and the hideous colours of decay, and finally became so accustomed to the horrible that if they came on a body they gave it no more than a passing thought.

In 1914 the German Army, according to plan, should have beaten both the French and the Russians. Apart from the obvious reasons there were two not so obvious ones why it did not. The army was not up to maximum strength because not enough of 'the right type' of officers could be found. And the German Navy was doing its best to beat the German Army; the navy was practically bankrupting the treasury in its fanatical, unrealistic spending.

In September 1914 the French resisted so violently and courageously at the battle of the Marne that the Great Plan received a setback; no quick victory would be possible after all. A negotiated peace might have been possible at this point, but no German was happy about this and least of all the members of the General Staff. No German Army could return home unvictorious; there was its pride to consider. So the war went on, with the General Staff becoming dictators of Germany.

The French held the Germans but at great cost. In their bright red pantaloons, perfect targets, they made their bloody sacrifice. Mounting one useless charge after another Joffre murdered many thousands of his countrymen—and Clausewitz from his grave helped him to do it.

It has been said that the German soldier is not so adaptable as soldiers of other races. Perhaps, but he soon successfully adapted himself to the tactics of trench warfare, although this form of fighting was not the ideal of the Germans and, moreover, never could be.

That winter of 1914 he was still cheerful, he still sang, he still possessed a sense of humour and he still drank.

On 4 November 1914, from a position near Beaumont, Alfred Vaeth, a student of philosophy, wrote to a friend:

'What you want most to know is whether I am still just the same as ever. I don't think, my friend, that I have changed in the least. I have experienced one great joy: that of seeing my conceptions of life and the world put to the test and finding that they have not failed me. . . .

'We have been through some bad times . . . and have endured many hardships, but I can honestly say that I should volunteer again all the same. Life here is hard; nearly everybody would be glad to go home, but there is much in it that is fine and valuable, and it is only the weather that often forces me to say: "I wish we could have peace and be at home again!"

'When we are not obliged to dig communication trenches we just lie about in dug-outs and clean our rifles and equipment—we can't clean ourselves as there is scarcely enough water even for drinking purposes—or stew apples (fetched under enemy fire), write letters, make notes or—which is what I like best—just dream and think about all sorts of things.

'We are a very thin line—one regiment against three French ones. If they had more pluck we should soon be done for—tired-out, grimy little crowd that we are. . . . The French have withdrawn a bit today. Before that we were only about 100 yards from each other. The unpleasant part of that was that one was always expecting to be blown up by a mine. I shouldn't like to die that way. I should prefer a fine, sunny day, when the barrage has cleared the way and the inspiriting order comes: "Fix bayonets! Up! March! March! March!" '

This was still the spirit that first winter. Let's get on with the war. Charge and put them on the run. It would be dangerous, but it would be glorious.

CHAPTER XIV

'The Attack Was Terribly Beautiful'

It has often been said that Britain (or France or Australia or Canada) gave the 'flower of her youth' in sacrifice in World War I, but no Allied writer has yet admitted that Germany also gave the flower of her youth. But she did. So many of her early casualties were students and graduates of various universities and colleges, young men of high intellect with soaring ambitions and sensitive natures. Why is it that we will not recognize that a German can have a sensitive soul?

The letters these young men wrote home sharply revealed their sensitivity, their emotions and their prayers. Dr. Philipp Witkop spent years collecting 20,000 letters sent home by German students who lost their lives in battle and in 1928 he published a selection of them . . . 'to form a living memorial by means of which these Sons of the Fatherland may survive in remembrance of their fellow countrymen as an example of devotion to duty, of self sacrifice and patriotism, and as a spur towards the realization of the ideals they cherished.' Dr. Witkop hoped, too, that they might also help towards the establishment of justice and a better understanding between nations. 'Then indeed the writers' last will and testament will have been carried out and their death will not have been in vain.'

A study of these letters reveals that these young Germans cherished many ideals. They wrote of their belief in God, a belief frequently made stronger by the sufferings they were enduring. They wrote of the justice of Germany's cause. They explained, a little naïvely perhaps, how life in Germany would be better after the war, for they would return home to set wrongs right. They described their delight in life and in creation, their joy of comradeship and their will to live, which was only matched by their readiness to die for their 'sacred cause'.

Not one of these students, most of whom were in their twenties, doubted for a moment that God was on Germany's side, any more than they doubted that Germany's cause was right. But they wrote in a reasoned way, not fanatically. Yet it is as a fanatic that so many writers have depicted the German soldiers of World War I. They were Huns and Vandals and they were variously described as 'fat Fritzes', 'stinking German sausages', and 'vicious thugs'.

German letters and literature have sunk to this form of abuse about the political enemies of Germany, but rarely if ever about enemy soldiers. The German soldier undoubtedly respected his opponent as a man, as a soldier and as a human being.[1]

'It has always been my ideal in war,' Lieut. Jünger wrote, 'to eliminate all feelings of hatred and to treat my enemy as an enemy only in battle and to humour him as a man according to his courage. It is exactly in this that I have found many kindred spirits among British officers. It depends, of course, on not letting oneself be blinded by an excessive national feeling, as is generally the case between French and Germans. The consciousness of the importance of one's own nation ought to reside as a matter of course and unobtrusively in everybody, just as an unconditional sense of honour does in a gentleman.'

The letters written home by German soldiers show many of them to be romantic, imaginative and even poetic. Men of this type hated war and detested its associations—the blood and suffering, the death and disease, the dirt and the squalor. But they all knew where their duty lay.

Not all the German Army was made up of men of this type. The militarism of the old German Army brutalized its men, but the old regulars were soon nearly all killed or out of action. The men who fought the Great War for Germany were the men who fought it for Britain—citizen soldiers, ordinary men in uniform, who only wanted 'to get it over with'. These Germans have been maligned. As real soldiers they deserve better from foreign soldiers.

Instead of the dangers and glories many young Germans hoped for, they found first of all only mud and work and sleep-

---

[1] Nietzsche said: 'You must have as enemies only those whom you hate, but not those whom you despise. You must be proud of your enemy, and then the enemy's success is your success also.'

less nights. The continuous exhaustion to which the men were subjected was partly the fault of the higher command, which had not yet grasped the spirit of modern trench warfare. In a short war of movement an officer could drive his men to the limit—indeed, he had to do so. In a dragging war, this could only lead to physical collapse. The immense number of posts and the continual digging were generally unnecessary in the early days of the war.

Belgium must not be treated as an enemy country, the German soldiers were told, so the troops were quartered in great draughty barns and complained as they bedded down that there was plenty of room in the big houses. Ernst Jünger, like others, thought military necessity should come first. 'We make ourselves ridiculous with our misplaced human kindness and might well have taken more care of our dignity.'

Eduard Schmieder, writing from Framonville in August 1914, was philosophical and idealistic. 'I have been smoking cigars while we lay under enemy shrapnel fire. And in those very moments I have once again vividly realized the beauty of the world and all the happiness which has been mine in life. In wartime one learns how beautiful, how rich our life is, in spite of small and great drawbacks. Each day brings gladness even when one knows that it will also bring fresh toil. After each battle one thanks God that one still has life, one values it so much. But we would all sacrifice it gladly for the Fatherland.'

In November he noted: 'There is blissful joy in every victory won for the sake of this beautiful German country.'[1]

'The modern Hun has made a cult of outrage,' an English author wrote in 1915. 'His excesses are deliberate . . . ordained by precept and practised by perfection.'

This was a vicious untruth, uncalled for even in time of war. Here is what one 'modern Hun', Walter Bohm,[2] student of philosophy in Berlin, wrote in January 1915: . . . 'One thing more dear Parents, and especially you, Mum: I asked you to spare me "snowball" prayers, amulets and so on. Don't be angry with me, please don't, because I quite understand your point of view. But I have received from God, in whom, in my own way, I believe more firmly than ever, two good weapons: my body, which is well trained; and an iron determination to

---

[1] A student of administration in Freiburg in Baden, he was born 10 October 1890 and killed before Lievin, 8 May 1916.
[2] He was born on 26 March 1894 and killed on the Eastern Front on 25 October 1915.

do my duty to my country, my Commander-in-Chief and my comrades on the one hand, and to myself and my family on the other. Supernatural means of protection I reject. Do you really think, Dear Mother, that the Law of Nature with regard to a bullet is going to be reversed in favour of such an unimportant member of the universe as I am? I am content if I can die in the consciousness that I have not lived to the disadvantage of anyone, that I have done my duty as a member of human society, and that I have never knowingly injured anybody.'

These sensitive letters were from students—as are most of those quoted in this book. The ordinary German soldier might not have been so articulate, but in that he was not so different from any ordinary soldiers and as the war went on any difference became muted.

True, the German soldier was not funny, as a Cockney soldier or an outback Australian or a Dublin Irishman could be funny. His humour was, and is, coarse, more so than most martial humour.

His ability to drink was proverbial. He would drain a stein at a draught and bang it on the table for more. One officer has deposed that his orderly once came to him in dismay to say that he thought his health was bad. Until recently he had been able to drink without trouble, but now, if he had four or five gallons, it seemed to make him queer.

The German soldier was a great singer, or more accurately, a great shouter of songs, generally of a lusty and simple kind. Most German military songs expressed elementary emotion soaked in treacly sentiment. When shouted to the accompaniment of beer mugs banging on the tables, as they were during the early part of the war, these sounds could be stirring and satisfying and the more men singing the more each individual soldier was pleased.

Startled by their inability to make sufficient progress, the Germans were soon forming assault parties—small groups of commandos. There was never a shortage of volunteers, but the men for these parties were handpicked nevertheless. They were some of the finest soldiers Germany ever produced, but their losses were high.

The first assault parties, which always consisted of three men, were formed in the Argonne Forest in 1914. They were specialists in rolling up enemy trenches. Their work was described by Prince Oskar of Prussia in his book *The Winter Battle in Champagne*.

Three men combined for attacks on trenches. The one in the middle, who was the strongest, carried two machine-gun protecting plates, hooked together, in his left hand and a pick in his right. The others, one with a large number of grenades and the second with a bayonet, followed close behind him on either side. They advanced along the bloody road striking, throwing and thrusting and spreading panic among the French.

Mostly they were young. Many a German, from theorist to veteran soldier, considered that troops composed of boys under twenty years of age, under experienced leadership, were the most formidable troops.

The attacks of these assault parties were at first always made from the flank, for even in the trench system this was the weakest point. But the French soon recognized the weakness and protected their flanks. The assault party needed a small cannon and in 1915 Krupps brought out a relatively light 3·7 cm. gun with a shield mounting.

Following this, assault parties were developed more intensively. The engineers were ordered to establish experimental assault units, which were highly successful. Captain Ulrich Rohr was one of the dynamic officers who inspired and organized the assault parties.

A tall, thin man, with a face described by his contemporaries as 'always ironical', Rohr had great tactical ability and technical knowledge. He moved continually between the trenches, munitions factories and chemical laboratories. The Nazi *Signal* magazine claimed that he created the modern soldier and his equipment. The steel helmet, the flame-thrower, the hand grenade, the concentric charge, the extended charge —with which barbed wire obstacles were removed—were all tried out, stimulated and perfected by Rohr.

Other Germans regarded the perfection of technical equipment as the factor which would win the war. Rohr regarded the perfection of the men as that factor. He summarized his ideas this way: All aids and machines will not achieve as much as a handful of brave men.

The assault parties photographed the position they planned to attack, built it behind the front and studied it. They quickly discarded the 3·7 gun because it did not hit hard enough; this led to the making of the 7·5 cm. infantry gun.

The first great achievement of the assault parties was the attack on the Schratzmannle, carried out within four hours on 12 October 1915. The Germans lost only four dead and eleven wounded. Then came the Hartmannsweilerkopf. It had been lost early in December 1915. Rohr's assault party, in collaboration with the 8th Reserve Battalion of Chasseurs, recaptured it on 22 and 23 December.

Franz Schauwecker, in his book *The Jaws of Death*, described the assault soldier vividly. 'Even in his exterior the "Western Front" soldier differs from the soldier at the beginning of the war. In his most perfected form the soldier of the assault battalion marches not with his rifle at the slope but slung over his shoulder. His knees and elbows are protected by pieces of leather. He no longer carries any ammunition pouches as he has his bullets in his tunic pockets.

'Strapped crosswise over his shoulders hang two narrow bags for hand grenades. The otherwise inevitable regulation high boots have disappeared on account of their heaviness and clumsiness; the men's legs are clad in light lace-up boots and puttees.'

The German excuse for their failure to win the war is that there were too few of them and that the armistice came before their lessons could be taught to the whole army, which was true.

Two new forms of artillery fire were introduced, both of which the Germans laid claim to having invented—the creeping barrage and sudden fire. Creeping barrage was a curtain of fire moving gradually forwards, followed closely by the infantry whose duty it was to overwhelm enemy infantry just after they had been forced to take cover from the creeping barrage.

Sudden fire marked the beginning of the modern break-through battle. It began without warning and achieved its full effect when the enemy had had no idea that artillery attack was imminent. Artillery was massed secretly and there was no experimental firing to find the range.

The Germans claim that the man responsible for perfecting these attacks was Colonel Bruchmüller, dubbed Durchbruch-müller (Break-through-Müller). Ludendorff certainly praised Bruchmüller highly as a brilliant artillery officer.

Perfection of attack was beyond the interest of many a German soldier. As early as March 1915, with the war in progress only seven months, Johannes Haas, a student of theology in Leipzig, was having doubts about the ethical problem of the war.

'Preachers in the pulpits at home dismiss the question much more easily; for us here the war remains a most difficult matter for one's conscience to decide about. When one is actually fighting, the instinct of self preservation and the excitement drown every other feeling, but when one is in rest or doing nothing in the trenches, then it is different. One looks with astonishment and horror at the more and more cunningly elaborate means devised for destroying the enemy. One is torn between the natural instinct which says "Thou shalt do no murder", and the sacred obligation "This must be done for the sake of the Fatherland".'

He was still thinking about the problem in April, when he wrote: 'This murdering is so senseless. The one consolation is that one is doing one's duty. I do think that we Germans have, more than any other nation, a stern sense of duty. And we stick to that in this ghastly war. The justification for militarism, which from the ordinary point of view is detestable, is that it has helped to encourage and strengthen this sense of duty.'

His letters show more optimism until late in November, when he became impassioned. '. . . In what way have we sinned, that we should be treated worse than animals? Hunted from place to place, cold, filthy and in rags, we wander about like gypsies and in the end are destroyed like vermin! Will they *never* make peace! . . .'

Richard Schmieder, student of philosophy, also of Leipzig, was equally as impassioned. 'When I heard the birds singing at Ripont, I could have crushed the whole world to death in my wrath and fury. If only those gentlemen—Grey, Asquith and Poincaré—could be transported to this spot, instead of the war lasting ten years, there would be peace tomorrow.'

Schmieder's reference to a long war shows that as early as this time some Germans had realized that no early peace could be expected. And already some were disillusioned about the 'great brotherhood' they had expected to find. Alfred Vaeth was one of them.

He wrote:

'We true patriots, who in peacetime derided Jingoism—the so-called "Hurrah Patriotism" (this reminds me of Byron's lines: "And when I laugh at any mortal thing, 'tis that I may not weep")—hoped that this community of sacrifice, this facing of a death common to all, would bring about an end to class distinctions. This is not the case. You do not believe it? I will give you an example. In the trench three privates are fighting over a loaf; inside the dug-out the officers have more wine than they can drink. It makes one's heart bleed. All honour to our regular officers, who as a rule take more care of their men than, for instance, the officers of the Reserve. . . .

'Oh Lord! One joined up with all sorts of hopes, and one experiences disappointment after disappointment! I can't understand some people at all. It is a joy to me that my comrades love me . . . It is no pleasure to me that I have been recommended for the Iron Cross, but what does please me is that when men of other sections have a dangerous job they come and ask me to go with them. . . . It is said that the young men of today are degenerates, but they are doing greater things than their fathers in 1870. Many of us have vowed that if (yes, if) we come back, the songs of triumph shall not be allowed to drown the notes of sorrow. . . . We shall not be beaten, but we may bleed to death. . . .'

Vaeth did indeed bleed to death—at Leintrey on 16 October 1915—but three days before his death he wrote:

'The attack was terribly beautiful. The most beautiful and at the same time the most terrible thing I have ever experienced. Our artillery shot magnificently and after two hours the position was sufficiently prepared for German infantry. The storm came, as only German infantry can storm! It was magnificent the way our men, especially the youngest, advanced! Magnificent! Officers belonging to other regiments, who were looking on, have since admitted that they had never seen anything like it! In the face of appalling machine-gun fire they went on with a confidence which nobody could ever attempt to equal. . . . The attack was glorious!'

So many Germans wrote about combat as if it were a revelation. Indeed, this is precisely what it is, but no other soldier has expressed himself so passionately and succintly about it. Or so seriously. There is often lightheartedness in British and Allied letters and diaries but rarely in German writing.

Hero Hellwich, a twenty-year-old student of political economy from Freiburg, wrote: 'It is not true that war hardens people's hearts. Anybody who comes back hardened must have been hard to start with. The effect of war is much more that of purifying and deepening. . . .' He was killed on the Somme on 20 December 1916.

Herbert Jahn,[1] student of mining and chemistry, Technical High School, Breslau, wrote: 'It is strange that for a long time I have been constantly thinking of being killed, though I have really no belief in premonitions. All the same this crazy idea has so far influenced me that I have written a farewell-letter and made a will. Both documents lie in my breast pocket. I have had amazing luck all my life so far, but I think the best thing of all has been the chance of taking part in this war— even if I am killed, for otherwise I should never have discovered the things I have learnt during the last ten months; and every day one goes on learning, every day one's horizon broadens.'

Others, less complex, asked only for flower seeds. Willy Holscher was writing to his parents: 'There is nothing very nice to look at round about my billet, and, as I don't know how long I may be stuck here, I want to grow some flowers. Please send me sweet-peas, convolvulus, sunflower, flax, mignonette etc.'

War was not all horror. On a pleasant summer evening when the British or the French lines were quiet, the Germans would lie about in the warm sun, play cards, read books, tend their rough gardens.

But these interludes were infrequent and fleeting—danger and death were only one patrol away. On 21 November 1915 a lieutenant took an entrenching party to a particular sector. One of his party, Landsturmmann Diener, a married man with four children, climbed on to a ledge in the side of the trench to shovel earth over the top. He was working when a shot hit him in the skull and he fell dead into the trench. His comrades, sobbing with rage, waited a long time behind the parapet to take vengeance. Their officer wrote: 'It is remarkable how little they grasp the war as an objective thing. They seem to regard the Englishman who fired the fatal shot as a personal enemy.'

There was really nothing remarkable about it, for sooner or later nearly every soldier saw the war subjectively, not objectively. It is difficult to feel objective about one's own survival.

After a time it was also difficult to take explosives seriously

[1] Born 3 February 1895, he died in the military hospital at Stenay on 10 April 1916.

enough. All soldiers become casual in their attitude to explosives. An N.C.O. picked up a toffee apple—the German name for a type of British grenade. He unscrewed the fuse and, seeing that the powder was smouldering, put the end of his cigarette into the opening. It exploded and wounded him in more than fifty places; he died soon after.

Then, once more it was Christmas—with parcels from home and perhaps an extra ration. But it was sometimes difficult to work up an appetite. 'We are up to our waists in ooze,' one soldier wrote to his father. 'It is enough to make one despair. On the right a dead body is coming to light—the legs only so far. Our gunner, Motullo, was killed by a shot through the head. Though his brain fell over his face to his chin, his mind was still clear when we took him to the nearest dug-out. . . .'

Both sides were aware of the need for some better protection for the head. The German spiked helmet—the *pickelhaube*—was of fairly tough leather but it could not stop flying steel.

The French were the first to introduce a steel helmet, originally only a small bowl fitting like a skull-cap. Then a committee of painters and sculptors produced an artistic creation with a bursting grenade on the front and a raised central crest. This helmet reached the front in 1915. During heavy fighting west of St. Quentin that year a noted German surgeon, Professor August Bier, operating on wounded at a hospital of the 18th Army Corps, noticed that 50 per cent. of the wounds were in the head. He discussed the matter with a medical colleague, Captain Friedrich Schwerd, and together they designed a steel helmet and sent in a suggestion that such a helmet should be issued to all ranks. In September 1915 Schwerd was called to the War Office to discuss manufacture of a helmet. He collaborated with a draftsman, Franz Marx, who had had much to do with restoration work on old armour and museum pieces and together they presented a design in the form of the Schallern—the ancient Gothic knight's helmet such as that worn by the horseman in Dürer's famous engraving, *Knight, Death and Devil*.

Their final design was sent to a steel works in Thale, where, in forty-two operations, a helmet was drawn from a single piece of tempered steel.

On 23 November forty sample helmets were subjected to artillery fire on the range at Kummersdorf; they could not be pierced by steel splinters or shrapnel bullets. General von Wrisberg, Chief of the General War Department, ordered the helmet to be introduced at once, not only as a piece of equipment for trench warfare, but as an item of general issue. At the end of January 1916 the first 30,000 helmets were issued to German troops engaged in fighting before Verdun. The head of the German soldier in his steel helmet became the symbol of the age. It was much stronger than the French helmet and infinitely more practical and comfortable than the British steel helmet, which the German described as an inverted washbasin. The only advantage the British helmet had was that in a brawl it could be used as a vicious cutting weapon, otherwise it was awkward, ill-balanced and depressing.[1]

---

[1] And it had not improved by World War II. The author, under shell fire, mortar fire and rifle fire often enough, 'lost' every steel helmet issued to him and took his chance in a slouch-hat. He sees no valour in this; he just happened to hate the damn thing. Fortunately for the British soldier the army now has a much better helmet.

CHAPTER XV

Bloodbaths of 1915–16

Throughout 1915 the Allied armies had made several great attempts to break through the German front and a spirit of defeatism began to permeate France. The Germans decided to move their main effort to the west—they had been expending much energy in the east. They intended to re-open the submarine campaign and at the same time strike against Verdun—deliberately selected because the French considered it impregnable. The Germans knew that the French might collapse if such a key fortress could be torn from them. If it could not be taken the Germans would still benefit, for the French would commit great quantities of men to its defence and thus bleed white their army. If the Germans did not win the battle, they could not very well lose it.

The Battle of Verdun opened on 21 February 1916. Like all previous attacks against entrenched fronts it failed, although it dragged on until 11 July—by when the Germans had suffered 281,000 casualties and the French 315,000. Logically, the casualties should have been in inverse proportion, but the Germans fought well.

German guns fired 1,350,000 tons of steel into Verdun. The laborious storming of three outlying forts and the gain of a few miles of ground, part of which had to be abandoned again, was the result of one of the most terrible battles of World War I. Technically, the Germans had not lost the battle, but some Germans were beginning to sense an inevitability about the whole conflict and some wrote about premonitions.

Johannes Haas's letters were full of such lines as ' "Let me go,

I long to see my Jesus so." It must be wonderful to see God in all His glory and His Peace. . . .'

He wrote his last 'letter'—it was only a scrawled note—on the day of his death in May.

'Dear Parents,

I am lying on the battle-field, wounded in the body. I think I am dying. I am glad to have time to prepare for the heavenly home-coming. Thank you, dear Parents. God be with you.

Hans.'

Other soldiers had basic complaints. For one the outstanding memory of the villages of Lorraine was the vain search for a water-closet. 'Baths were unknown . . . even in the most magnificent mansions. Much as I esteem the French, I cannot help thinking that this is a characteristic side of their life. I know indeed that hostile races always call each other dirty,[1] and that the French called us "sales Boches", but I feel we were fully justified in returning the compliment.'

Out of the line the Germans enjoyed themselves in the way that the British or French did. The officers especially made up parties and motored to towns well away from the front 'to see the women for once'. Yet not all officers were glad to leave the trenches, or of reading and going for long walks. At least one made a collection of beetles and, of course, there was always the mess, where as a Lieutenant Jünger wrote, 'in the evenings there soon grew up that cheerful, careless spirit that is characteristic of a body of Prussian officers.'

But by 1916 the army had changed in a subtle yet definite way. Two years of war had killed many of the peasant soldiers, the idealistic students and pseudo-aristocratic Junker officers. Now the army was a mixed mass of urban and rural men, officered by professional men from the middle classes. Some were no less brutal and overbearing than the pure Junkers: some succeeded in surpassing the Junkers whom they were aping.

[1] Brigadier General J. H. Morgan quotes a former C.I.G.S., General Sir Archibald Murray, as saying that when he and his staff took over a beautiful country house after the battle of the Marne they found it almost uninhabitable. The German officers who had occupied it had systematically defiled every bed in the house. (In his book, *Assize of Arms*, 1945.) Other British officers have testified to 'German filthiness' in buildings they had taken over.

Young German officers could be as high-spirited as British officers. Two of them had taken a magnificent coach from an abandoned Flemish mansion and somehow had got it as far as Lorraine. From their quarters they set off in it for a grand expedition to Metz, to live life as it should be lived. But they had not noticed that the coach had no brakes, having been designed for the plains of Flanders, not the hills of Lorraine. Before they were out of their village they had begun to roll and soon horses and coach were in mad career down hills and round sharp bends. The coachmen jumped first, then one of the young officers—into a heap of farm machinery. The other officer stayed put amid the silken upholstery until the horses threw the coach clear, down a bank and into a wall. Then he went out through the window.[1]

But these carefree if hazardous incidents did not make the summer of 1916 any less grim, for it was on 1 July that the French and British launched the battle of the Somme. The Germans knew it was coming. Lieut. Jünger wrote: 'We knew that we were on the verge this time of a battle such as the world had never seen. Soon our excited talk rose to a pitch that would have rejoiced the hearts of any freebooters, or of Frederick's Grenadiers. A few days later there were very few of that party still alive.'[2]

Massed French and British artillery pounded the Germans for seven days before the Somme offensive. A German soldier wrote: 'I believe I have found a comparison that exactly conveys what men experienced in artillery fire. It is as if one is tied to a post and threatened by a fellow with a sledgehammer. The hammer is swung back for the blow, now it whirls forward, till, just missing your skull, it sends the splinters flying from the post once more . . . and again . . . and again. . . .'

When the artillery stopped there were infantry attacks, which were stopped by both sides with machine-guns and more artillery attacks. . . .

---

[1] One young officer wrote: 'The war left one with two memories, as I am sure every outspoken soldier of it will agree, that were always recurring. One, when one was faced with the worst moments it had to offer; the other, when the bottle went round as madly and merrily as ever it did in times of peace. It was only because these black and red threads were interlaced in fairly equal proportions that the experiences of the war were tolerable.'

[2] Previously, Jünger had written: 'On the way to the station back to the front, I met three girls in light summer dresses, with tennis rackets in their hands, laughing as they went. It was a brilliant farewell life gave me and one that I often thought of when I was back in the line.'

Jünger wrote:

'On and on! Some of the men collapsed as they ran, for we were compelled to force the last ounce from their exhausted bodies. Wounded men called to us on left and right from the shell-holes and were disregarded. On and on, with our eyes fixed upon the man in front, along a knee-deep trench formed of linked-up shell-holes of enormous size, where the dead were almost touching. Our feet found little purchase against their soft and yielding bodies. Even the wounded who fell by the way shared the same fate and were trodden beneath the boots of those who still hurried on.

'The sunken road now appeared as nothing but a series of enormous shell-holes filled with pieces of uniform, weapons and bodies. The ground all round was ploughed by shells. You could search in vain for one blade of grass. This churned up battlefield was ghastly. Among the living lay the dead. As we dug ourselves in we found them in layers stacked one upon the other. One company after another had been shoved into the drum-fire and steadily annihilated. The corpses were covered with the masses of soil turned up by the shells and the next company advanced in the place of the fallen.'

I wonder what Hindenburg, who became Chief of the General Staff on 29 August, would have said had he seen the carnage. He was fond of saying that war to him was as refreshing as a mineral-water cure. But then Hindenburg was never at the front, nor was he ever in danger. Both German and Allied soldiers of the ranks were often shocked by the unwritten understanding of the General Staffs not to bother each other. Retaliation would be so easy, so neither side gave offence to the other. British H.Q. remained for two and a half years in one place.

This terrible 1916 battle of attrition, sheer lunacy, cost each side more than 600,000 in killed, wounded and prisoners, before it ended on 18 November. One German who died was Hugo Müller, a law student of Leipzig, aged twenty-four. The day before he died in the Ancre Valley he sent his family a French field postcard taken from a dead French soldier. Müller had seen many cards and letters written by French soldiers. 'To my astonishment I never found any expressions of hatred or abuse of Germany or German soldiers. On the other hand, many letters from relations revealed an absolute conviction of the justice of their cause, and sometimes also of confidence in victory.'

British and French troops, it should be said, were equally as astonished when they found that the Germans apparently sincerely believed in their cause.

A letter from Hans Stegemann, a forester, of Eberswalde, killed on 20 September on the Eastern Front, shows this. Stegemann, a fine and gallant soldier, survived several bloody battles against the Russians, but wrote that he had learnt one thing 'in these terrible days'.

'Even if we are killed death does not triumph over us, for the German soul will conquer, the German spirit is invincible throughout all eternity. May God preserve our Fatherland!'

Another hard winter came, cold and rain in the early part, then cold and frost and snow. But winter no longer halted fighting and a battle was no longer an episode that spent itself in blood and fire; it was a condition of things that dug itself in relentlessly week after week and even month after month. The terrible German losses, out of all proportion to the breadth of front attacked, were principally due to the old Prussian obstinacy with which the tactics of the line were pursued to their logical conclusion. One battalion after another was crowded up into the front line already over-manned and in a few hours pounded to bits.

Many men died in night raids, large and small, all along the front. These nocturnal fights, often at the wire, were short and murderous, a violent shooting, stabbing and slashing, weird in the gloom—then both parties running before machine-guns from both sides mowed them down indiscriminately.

A patrol led by a lieutenant on the morning of 5 March 1917 killed a young lieutenant of the Royal Munster Fusiliers. The German officer reported that he was very well clad and his features were intelligent and energetic. 'It affected me,' he wrote privately, 'to find the address of several London girls in his pocket-book. We buried him behind our trench and put a simple cross at his head.'

Englishmen could be affected, too. A private of the Coldstream Guards wrote:

'We had a ten minutes' truce with the Huns last week. They made a night attack and we drove them off and when the dawn came a wounded man was seen among the dead.

We called out to him and told him to get to our trenches if he could. But he could not crawl. At last a lull came in the fighting and we shouted to the Germans to come and fetch their wounded.

'At first they seemed very dubious, and would only show their helmets; but we promised not to shoot, and a man who wore the Iron Cross advanced boldly up to our entanglements and proceeded to assist the wounded man. Another man followed shortly, and amid the cheers of the Coldstreams they carried him off.

'Before going, the first man saluted and said, "Thank you, gentlemen, one and all. I thank you very much. Good day."

'This incident upset me for a time, and I wished that we might all be friends again. He was a handsome fellow, and big, and by far the most cultured and polite German I have heard or seen out here.'

Charlie Harrison, an Australian infantryman, told of an encounter with a German in a trench raid.

'I lunge forward, aiming at his stomach. It is a lightning, instinctive movement. In that second he twists and reaches for his revolver. The thrust jerks my body. Something heavy collides with the point of my bayonet. I become insane. I want to strike again and again but I cannot. My bayonet does not come clear. I pull, tug, jerk. . . . I hear him shriek. . . . We are facing each other—four feet of space separates us. His eyes are distended; they seem all whites and look as though they will leap out of their sockets. There is froth at the corners of his mouth which opens and shuts . . . He joins me in the effort to withdraw . . . I try to kick him off. He shrieks . . . I kick him again and again. . . . It is too much for me. Suddenly I drop the butt of my rifle . . . he collapses, his hands still gripping the barrel. . . .'

Harrison then ran away, but becoming apprehensive at being unarmed, he returned to the German.

'I move to seize the butt of my rifle . . . He grabs the barrel with a childish movement which seems to say: "It is mine, you may not take it away! . . . My tugging and pulling works the blade in his insides. Again those horrible shrieks. . . . Suddenly I remember what I must do . . . and pull back my breechblock. He stops his screaming; he looks at me, silently now. He knows what I am going to do. A white Verey light soars over our heads. His helmet has fallen from his head. I see his boyish face . . . he looks like a Saxon;[1] he is fair under the light and I see white down against green cheeks. . . . I pull my trigger. . . .'[2]

Yes, a German soldier dies like other soldiers and he knows how to die.

How many infantry soldiers of any race can honestly claim never to have killed a helpless enemy? The fury of action is responsible for such an action. When a man has reached killing heat he cannot suddenly be switched off and cooled. One German officer records such an incident.

'A figure crouched, wounded apparently, three metres in front of me in the middle of the pounded hollow of the road. I saw him start at the sight of me and stare at me with wide-open eyes as I walked slowly up to him holding out my revolver in front of me. To me the mere sight of an enemy in tangible form was a release. Grinding my teeth, I pressed the muzzle to the temple of this wretch, whom terror now crippled, and with my other hand gripped hold of his tunic. With a beseeching cry he snatched a photograph from his pocket and held it before my eyes—himself, surrounded by a numerous family . . . I forced down my mad rage and walked past. . . .'

It has often been said of the Great War that an infantry battle degenerated into mere, dull butchery. But the individual counted, even in trench warfare, even in this bloodiest, wildest and most brutal of warfare. Here, two individual enemies confronting each other suddenly in a narrow trench, could decide the result of the fight by their action. Where would be the

[1] 'You will not find a man in the whole army who can be relied upon so implicitly to do his duty simply and without fuss as the man of Lower Saxony. When there was need to prove, "Here stands a man, and if need be here he falls . . ." not one of them ever wavered.' Lieut. Jünger.
[2] Harrison had the extraordinary and unnerving experience of taking prisoner the brother of the man he had killed and of watching the living man with his dead brother. His account of the incident is one of the most moving and truthful in all the history of war.

success of war if it were not for individuals for whom the thrill of action intoxicates and hurls forward with irresistible impetus?

There was very little difference in junior leadership between British and German. Even in 1917, many young officers of both sides spoke and wrote of the chances of 'winning a glorious death', though older men had long since realized that glory was dead. Both led with dash and verve, appreciating that danger was the supreme moment of career, the chance to show manhood at its best. Honour and gallantry made them the master of the hour. It is not mere poetic extravagance to say that many young officers regarded as sublime the facing of death at the head of a platoon or company of men.

But there was no pretence of equality in the German Army out of the line. Men were kept apart from officers not only in the obvious places but in churches, beaches, hairdressers, theatres, stairways, lavatories and brothels. Feeling against this rose so high that in March 1917 Ludendorff sent out an order warning officers to watch their behaviour. He went so far in this order as to agree that the men had justifiable complaints. After sharing the hardships of the trenches with officers the soldiers resented artificial barriers when on leave. The more idealistic among them had hoped for a democratic fraternity forged by the brotherhood of war, but most were soon disillusioned as they saw the class process continuing right through the war. Many officers continued, even in 1918, to give expensive dinners prepared from army rations. Ludendorff tried to stop this, too.[1]

Gradually, and in Picardy especially, the qualities which had raised the Germans to greatness fanned themselves to white heat and then, inexorably, they were drowned in the mud and blood.

One of the worst features of the war was that a helpless wounded man knew for certain he could drown in a mud-hole. A suffusion of blood on the surface of a shell-hole here and there showed that a man had vanished.

Spring was not much better, for collapse of the frozen trench walls brought to light men who had fallen in the previous autumn's fighting. But this was a minor horror compared to the British offensive of late spring, 1917, when the battle of Messines was launched—under cover of 2,226 guns and nineteen mines packed with a million pounds of explosives. The German Army never did find out how many men it lost when those mines went

[1]Better food for officers had long been the English practice, but many an individual officer shared equally with his men.

up. Next, on 31 July, after a two-weeks' bombardment, the Third Battle of Ypres was launched.

The battlefield was reclaimed swampland. Under the artillery fire and with ground-water and rain soon filling the craters the area became one vast bog in which soldiers of both sides floundered, struggled and drowned until 20 November, by which time the British had lost more than 380,000 men. The Germans suffered, too, and they lost a few positions—but they held. They held.

George Bucher, an infantry officer, wrote:

'There was an absolute downpour of earth and shell splinters . . . Three men were plastered on the walls of the trench or lying in fragments on the ground . . . There was a terrific explosion and a hissing column of flame and earth rose from the trench . . . a dug-out and four men in it had ceased to exist. I arrived at the company commander's dug-out just in time to help carry Lieutenant Kranz down the steps. He was already dead—a big splinter stuck out from the rent in the crown of his head.

' "I'm taking over command of the company," young von Mall said. That twenty-year-old was responsible for 160 men. I saw his calm, steady hand grasp the telephone . . . the situation was beyond our control. The bombardment raged with undiminished intensity; we reported to von Mall; twenty-seven dead so far, all mutilated horribly.

'By the evening the parapets had disappeared. . . . Forty-one dead, all blown to shreds. All through the night the soil of Flanders was lacerated by most furious shell fire. In the morning we reported fifty-nine dead, all unrecognizable. More than twenty severely wounded men were lying in the dug-outs. . . .

'About midday the ground heaved and rocked. I staggered out of my shelter and worked my way along the ruins of the trench while shell splinters hummed around me. Where the company commander's dug-out had been twelve steps deep and reinforced with baulks of timber was now a huge smoking crater. There was nothing to be seen in it but wreckage and a little blood-soaked earth. Young von Mall had been no coward . . . The third night had come . . . We laid the remains of our eighty-four dead in the huge crater but not for a moment did the shells leave them alone.'

On the fourth day a very young soldier had had enough. He climbed out of the trench with two grenades from which he had taken the safety pins and told his comrades what he thought of the war. He intended to run towards the British rifle fire and throw his grenades at them, but he would throw them at his comrades if they tried to stop him. They let him go. . . .

Later somebody came running to Bucher to say that his friend Sonderbeck was wounded and asking for him.

'Blood was streaming from him. He did not shriek—but his hands were clutching a ghastly fragment of himself, his severed leg which still wore a talisman boot. It lay across him—he held it to him as a mother might hold her child. . . . I tried to take it away from him but he held on to it fiercely and moaned imploringly. . . . Nothing could have saved him.'

As on many other occasions, the British were too confident that the artillery had killed every last German.

But forty of Bucher's company were still alive and these survivors with others inflicted dreadful casualties on 'the English Tommies of furious, superhuman courage whose bravery compelled my admiration'. In the end the Germans retook most of the ground the British had captured.

Fairly frequently, at parades behind the lines and sometimes in the line itself, soldiers were awarded the Iron Cross for bravery. Altogether, for the war of 1813, that of 1870-1 and for the 1914-18 war, 219,000 First Class crosses were awarded and 5,500,000 Second Class crosses. The comparable British decoration for the First Class Iron Cross is the Distinguished Conduct Medal (instituted 1854) and for the Second Class, the Military Medal (instituted 1916). During the Great War the M.M. was awarded 115,429 times and a bar to the medal 5,965 times; the D.C.M. 24,571 times with 478 bars.

Because so many Iron Crosses were awarded there has been a tendency to sneer at it as 'having been brought up with the rations'—a criticism also levelled at the M.M. Such a slur is not justified. The men who won the Iron Cross well deserved it. It is a pity that each award was not inscribed with the name and regiment of the recipient, in the British fashion.

Wound badges were as highly valued as the Iron Cross. These had no ribbon but were worn on the breast like the star of an order. They were issued in black metal for one or two wounds, in silver for three or four and in gold for five or more.

CHAPTER XVI

The Only Undefeated German Leader

On 20 November 1917 came the revolutionary battle of Cambrai, in which the British Army used 381 tanks during the first great tank battle of history. The Germans were temporarily demoralized by the psychological effect of the great lumbering monsters. They travelled at only three miles an hour but were so huge and deliberate and apparently invulnerable that many Germans despaired. It was a great victory for the British, although the success was nullified because the British General Staff had not expected such a success and had not made plans to follow up. At the end of the day's fighting British casualties were about 4,000, but by the time the Germans had stabilized the front, 45,000.

Much of the initial fighting took place around Flesquières, where Germans fought with great gallantry. The British Commander-in-Chief, Sir Douglas Haig, reported: 'Many of the hits on tanks at Flesquières were obtained by a German artillery officer, who remained alone at his battery, and served his gun single-handedly until killed. The great bravery of this officer aroused the admiration of all ranks.'

On this day batteries of Field Regiments 282 and 108 fought at Flesquières. The Germans do not know to which regiment the unknown hero belonged. But British and German soldiers all spoke of a battery stationed to the west of Flesquières which continued to shoot in the midst of murderous fire. It hit tank after tank, and took heavy punishment in return. One by one the crew went down until only one man remained at his post, drenched in blood and blackened by smoke. He loaded, aimed and fired. Then he, too, was killed. The Germans claimed that the battery wrecked forty-nine British tanks.[1]

To many a German officer it had become more and more clear as the war progressed that all success sprang from the sort of individual action provided by the officer at Flesquières, while the mass of troops gave weight and impetus of fire. These officers, soldiers by inclination as well as by conscription, devoted much time to the training of shock troops—trying to build on what the assault parties of 1915 had begun. Their attitude was that it was better to command a resolute section than a wavering company, but if they could get a resolute company so much the better. Unfortunately, shock troops needed to be handpicked and by 1918 Germany had too many formations for which to find a hard core to be able to pick them out and put them into select companies.

By 1918 the German Supreme Command knew that only a great offensive could break the crushing grip imposed by the naval blockade. All Germans were ready for an offensive. Many soldiers who had been wounded in earlier battles were back in the line. The soldier who could go back time and again indeed had nerve, for every new and frightful impression seared itself into his brain, adding to the crazy complexity of fearful memories already there. The Germans went back—time and again. There are authenticated cases of men returning to action after as many as twenty wounds—that is, wounded on twenty separate occasions, not merely with twenty splinters from the one grenade.

Great preparations were made and on 21 March the Kaiserschlacht was launched—mostly against the front of the British Fifth Army, commanded by General Gough who was later blamed for the German success. Initially the attack was violently successful and the Germans were jubilant.

The Allied situation became so desperate that on 26 March Foch was appointed Commander-in-Chief of the Allied Armies. By 5 April the German attack had run itself to ground and was left with an extensive salient with its apex nine miles east of Amiens. On 9 April the Germans launched another powerful attack—this time on the British First Army along the Lys River

[1] When German artillerymen erected a Monument of Honour in Cologne in 1936 in memory of their 150,000 fallen comrades of the Great War the sculptor was commissioned to represent this unknown artilleryman holding the last hand grenade in his hand while he still defended his gun after firing the last shell.

—after scattering the Portuguese Army like chaff. This attack also petered out and by 30 April the Germans merely had another salient. And salients are terribly vulnerable to enemy artillery.

On 27 May they launched their third great attack—against the French this time. They stormed the ridge of Chemin des Dames and within thirty-six hours they had pushed a large bulge in the line between Reims and Soissons. They made several attacks right up until 6 July on this area, then came to a halt. Between 21 March and August each side had lost a million casualties.

The Germans killed many prisoners during their great offensive of 1918. A German writer records: 'No quarter was given. The English hastened with upstretched arms through the first wave of storm troops to the rear, where the fury of battle had not reached boiling point. An orderly of Lieutenant Gipkens shot a good dozen or more with his 32 repeater. I cannot blame our men for their bloodthirsty conduct. To kill a defenceless man is baseness . . . On the other hand, the defending force, after driving their bullets into the attacking one at five paces distance, must take the consequences. A man cannot change his feelings during the last rush with a veil of blood before his eyes. He does not want to take prisoners but to kill. He has no scruples left; only the spell of primeval instinct remains.'

The Germans were not always the methodical, competent troops they appeared. Their artillery, like that of all armies, occasionally shelled their own men, as in July 1918 near Puisieux, where a company was practically annihilated. A platoon commander, with a direct hit in the loins from a shell, was a shapeless mass. One man had both hands severed at the wrist. Blood and brains and pieces of flesh were everywhere and at once collected swarms of flies. The company commander sent protest after protest to H.Q., demanding either the cessation of the firing or the presence of artillery officers in the trench.

After all this it seemed impossible that the Germans could survive another offensive. Their losses had been enormous and were now irreplaceable; boys were being pushed in to do men's work. But the Allies had fresh troops pouring in at the rate of 250,000 a month—Americans.

On 8 August, in a major attack for which elaborate preparations had been made, the Allies achieved their greatest triumph since the Marne, nearly four years earlier. This was the Battle of Amiens. At a cost of 12,000 men, two attacking armies—largely spearheaded by Australians—killed and wounded 13,000 of the enemy, captured 15,000, took 400 guns and drove right through the German front.

But the Allies were not sufficiently prepared to follow up this success with relentless exploitation. By 10 August German resistance had stiffened as many reserve divisions were thrown in. Many of the troops were boys, some so young that tough Australians could not shoot them, but booted them in the bottom and sent them rearwards as prisoners.

On 11 August, after severe fighting, the Australians captured Lihons, but not long after this the Germans launched a series of determined counter-attacks, supported by heavy artillery. The German ability to recover and hit back, as they did time and again, was one of the most astonishing aspects of the war.

These vigorous counter-attacks were a sure sign it was time to end the battle, so it was decided to postpone operations until 15 August. The total casualties of the great battle were: French 24,232; British 22,202; German, about 75,000. The French captured 11,373 and 259 guns and the British 18,500 and 240 guns.

To the Germans of all ranks the battle was more of a catastrophe than the Allies realized. General Ludendorff was to write that 8 August was 'the black day of the German Army in this war'. German despondency was understandable. The great gains of March had been lost; every letter from home told how hungry the soldiers' families were; German armour could not match Allied armour. A German prisoner said: 'The officers and men in many cases come to consider the approach of tanks a sufficient excuse for not fighting. Their sense of duty is sufficient to make them fight against infantry, but if tanks appear, many feel they are justified in surrendering.'

Nevertheless, fighting continued, with the war now in its final phase. Battle followed battle and the German line was forced back and back until the Armistice on 11 November.

Meanwhile, despite the generally superficial unity in the General Staff, sharp conflicts and jealousies occurred. In 1918 no staff officer would hold a conversation with another unless he had a witness.

The often expressed statement that 'Germany lost the Great

War' is meaningless. Politically she was beaten to her knees and made to grovel, but the German Army was not beaten and never at any time felt itself beaten. It was overwhelmed, which is something different.[1] Many officers and men were astonished and angry at surrender, many came out of the holocaust more militant militarists than ever before. Lieutenant Jünger expressed the feelings of these men very clearly. 'The idea of the Fatherland had been distilled from all these afflictions in a clearer and brighter essence. That was the final winnings in a game on which so often all had been staked; the nation was no longer to me an empty thought veiled in symbols. How could it when I had seen so many die for its sake . . . ? And so, I learned from this four years' schooling in force and in all the fantastic extravagance of material warfare that life has no meaning except when it is pledged for an ideal, and that there are ideals in comparison with which the life of an individual and even of people has no weight. . . . German lives and Germany never shall go under.'

Jünger was writing contemporarily. In 1942, *Signal* magazine, looking back to November 1918, stated: 'To have created the new warrior, who dared to advance against the products of war techniques, was the proud achievement of the German infantry. The German Army, crowned with glory, could lay down its weapons unashamed, because it passed on to the coming generation a legacy of the spiritual kind, the science and teaching of the new man.'

Signal's language was extravagant, but it did no more than justice to one small part of the Germany Army, except that this small part did not lay down its arms at all. It was led by the most outstanding German soldier of the Great War—and one of the greatest military geniuses in history—Colonel Paul von Lettow-Vorbeck. Regrettably, he is little known other than to some military historians and to specialists on East Africa.

Von Lettow-Vorbeck began the war in East Africa with 216 white officers and men and 2,540 native troops. His maximum strength, including bearers, never exceeded 20,000 and he had to improvise with everything. He had not a single modern rifle; he had no depot and no field hospital.

Yet he kept more than 300,000 British and Allied troops

[1] The Germans left a million soldiers in the East to keep the conquered territories subdued. It is sobering to think of the difference this number could have made if flooded on to the Western Front.

chasing him over an area half the size of Australia. They never defeated him and never caught him, but he inflicted 60,000 casualties on them, including 20,000 dead. The British and their Allies sent no fewer than 130 generals into action against von Lettow-Vorbeck and their campaigns cost about £150,000,000. Von Lettow-Vorbeck remained a colonel; he also remained the only undefeated German leader of the war.

When faced with the crisis of defending German East Africa without possibility of reinforcements from Germany and with little chance of getting supplies, the colonel was aged forty-four; he was greying and he had only one eye. But with that eye he saw more than most men see with two. He showed what he was made of on 3 November 1914 at Tanga, the day the British landed 'to occupy' German East Africa. By 10 a.m. they had 4,000 men ashore from the transports and outnumbered the German force four to one; his officers urged von Lettow-Vorbeck to open fire.

'A little longer,' he said. By noon the odds had grown to six to one. The colonel wanted a little longer yet. The odds were at least eight to one by 3 p.m. when the Germans launched a single, narrow-fronted attack which drove the British and Indian troops back from Tanga township with heavy losses.

Von Lettow-Vorbeck hoped that the British would counter-attack. This they obligingly did—in the only part of the field where a mass attack was possible. In addition to his frontal defences, the German commander had machine-guns on ridges on both flanks of this area. . . .

At 4.35 p.m. the British counter-attack began—with several waves of English and Indian troops advancing steadily towards the German positions ahead of them. Not a shot was fired. When the first wave was 100 yards from the German positions a British whistle blew and the bayonet charge began. At 50 yards the German machine-guns in front opened up and the attack stopped dead for a few minutes until the following infantry, hurdling the dead and wounded, seemed about to overwhelm the German line by sheer weight. At that moment von Lettow-Vorbeck signalled the order to his flank gunners to open fire; the effect was devastating and demoralizing. Several British officers rallied men for charges, but none could get started. A British colonel saw that the flanking guns were the main menace and, rallying the remnants of a company, he led a charge up the ridge; he and his men were shot down on the crest. The colonel himself, wounded, crawled forward but an African soldier shot him through the head. Von Lettow-Vorbeck often spoke of the bravery of that British officer.

Fighting continued throughout the night, the British commander leaving it until daylight before making the decision to evacuate. Unhindered, the German machine-guns raked the boats taking the troops to the waiting ships. In all, British losses were at least 2,000 dead and probably another 2,000 wounded. Naturally enough, in Britain the débâcle was hushed up and figures were never released, but the casualties were among the most one-sided ever inflicted on a major power. Von Lettow-Vorbeck lost fifteen German and fifty-four native soldiers.

For the next eighteen months the British did not seriously threaten 'that Prussian', as they called him, but he threatened them. He attacked the 440-mile Mombasa–Lake Victoria railway and in two years destroyed twenty trains and tore up the line scores of times. The British had to build hundreds of blockhouses in their efforts to defend the line.

Ammunition was always a problem for the Germans. In April 1915 a supply ship cleared the blockade but ran aground near Tanga. The Germans salvaged some of the cargo and for months afterwards every German in Tanganyika took apart rifle cartridges to remove wet powder and fit new caps.

When clothing supplies gave out the Germans spun cotton by hand and made new clothing; they made shoes from buffalo hide. They gathered wild rubber and vulcanized it with sulphur to make truck and bicycle tyres. When not enough captured petrol was available they distilled a crude fuel from coconuts. These Germans, under von Lettow-Vorbeck, became some of the most versatile and enterprising guerrilla fighters ever.

In February 1916 about 45,000 South African troops, led by General Smuts, attacked across the Kenya frontier. Von Lettow-Vorbeck gave battle and beat the South Africans decisively. The next British steps were to bring in more native troops—from Kenya, the Gold Coast and Nigeria—and to build a railway to the Tanganyika frontier to supply their forces. By August 1916 weight of numbers had pushed the Prussian back into the southern half of Tanganyika, but it was no victory for the Allied force, because the white troops were going down in hundreds with malaria and other diseases, while the toughened Germans and their native troops were fit and well.

The Allied attack had lost all momentum, but Smuts wrote to von Lettow-Vorbeck urging surrender to avoid further bloodshed. 'That Prussian' replied courteously that the war would continue. Soon after, he wrote to Smuts again to ask about a note found on a dead South African officer to the effect that no German prisoners were to be taken. Smuts denied, truthfully, that any such order existed. For his own part, von Lettow-Vorbeck released all his prisoners if they gave their word not to fight again. He had neither the food to keep them alive nor the guards to keep them captive, and he had no base compound in which to keep them. At all times he scrupulously obeyed the rules of warfare. Smuts respected his enemy so much that he allowed the Germans to receive mail from home and even had it delivered to them.

Late in 1917 trouble closed in on von Lettow-Vorbeck on all sides. The Belgians sent a column from the Congo; the Portuguese moved in from Angola and Mozambique; a Rhodesian expedition headed from the south-east and a big British-South African attack was being mounted in the north. At this point the Prussian had 4,000 men—but what men they were! Seasoned, hard, loyal and with no discrimination whatever between black and white troops.

For practice more than anything else, they attacked the terrified Portuguese garrisons and always won. They ambushed other enemy patrols and wiped them out. But nobody ever trapped or ambushed any of von Lettow-Vorbeck's men. On 18 October 1918, now back in Tanganyika, the Prussian, buoyant and adventurous, struck south into Rhodesia, where he captured one military depot after another in a series of lightning raids. On 13 November he was ready to attack Broken Hill, the main centre of Northern Rhodesia. Then, to his astonishment, he heard from a captured British soldier that an armistice had been signed. Confirming the report, von Lettow-Vorbeck first planned to make for Portuguese East Africa where he could have kept several divisions busy for years trying to winkle him out. But on consideration the colonel concluded that he must, in honour, conform to the armistice.

Bitterly disappointed, he disbanded his bearers and reported himself to the nearest British senior officer—two weeks after the armistice. 'I am not surrendering,' he said. 'I am merely putting myself at your disposal.' He and his troops were allowed to retain their weapons in recognition of their achievements. This gallant and humane soldier must for ever hold a unique place in military history.[1]

[1] Von Lettow-Vorbeck—who lost his two sons in the 1939–45 War—never did get much publicity in Britain, although British veterans of East Africa stood and sang 'For He's a Jolly Good Fellow' when he attended their rally in London in 1929. It is pleasant to record that in 1945, when von Lettow-Vorbeck was poverty-stricken in shattered Germany, Field-Marshal Smuts suggested to a few wealthy British and South African friends that they pay him a small pension in appreciation of his gallantry. Despite Smuts's death, this pension was paid until von Lettow-Vorbeck himself died on 9 March 1964—eleven days before his ninety-fourth birthday.

CHAPTER XVII

Two Classes of People—Soldiers and Swine

For the German soldier the most profound human experience of the World War was the comradeship—the human bonds uniting him to his fellows in his misery and during the fighting, the feeling of an indissoluble community of destiny in the face of a hostile world superior in material resources. It was from this spiritual and mental factor that the Socialist idea on a national basis was born.

But while the common soldier[1] was inarticulate the generals had much to say and they said it at length. They produced a flood of literature, some of it apologia, some of it justifying, much of it vainglorious. Everybody had to explain what had gone wrong, best achieved, it seemed, by vilification of colleagues.

The General Staff strove hard to avoid being identified with the German defeat and Hindenburg, whose nominal responsibility it was, found several scapegoats. The first one was not even a military man, but a Catholic from the south of Germany. He was Erzberger, an advocate of peace, and a true patriot. He tried to represent the beaten army and for his pains—and painful his job must have been—he was later assassinated by soldiers.

The Allies made a major mistake in agreeing to negotiate with Erzberger. Hindenburg should have been forced to report

---

[1] One such common soldier was Corporal Adolf Hitler of the 16th Bavarian Infantry Regiment who, it is reputed, won the Military Service Cross with Swords, the Regimental Diploma for Gallantry and the Iron Cross first class. Whatever later faults he displayed, Hitler was a brave and competent soldier. At the end of the war he was in a military hospital in Pomerania, half blinded by poison gas.

to Foch and to hand over his sword in ceremonial surrender—
as the Germans made Napoleon III do after the French defeat
at Sedan. Had this been done the Germans would have understood that they were beaten; being a martial race they could
have appreciated the military gesture. There was no such formal
surrender, merely a shabby political encounter.

Throughout history beaten generals have had an unhappy
time. Many have been exiled or gaoled or executed by a variety
of means—beheading, hanging, shooting. A thoroughly beaten
general has no career left for him. In modern times the usual
practice is to promote him and pension him—then forget him.
But after World War I the German generals still had honour in
the eyes of the public and of the army. Hindenburg and Ludendorff, the two great military architects, did not admit a single
error. They supported the propaganda department created to
spread the belief that the German Army had been 'unconquered
in the field; beaten at home'. This slogan was served up so
repeatedly and with such an air of authority that few people
questioned it. The story was that the politicians had stabbed
Germany in the back while the attention of the generals had
been fixed on the war.

Only a few men spoke out against the developing myth. One
officer told the Reichstag: 'Nobody would have dared at the
beginning of the war to expect from the soldier what he afterwards had to endure for years. There were no limits, till the
moment arrived when a quick breakdown commenced. Not to
have seen this was a psychological error on the part of the
Supreme Command . . . who lost at last all estimate of what was
attainable.'

But heretics like this were brushed aside. After a tradition of
victory, after many years of believing in German invincibility,
the public was anxious to accept an excuse, any excuse, for
defeat.[1] The Germans, civil and military, were equally ready to
believe that the Allies had been the aggressors and the Germans
the innocent victims.

This surprised the Allied propaganda experts, who had been
bombarding the German troops with political leaflets. The
troops were tired and hungry and short of munitions and they
had all kinds of complaints, but they so resented the leaflets
that they did more harm than good. Propaganda may influence

[1] Much later Captain Schmidt, in a book on war profits and economy,
charged that the 'untamed profit-intoxication of the privileged decisively
contributed to our breakdown in 1918'.

civilian populations, but it has little influence on real fighting men. If anything it increases their corporate morale rather than lowers it.

German postwar vengefulness showed itself in many ways. As early as 25 September 1919 the *Deutsche Zeitung* carried an article exhorting 'workmen of Germany' to kill British occupation troops. 'KILL THEM. THE LAST GREAT JUDGMENT WILL HOLD YOU BLAMELESS' (Paper's capitals).

Gustav Stresemann, in a speech to the National Assembly on 8 October 1919, was hinting at the next war. 'This Alsace and vast tracts of Lorraine are German regions and their inhabitants are of German blood. The tricolour may float above Strasbourg cathedral, but that imposing edifice was born of German spirit . . . It all bears the impress of the German character and is animated by German spirit. That is why we shall never forget that Alsace-Lorraine is German, that it will always belong to us in spirit and that our task will be to preserve for Germany this spiritual patrimony.'

He was merely echoing the sentiments of all Germans. The German people and the army never did believe they were beaten, so the stipulations of the Treaty of Versailles, ratified on 10 January 1920, came as such a surprise to them.[1] To block German attempts at supremacy in Europe, the Germans were told to stay in their own national area; they had to leave Poland and the Danubian lands—all sharp blows to German pride.

Many Germans genuinely believed that some mistake had been made in the Treaty and that soon it would be put right. The reparations Germany was called upon to pay were considered a mere matter of form, consequently the Germans had another shock when the money was actually demanded. The Treaty of Versailles did not break the Germans; it united them. Germany was like an angry and puzzled boxer who genuinely believed that the referee had awarded the fight to the wrong man and was, therefore, eager for a return fight to prove his point.

She had, after all, fought harder and more completely than any other country and though the war cost 164 million marks, not a penny of it came from extra taxation.[2]

---

[1] The Armistice had lasted no less than fourteen months—from 11 November 1918. Until the ratification of the Treaty of Versailles, hostilities had merely been suspended.

[2] After six years of peace Germany had recovered from the war more completely than any other nation—a tribute to hard work and enterprise—and to the Treaty of Versailles!

Soon after the peace the infamous Free Corps had come into existence. These were bands of demobbed and unemployable officers and they forayed across the country putting down democratic upsurges. Bloody-minded and brutal-handed mercenaries, they were guilty of shocking atrocities and were the spiritual predecessors of Hitler's S.S. and Gestapo.

In 1919 the Free Corps was transferred to the Baltic, where it fought the Poles—sub-humans by German standards—for nearly two years. Later, they carried out a political putsch, but were not punished and continued their reign of terror.

War crimes had been alleged against nearly 3,000 German officers and many men, but only twelve were actually brought to trial—charged with murder and cruelty to British prisoners-of-war. The whole proceeding—at Leipzig in 1920—was a farce and the maximum sentence was two years' gaol. The men tried became public heroes.

The Control Commission for the Disarmament of Germany was functioning and its members did their duty as best they could, but they were thwarted at every turn.

The German Officers' Corps was the most potent element in the community during the whole time the Control Commission was stationed in Germany.[1] Every German regimental mess met in secret. Even more remarkable, the courts of honour still met and meted out a form of justice that covered every officer not only in the army but in the reserve as well.

The police were also powerful. The Security Police, from the colour of their uniform, were known as the Green Police, and in Berlin itself they were ex-Guardsmen to a man, just as the Blue Police all over Germany were all ex-servicemen.

During the years of the occupation there was much trouble between former German soldiers, mostly officers, and occupation troops. 'Incidents' were commonplace.

The German Army itself was not happy. Under the Treaty its numbers were limited to 100,000—though it soon found ways of circumventing this restriction.[2] For a time German officers dared not wear uniform in public, for town mobs spat at them and tore off their epaulettes. This was reaction. So many people

---

[1] Until 1927.

[2] In returns supplied to the control commission on 17 February 1920, the German Government admitted the existence of 470,560 effective troops—370,560 more than the Treaty establishment. This did not include the masked military formation, the Security Police, of about 60,000, the infamous Free Corps, or the huge improvised militia.

thought that the army should never have surrendered. The reaction did not last long.

In the German '100,000 army' of 1920 and also in the German Police Force were the so-called 'traditional companies'. They were companies like any others, with the difference that it was their task to keep alive the memory of a former military unit famous in Germany's past. No meritorious regiment was forgotten. The souvenirs, the old weapons, flags, uniforms and pictures were preserved in the billets of these companies. Customs were also observed which recalled the old units.

Many soldiers wore a narrow ribbon with an embroidered inscription on their sleeve. There was, for instance, a light blue ribbon which preserved the memory of a regiment which stormed a hill near Gibraltar.

During their instruction the men of these traditional companies were made familiar with the history of the regiment which they represented. Almost every German regiment had its own march. The Ninth Infantry Regiment used the Dessau March, to honour Prussian valour at Turin in the eighteenth century.[1]

In 1920, a German Staff Officer revealed that the senior cadets at officers' training schools practised orgies of torture on the junior boys, sticking them with knives and needles, sewing their trouser buttons into their flesh, tying the victim up for hours in a kind of improvised pillory with his limbs extended until he collapsed, and numerous other ingenious malpractices.[2]

Boy cadets—the youngest were only ten years of age—had been especially well indoctrinated. From rising in the morning to lying down at night they did everything as a drill. The last order at night was a shouted 'Attention! Go to sleep!'

All ranks were told in as many words that only two classes of human beings existed—soldiers and swine. This attitude was not new and it never ended.

Foreign observers were apt to say that it was only the monarchical idea to which the German soldier owed his élan and which formed the basis of German discipline. When William II abdicated, these people thought that the living tradition of the German Army was interrupted. They were to

[1] In most armies patriotism in the army is only an indirect motive for fighting and most soldiers would be embarrassed by repeated references to it, but in Germany patriotism was stressed on every possible occasion.
[2] *Das alte Heer*, by a German Staff Officer, published Charlottenburg, 1920.

learn that the German Army drew its strength from the soul of its people, for every German was a soldier at heart, and during the 1920s the old respect for the uniform had returned.

If an officer walked along the pavement he had the right of way; he never waited in a queue at a box office and he was always served first in any establishment. In law, it was no mere figure of speech to say that a German officer had only to allege that the victim had 'insulted' him and he was practically assured of acquittal. In a public scuffle if an officer omitted to cut down a civilian he would be tried by a court of honour and deprived of the right to wear a uniform and made an outcast. Most officers so treated committed suicide.

The 100,000 army was an excellent training ground for officers and many innovations of a tactical and technical nature were tried out. But nobody, least of all the foreign experts, considered it possible to wage war with this army.

One of the General Staff's first reforms was to re-organize the Service Corps and invest it with more distinction than it ever had before. Nobody had wanted to serve in the Army Service Corps; an officer who did so was a social outcast. The General Staff changed that; it was another example of the German ability to profit by mistake.

Some sober, analytical Germans still existed, but few dared to speak out openly. In 1921 one of them published in Stuttgart a fascinating and now very rare book. It was *Die Tragödie Deutschlands, von einem Deutschen* (Germany's Tragedy, by a German). The reason for the author's anonymity will become obvious. He wrote, in part:

> 'The war has been conducted by us without the slightest chivalry, without the slightest nobility and with the most appalling hatred. That is why the moral brutalization which the war produced among us now knows no limits.[1] The instincts of an unlicensed soldiery dominate today the whole of our public life. The hand grenade . . . the revolver and the rubber truncheon take the place of argument, murder has become the recognized instrument of politics . . . That the craft of war brutalizes there can be no doubt. And it brutalizes the young far more than the old . . . It

[1] Not long before the book was published the Blücher family tomb at Wahlstadt, Silesia, was broken open and next morning the skeleton of Blücher was found on the snow beside the tomb. Robbers had expected to find his decorations which had reputedly been buried with him.

simply brutalized the very soul of the German people. Nowhere was this brutalization more apparent than in matters of sex. During the war hundreds of thousands of children were born infected with syphilis. The officers set the example in this unbridled licentiousness. Special brothels reserved for officers flooded every place occupied by the army. The brothel system was simply nauseating . . . All self control and sense of discipline in Germany disappeared. The German people, steeped in war, became dirty to the very depths of their souls. . . . The Press systematically and under official direction, indoctrinated the whole people with a cult of hate, brutality, blood-lust and cruelty.'

Long before Hitler came to power, long before anybody suspected that he might come to power, the army was regaining its strength, thinking deeply, planning ahead, under its Chief of Staff and organizing genius, General Hans von Seeckt,[1] to whom war was 'the highest summit of human achievement; it is the natural, the final stage in the historical development of humanity'.

[1] As a young lieutenant, von Seeckt, on duty with a company of troops at the public lying-in-state of Emperor William I in the Berlin cathedral in 1888, ordered his men to fix bayonets and charge into the crowd, which had become so great as to break some barriers. There was no riot, no intention to riot. The silent, undemonstrative crowd was there to pay its respect to the monarch. For his act von Seeckt was acclaimed 'a true soldier'.

CHAPTER XVIII

Psychological Preparation for War

One of the most important features of the Second World War was the German's clever use of psychology[1] to revitalize military strategy and tactics to meet the demands of total war.

Even now, few people fully appreciate the thoroughness of Germany's psychological treatment of its armed forces—and for that matter, of its entire population. The High Command used psychology to choose the most competent man for the right place, to bolster morale, to accustom the troops to the stress and strains of technical warfare, to ease combat-shock, to heighten military efficiency, and to control the officer-man relationship.[2]

That the Germans were conscious of the need for a psychological approach to war is shown by the nearly six hundred books written wholly or partly about the subject. It is short-sighted to dismiss the subject as mere quackery. The Germans considered a man's social-emotional qualifications an important part of the study to determine his potential ability as a leader and fighter.

[1] Psychology played a small part in German preparations for the First World War, though they had sent a team to study problems of panic in the Russo-Japanese war. During the 1914–18 war Ludendorff issued several edicts on the need for 'a morale service', and urged 'patriotic education of the troops'. A few psychologists were invited to study the strains of combat, but not until the middle of the war were they actually asked to use their skill in selecting army specialists. They psychologically tested drivers, airmen and gas warfare technicians.

[2] Some sort of psychological study seemed necessary. In 1923 the number of suicides in the army was 111 per 100,000 and in 1924 it rose to 160. Suicides among the civilian population amounted to 23 per 100,000. (*Finanzpolitische Korrespondenz*, 25 May 1925.)

As early as 1926 a German officer and a noted military writer and psychologist—he subsequently fled to the United States—predicted what the leader of the future would be like. 'He will be a military psychologist, a sort of aggressive pacifist withholding the use of armed force until all other means of warfare have failed to realize their aims.' He strongly implied that 'pacific aggression' could bring victory even without the actual waging of war. It was precisely this sort of 'pacific aggression' which gave Hitler his early victories, such as over Austria and Czechoslovakia.

Psychological 'study' in the British and American armies was largely based on intelligence tests. The Germans were more concerned with character—the social, emotional and temperamental qualities which go to make up a man and which do not necessarily come to light in a pencil-and-paper intelligence test.

German morale-building did not begin and end with Y.M.C.A. recreation huts and lectures on the dangers of V.D. To the Germans a soldier's morale was based on community, religious and familial values and the army took them all into full account.

After the war a group of young officers advocated the introduction of aptitude testing into the professional nucleus army and immediate use of psychology in military education and training. The idea was adopted, but apart from one or two professional psychologists the work was given to ex-officers who were more enthusiastic than competent.

However, in 1929 an army psychology research institute was founded, with Hans von Voss, a retired colonel, as military commander and M. Simoneit as scientific director. The seven professional psychologists who formed the staff of the institute began something which was to build up to an immense and complex organization.

But they had a difficult beginning. Even General von Seeckt had little use for psychologists in the army. But like all the other misbelievers, von Seeckt came to realize that psychology was the most important aspect of military leadership. He and others, like General Marx and Admiral Hansen, had argued that commanding officers, through long experience, were the best judges of men in the forces.

Still, everybody agreed that a new type of soldier was needed. Up till now military skill and blind obedience were all that had been required of a soldier. A soldier who thought for himself was not merely unorthodox; he was dangerous. Every soldier was expected to be at all times within sight of an officer, preferably his company commander.

But the savagery of the Great War destroyed company formation. When called upon by circumstance to produce initiative and to act independently many a German soldier was helpless. Droves of prisoners were taken in this way. Hence a new type of soldier was needed, one described by the psychologist K. Hesse[1] as 'a warrior willing and able to subordinate himself yet be capable of independent action'.

This transformation came about during the Reichswehr period (1919–33) when the army tried to develop qualities of leadership together with military skill. A will-to-live in order to accomplish a task replaced the old will-to-die creed.

Even so there was still much brutality in the army. It was still routine for an officer or an N.C.O. to punch or kick a soldier.

Simultaneously with practical developments in the army some people were drumming up enthusiasm for militarism. Hindenburg was one of them. Speaking to an organization called the Steel Helmet of Gross-Schwülper on 19 September 1927, he told them, 'You are all young men and you have played to me the *March of Entry into Paris* well. I hope that one day you will be playing this military march where you should, at the same spot where I was in 1870.' (In 1870 Hindenburg was on French soil.)

In 1931 the Reichswehr Ministry's Press department issued this statement:

'The Army's future depends on the fact that the warlike spirit is kept awake; that in the midst of a world bristling with arms the only man who is respected is he who is resolved to defend himself against an attack . . . To assert military thought in the education of youth . . . to lead actively the fight against anti-militarism which undermines the cultural and moral bases of our national life, to enforce the interests of the army . . . these are the permanent tasks which occupy the Reichswehr Ministry'.

Schoolteachers knew their duty to the Fatherland, but in case they were unsure General Horst von Metzsch spelled it out for them. 'It must be the teacher's ambition that his "good" pupils become soldiers. The joy in obedience can be implanted *ex cathedra*.'

There was a principle for military education, too, as defined

[1] He later became an official Nazi war correspondent with the rank of colonel.

in the *Directions for Training in the Army*, published the same year. 'The individual soldier must be educated so that he is able to accomplish his tasks in battle even if left to himself. He must know that he alone is responsible for his acts and failures.'

This was revolutionary stuff for an army that had up to now been rather hidebound. It is revolutionary enough for any army to encourage independent thinking in the ranks, for firm discipline and obedience to orders is the simple key by which an army or an infantry section wins its fight. But the same Directions pointed out that the soldier must have a balanced outlook and that a 'brash feeling of knowing-it-all should not replace discipline'.[1]

Hesse, in his *Aptitude Testing in the Army*, which became an army textbook in 1930, formulated test methods called 'command series' and 'leadership tests'.

In the command series the candidate would be given a series of orders, perhaps fifty of them, to be carried out during the day. Such qualities as alertness, quick thinking and memory would be tested in this way.

In the leadership test the candidate was given charge of a group of soldiers and told to instruct them in the assembling of a piece of equipment. Then he would have to lecture to his group on a subject known to interest him. The psychologists would not so much study the candidate as the men under his instruction. If they were interested and responsive the candidate would get high marks.

Generally, the tests were supervised by an army colonel, a medical officer and three psychologists. In groups of four and five, the candidates would spend at least two full days undergoing the tests. An annual average of 2,500 candidates were examined in the years 1930–2.

Hesse insisted that the army needed men capable of becoming leaders in an emergency. The psychological effects of new weapons required personnel with never-failing nerves, so that the selection of specialists had to go beyond the mere examination of intellect and skill and had to concentrate on the analysis of the whole personality. He wanted a characterological approach to selection, despite its apparent shortcomings.

---

[1] 'The barrack square is no place for excessive sentiment and yet living men drill on it. The human heart cannot be forced without damage being done to it and however strange it sounds, brutes and soulless arithmeticians prove a failure on the barrack square even earlier than in my lady's boudoir.' A writer in an army magazine.

When selecting officers and specialists, German military psychologists were mainly interested in the soldier's readiness to apply his will to a certain act—something they called *Einsatzbereitschaft*, rather than his ability for performance which could be objectively tested. Naturally, it was not possible to measure a man's future application of will and courage, so the Germans depended on a characterological examination of the whole personality.

Even straightforward performance tests were designed to test a man's will power, staying power and mental energy. It was ordained from the top that formal knowledge was to be regarded as very secondary to 'spiritual qualities and emotional attitudes'.

The Germans went to great lengths in their testing. While the candidate was relating his life history his expression was analysed. His facial movements were studied by a movie camera concealed by a wall chart. He was then asked specific questions, subjected to sudden and painful stimulations and ordered to work an ergograph. His resulting facial expressions were later studied.

Body movements, such as scratching the chin or the position of the lips while thinking were also noted. Even the candidate's voice was listened to intently. Monotone, hard timbre and staccato accentuation were considered indicative of calm and determined will power.

The psychologists depended greatly on the candidate's appearance and carefully noted down their first impression of the man they were examining. For instance, if he was neat they labelled him probably careful, reliable but parsimonious. He would be prone to vanity, but this was harmless. He would need to be checked to see if he was merely a bluffer and if he had an overdeveloped desire for recognition.

They did not necessarily approve of a man with robust physical appearance. This usually showed powers of endurance and energy but such a man might also be light-minded and supercilious; he could be very egotistic, pretentious and scornful. Such a man, the psychologists believed, could prove a menace in commissioned rank.

The best men of all, the men with iron nerves, intense resolution and mental resilience were put into *élite* corps, such as tank attack gunners. The Germans never talked about 'defence against tanks', as the British and Americans did; they spoke about 'attack against tanks'. The psychologists again.

General H. Franke listed as the soldierly virtues, self-discipline, secrecy, loyalty, readiness to sacrifice, courage to acknowledge guilt, resolution, willingness to share responsibility, and national pride. As Franke was one of the army's foremost theorists and editor of the official *Handbook of Modern Military Sciences* his opinion obviously carried weight.

Military life in Germany in the 'thirties and on into the war did not mean merely army service. The Nazis intended it to be the way of life of the entire German nation. In *Soldatentum*—a military journal—in 1934, Simoneit wrote that 'the most noble task of military psychology is the indoctrination of the German people with traditional soldierly virtues'.

Koeber wrote in *Young Germany: The Hitler Jugend*: 'The driving motive of the Hitler Youth is to produce a new type of militant young German . . . and to make one militarized corporate body of the whole nation.'

History, as a subject, was presented as the development of the political, spiritual and ethnic unity and destiny of the German people. It emphasized the political and military struggles experienced to accomplish this aim.

Writing in *Soldatentum* in 1934 H. H. Grunwaldt, an army psychologist, showed the difference between the German and British attitude to war—at least the difference as the Germans saw it. Grunwaldt related the story of a British colonel who, sometime during the Great War, to inspire his men to attack, threw a soccer ball towards the German lines and yelled, 'After it, boys!'

The humourless Grunwaldt said: 'The German does not consider war as a sport but as a sacred duty—in which the flag can never degenerate into a soccer ball.'

He was right; it never could. After centuries of militarism war for the German was not an unpleasant ordeal to be finished with as soon as possible, but a religion. And one does not mock one's religion by kicking a soccer ball at it.

The Third Reich was founded on terror and implemented by force—yet the Germans accepted it as implicitly as they had accepted militarism for centuries.

CHAPTER XIX

1933-9—The Nazi War Cult

From January 1933—the month Hindenburg called on Hitler to become Chancellor—Germany abandoned any pretence of keeping to the Versailles conditions and began mobilizing for war, but until July 1934 she did so with some restraint. Then the barriers came down and mobilization became blatant and open. Hitler, now Führer, was merely copying Frederick the Great,[1] in getting ready for war before declaring it. It was sound practice. It had worked before and it would work again.

In 1935 a conscript army came into being. Older people particularly favoured it. As one writer pointed out poetically, 'They knew from their own youth that blossoms with a more delicate fragrance and of purer colour are produced on the meagre soil of self-renunciation than are to be seen on the flowers growing luxuriantly in very rich earth.'[2]

With officers badly needed for the army, specially selected police officers were enlisted. But these men from the lower middle classes, many of them highly efficient, were sent back to the police force once a new crop of Junkers-type officers were available for duty.

[1] At this point, so long after Frederick's time, it is interesting to read a modern, foreign assessment of him. It was made by Brigadier-General J. H. Morgan in *Assize of Arms*, 1945. 'Filthy in mind and body, brutal, perverted, cruel, treacherous, the true character of Frederick the Great and his corrupting influence on the German people has been wholly obscured from Englishmen by the panegyrics of Carlyle who prostrates himself, and prostitutes his intellect before the image of the debased soldier with that idolatry so peculiarly characteristic of men of letters bewitched by men of action.'

[2] *Signal*, May 1943.

In the new German Army that came into being between the wars it was stressed that the officer's origin and family background were not considered important, but this was mere lip service to an impossible idea. The Officers' Corps remained a militant, selfish clique until many casualties did open the way for officers from lower classes. Throughout the Reichswehr period the Officers' Corps blocked every attempt to commission men from the ranks.

The indoctrination of an officer in peacetime was thorough. First of all, for six months to a year, he was required to serve in the Labour Service, which was supposed to teach him 'humanity', subordination and manual labour. Then, as an officer-candidate, he entered the army proper. His rank was that of a private with privileges—such as dining in the officers' mess.

During this period he was under the patronage of a father-adviser, an elderly officer whose duty it was to iron out difficulties for the young officer-candidate and to set him a model of behaviour and soldierly bearing. After a year's training the officer-candidate was promoted to non-commissioned rank, after which he was sent to an officers' school. Then followed four months at an arms school.

Finally, after at least two years and three months in the army and having qualified in two examinations, he was commissioned second-lieutenant.

Throughout the education of the German soldier—at least from 1935 onwards—no mention was ever made of the word 'defeat' or 'retreat'. Allied to this was the theory that no German soldier would ever contemplate desertion. And, in fact, very few ever did. Those who did desert left from camp or barracks, rarely from the line and under fire. I believe that this was directly a result of the intense indoctrination in patriotism and comradeship.

It is a remarkable fact that the German Army had no detention barracks or guardhouses during this build-up period. This is unique among armies. The military ideal abhorred the idea of one German soldier guarding another. This is not to say that no German soldier ever committed a crime. But if it was so serious as to warrant gaol then clearly the man had forfeited his right to be a soldier and should be dishonourably discharged at once. When this happened the man was told that he would be for ever barred from the army, which, to the proud German soldier, was humiliating and degrading. A man who had committed a crime was ignored by his comrades while he waited for his discharge to be signed. I am speaking here of military offences—going AWL, stealing from a comrade, abusing or striking a superior, attempting suicide, being caught in a homosexual act, deliberately damaging military equipment, being drunk and so on. The German Army of the 1930s had no degrading penalties, but during the war a man could be demoted to the rank of second-class soldier or posted to a punishment battalion.

The stimulation of morale was considered a complex problem, but its many facets were all triggered by tradition. Right from the beginning of the rebuilding of the new army, tradition was given even more importance than in the 1920s. Each regiment was assigned the tradition of an old Imperial regiment and expected to live up to its ideals.

The enlisting German soldier was told, almost in as many words, 'You are highly privileged to become a soldier in the German Army. You are being permitted to join a sacred brotherhood'. Later, when fully trained, the soldier was encouraged to develop a feeling of superiority over men not fortunate enough to be admitted to the army and over soldiers who were still recruits.

Throughout the 'thirties the emphasis on psychology did not flag—nor did controversy over it. In 1935 a writer in the *Militär-Wochenblatt* argued that the oversight of wrong solution of psychological problems, the careless treatment of soldiers' and civilians' minds had brought Germany to defeat in 1918. Infantry schools, he said, should introduce psychology into their curriculum and he advocated that young officers should be taught to regard and treat the soldier as an individual and a member of 'a greater community with a mind of his own'.

These views brought fire from officers' groups. One officer, a Major Schack, wrote in the same magazine that psychological theories were nonsense and merely made complex a simple duty. All an officer had to remember for himself and for his men was a maxim of Frederick the Great—'You must die stalwartly'.

But weight of opinion was against officers like Major Schack and the psychological approach to selection and training was intensified. For instance, it did not take the German military psychologists long to find out that good chauffeurs did not necessarily make good tank drivers and that good commercial aviators did not necessarily make good combat pilots. For this to happen, a man's technical skill had to be supplemented by the sometimes nebulous 'soldierly qualities'.

Tank crewmen were very carefully chosen. They were required to have a high degree of individualism and ability for independent action, a mechanic's devotion to his machine, a readiness to sacrifice and an absolute devotion to the country's cause.

The Germans now knew, better than anybody else, that the next war would be a technological one with terrific strain on the nerves of soldiers, particularly those in special services, such as paratroops, and tank crews. It was mainly due to strict selection followed by equally strict training that the German Panzer Divisions were so efficient and successful.

In fact, selection under the Nazis began long before a young man joined the army. All boys—and girls, too—from six to eighteeen were closely observed in school, in Hitler Youth and any other official organization to which they might belong.

Members of Hitler Youth were specially examined to determine general conduct in service, such as their orderliness, reliability, subordination and punctuality, attitude towards superiors and comrades, intellectual capacity and leadership qualifications. Results of complex tests were tabulated, analysed and filed—to be produced when the youth entered the forces. By now the Nazis had coined the expression 'total education' to describe what amounted to the sum purpose of existence—to serve the state. The climax of total education was army service.

The year 1936 was momentous for the army. The Rhineland was militarized again and in the same period Germany intervened in Spain, largely so that her officers could study the lessons to be learned from modern conflict. For 1936-7 at least 67 per cent. of the German budget was spent on armament. Nobody complained.

By 1937 the war cult was reaching its peak. That year Alfred Rosenberg, later to become Nazi Minister for Eastern Territories, preached: 'The German nation is just now about to find its style of life for good, a style fundamentally different from what is called British liberalism. It is the style of the marching column, regardless of where and for what purpose this marching column is to be used. It is a mark of the German style of life that no German nowadays wants to feel himself a private person. That is the explanation of why Germany is uniformed and marching in columns.'[1]

Hitler had restored to officers their old accustomed social seniority and prestige. In fact, they had the very highest rank in society, even above Nazi party officials.

The Nazis created a great devotion to the uniform and all its trappings. To a people still smarting under defeat, a uniform was something flamboyant and ego-building. It inspired the Germans with tremendous confidence, and made them into bullies. No German who had a uniform to wear, any uniform, would have been seen in public in mufti, although officers and even ordinary soldiers of other nations wore mufti increasingly when off duty.

The lines

> *Der Soldate, der Soldate,*
> *Ist der erste Mann im ganzen Staate*

became almost a creed.

The psychologists were completely in the ascendant. By 1939 the army had about two hundred psychologists on its payroll. But it made use of the thousands who remained in universities and in private practice and drew on their services whenever necessary, which was frequently.

Many top-ranking men were assigned specific research programmes, such as the problems of homesickness among conscripts; Service homosexuality; religious ethics. The two hundred uniformed psychologists had high status and, in some cases, very high rank and their qualifications were uniformly impressive.

To be sure of a candidate's suitability as an army psychologist his whole personality was investigated; his professional and general knowledge; his practical talent in research work; his character and ability to deal with ordinary soldiers, even his home life. He had to undergo serious examinations and to be approved by several interviewing boards.

Once in the army the psychologist was compelled to undergo strict military training and to become a competent soldier. This rule had two purposes: to show the psychologist what was expected of a soldier and to show senior service officers that a

[1] One of the most significant and revealing statements ever made by any Nazi.

man posted as a psychologist was not merely some sort of intellectual freak or a scholarly eccentric.[1]

The army psychologists' idea of what made a good leader is interesting. His character, they said, should contain these traits: determination; positive will; operative thinking; mental elasticity; mathematical thinking and character—a rather nebulous term subdivided into integrity, selflessness, idealism and well-controlled self-esteem.

Positive will and determination might appear to be synonymous terms, but in Nazi language, will was the 'habit of voluntary response to the command of a superior leader'. Determination was the 'drive and ability to achieve a pre-determined goal'.

The psychologists saw two major pitfalls: fatigue produced by great responsibility and accumulation of work (they pointed to Ludendorff as a prime example) and over-estimation of one's own personality, which could lead to a breach between superior and subordinates.

By 1939 the tests to which officer candidates were subjected were many and varied. In one of the most interesting the examinee was seated on a chair with his feet against a rail. He then had to pull with both hands on a spring exercise expander fixed to the wall. A steadily increasing electrical current coursed through the expander. The examinee had to hold out as long as he could against both stresses. But there was more to it than a mere test of strength and will power. An unseen camera recorded all the candidate's facial expressions and these were later studied and assessed.

The army was satisfied that the tests were 98 per cent. accurate; in short, that only two per cent. of men chosen to be officers were subsequently found to be unsuited to command. This was, compared with British, American and French experience, a minute percentage.

Senior Nazi leaders at least benefited from suggestions put forward by the army psychologists. They were to get enough sleep—at least six hours and up to eight hours a day, without

[1] Before the war and during the early stages of it the American Army regarded German emphasis on psychology with derision and considered that many of the psychologists were charlatans. They might have been unorthodox, but they were not charlatans and gradually the Americans took the problem seriously. In 1942 they prepared an exhaustive report on the subject; this report soon became the basis of the United States Army's own approach to military psychology.

interruptions from staff. They were to be given regular 'total rests' away from duty. Total rest, however, did not mean loafing; they should go mountain climbing and from time to time were to be 'regenerated' by such activities as tennis.

The selection of men qualified to become leaders took first place among all measures taken by the state, 'to insure the maximum development of the German people's fighting spirit and striking power'.

By 1939 the German Army was studying its men more than any other army has ever done. The psychologists warned of the various hazards and problems facing the new soldier and made many recommendations which the army, not without a struggle in some cases, adopted. For instance, the psychologists suggested that recruits be welcomed with music and an intimate man-to-man talk by a hero-type officer. Disturbing influences and frustrations—barrack-room bullies, sexual deprivation and many others—were handled carefully.

The commanding officers and psychologists of a unit had the onerous task of giving the soldier advice on his sex life. The German soldier's sex life was no more restricted than that of any other soldier, but few armies have gone to the trouble of giving its troops 'sexual deprivation therapy'. Unfortunately, nobody in Germany has ever published a paper on the success or otherwise of this treatment. It could be very illuminating.[1]

The relationship between officers and men was now excellent, largely as a result of the principle which stated that an officer must seem to be a teacher rather than a superior. Colonel Scherbening, writing in *Soldatentum* in 1939, pointed out that the officer–man relationship must be based on the soldier's confidence in the officer's intellectual capacity and character. During inspections the officer should look into the eyes of his

---

[1] At the end of the war, in 1945, a Jewish writer Samuel Igra—whose views at this time must inevitably be open to suspicions of prejudice—claimed that sexual perversion had always been rife in the Prussian and German Armies. He called it 'Germany's national vice'.

'German homosexualism is a manifestation of primitive savagery, of physical lust for which the female is too refined an object of gratification,' Igra wrote. . . . 'The deliberate relegation of German womanhood to an inferior position . . . lies at the root of those moral by-products that are the offshoots of German militarism.'

Certainly many leading Nazis were perverts, among them Ernst Roehm, Baldur von Schirach, Reinhard Heydrich, Julius Streicher, Edmond Heines, group-leader of the Breslau storm troops . . . Hitler's adjutant, Brueckner, and his secretary, Maurice.

men to detect personal problems. And he should solve those problems no matter to what trouble he was put.

An officer was taught never to ridicule a man in front of others and he was required to congratulate every man in his command on his birthday. At conferences with non-coms and even with privates he had to cultivate 'a casual friendly atmosphere', in part by offering them cigarettes.

Despite all this relaxation, he nevertheless must have a strong will and firm personality, firm enough to command unconditional response to his orders. The technique of giving orders—not merely drill commands—was given much emphasis in officers' training.

The Germans had a pattern for the ideal non-com, too. They saw him as a simple, straightforward and unsophisticated man, painstaking and reliable, but intellectually and emotionally limited. Even so, he had to be trained to develop his personality and to be able to assess the varying capabilities of his men.[1]

In a highly revealing handbook in 1942 the army pointed out that 'today's youth is critical and sensitive and a new type of non-commissioned officer is necessary to control him'.

Control was one of the most important aspects of study in the new Nazi army. Between 1933 and 1939 the Germans carried out large-scale experiments in artificial panic induced among soldiers and civilians—even among schoolchildren. What they learnt from these experiments was applied to making the German soldier as panic-proof as possible.

In training, German troops were systematically subjected to panic-producing influences, so as to immunize them against panic in action. Copying Soviet training methods, the Germans held at least one-third of all training by night. Specially trained small units deliberately tried to incite panic among the troops and occasionally they were successful. It was then the duty of officers and non-coms to quell the disaffection, by force of arms if necessary. Sometimes if a commander believed that morale and control were slipping, perhaps because of exhaustion, hunger and prolonged bombardment, he would release a 'good news bulletin'—not necessarily factual—to restore the men's equilibrium.

[1] This was revolutionary stuff. There was opposition from many officers and N.C.O.s, accustomed to brutality and liking it. But the orders from 'above' were followed up and if an officer or N.C.O. could not or would not conform to the new pattern he was transferred to punitive units where his talents could be better used.

Even the most severe critics of the German Army could not accuse it of ever having panicked. German war diaries are meticulously kept, but I have been unable to find any reference to loss of control, even by the smallest formation.

It is not in the German nature to panic in the modern French fashion, but in any case indoctrination against it was particularly thorough after the psychologists had advised on methods to prevent it. Army Regulations contained the most detailed instructions for field officers on how to detect precipitating causes of panic and on how to deal with it.

'Natural cowards'—the adjective is that applied by the army —sometimes got into the army before they could be detected, but when one was spotted he was discharged the moment a psychologist verified that he was not merely putting on an act to be discharged. This, however, would have been highly improbable.

For some reason, in 1939, a Berlin garrison psychologist named Deegener was called on to define an imbecile. He dutifully went to work and came up with a classic definition. 'The term covers morons, simpletons, semi-Aryans, habitual criminals, intellectual pacifists and conscientious objectors, former Communists, atheists, and egotists incapable of understanding the Nazi ideal. It is doubtful if education, friendly advice or punishment could cure any of these men.'

With all doubtful cases weeded out, watched or under guard, when the war came in September 1939 the Germans—civilians and soldiers—were as physically and as psychologically prepared for it as any nation has ever been. They were crusaders, the Nazis told them, setting out to save Europe. The army, from General Staff to boy cadet, was ready for the adventure. The public acknowledged the absolute premiership of the military and accepted it without criticism.

The Nazi machine taught—and all Germans believed—that war was sublime and 'the father of all things', as one textbook expressed it.[1] This was logical teaching, for how can a nation which preaches that war is wicked possibly create an efficient army?

---

[1] Mussolini lent his weight to the thesis when he said: 'Only war brings human energies to their highest tension and ennobles those peoples which dare to undertake it.'

CHAPTER XX

Soldiers and Nazi Thugs

To the average man, the German soldiers of 1939–45 were Nazis, and therefore brutal sadists. I am no apologist for the Germans and especially not for the Prussianistic of them; they are fundamentally a hard race but it is wrong to allege that the entire army was one of sadists. With few exceptions the horrible crimes perpetrated against occupied peoples and military prisoners were not the work of fighting units of the German Army, though collectively the army must take the blame for them.

These crimes were the work of special formations whose duties were punitive or worse. I am not here concerned with these units, but they cannot be ignored, because they tended to despoil the overall manly tradition the German Army had so painstakingly built for itself.

The Leadership Corps, the Gestapo, the S.S. (Schutzstaffeln —Nazi Party troops) and the S.D. (Sicherheitsdienst—security service) were the instruments of Hitler's tyranny both in Germany and outside it. The thirty-six divisions of the Waffen-S.S. —the Nazis' own army—terrified all occupied Europe. Special S.S. units were responsible for mass shootings of hostages and for such brutal massacres as that of Lidice in Czechoslovakia, which was obliterated, and Oradour in France, where they burned 645 women and children in a church. They were present at the destruction of the Warsaw ghetto.

The S.S., the S.D. and the Gestapo were responsible for the massacres of British, American and Canadian prisoners-of-war and for brutal treatment of other military prisoners. As early as May 1940 the Waffen-S.S. earned infamy at Paradis in the

Pas-de-Calais, where they massacred survivors of the 2nd Battalion The Norfolk Regiment. Throughout the war they committed one crime after another.

These brutal criminals were Germans, but they were not German soldiers in the accepted sense. The Waffen-S.S. was not even part of the Wehrmacht and most soldiers detested them.

The bulk of the S.S. was riffraff, recruited from every corner of Germany and of Europe—although there were the misguided idealists and other older, educated men who should have known better. One of the S.S.'s chief tasks was to watch the generals to see that they obeyed party orders. The anti-Hitler putsch of 20 July 1944—when an attempt was made to kill Hitler—was suppressed by the S.S.

The 'general duty men' of the S.S. staffed the Nazis' three hundred concentration camps. All S.S. men were specialists in '*Schweinerei*'—filthiness.

The Waffen-S.S. was the main Party organization—a large, fully military formation developed out of what was first Hitler's bodyguard and later became the Nazis' private army. The '*élite*' S.S. men were men described by Himmler as the 'wish-picture of the Nordic prototype'. Many of the S.S. regiments were wiped out in the Russian campaign—they were engaged only because of the shortage of regular troops—and subsequent replacements were promised many privileges. The S.S. units were supposed to be shock troops of the first order, but reports from several fronts claimed that their standard was below that of ordinary regular troops.

When Hitler assumed supreme command of the army in December 1941 the Waffen-S.S. was given greater publicity and its leaders, all staunch and often notorious Nazis, were given higher ranks. The Waffen-S.S., after this time, saw less real action, although they were occasionally involved in fierce fighting. However, many times they merely occupied enemy positions captured with difficulty by ordinary troops. This led to acute resentment against the Waffen-S.S., perhaps not always justifiably.

Throughout military history it has been noticeable that support and rear echelon troops have been guilty of greater excesses than front-line troops. Front-line troops do not have to prove their courage; they live it. Perhaps the follow-up men get a vicarious martial excitement and justification in maltreating the enemy.

Men of German fighting units were accused of rape and they

were guilty of it. What army advancing into enemy territory has not been guilty of rape? Some of the worst cases are to be found in the pages of British military history—and against women of Allied, not enemy, countries at that.

The Nazis fought a total war and the rights and wrongs of massive bombings of cities is outside my theme. The Germans started it, but in the end all the deaths and damage they caused were infinitesimal compared with the destruction inflicted in return by Allied bombers. I am not condoning the Nazis' foul and fantastic crimes. I am presenting the German Army, many of whose members were not members of the Nazi Party at all and most of whose members were not even aware of Nazi atrocities.

It is, however, important to point out that German soldiers had a completely different attitude towards Russian troops from that which they had for other enemies. They regarded Russians as vermin to be stamped out. This was an outlook comparable to that held by British and Australian troops about the Japanese.

Many instances of brutality to Russian prisoners have been verified. Some were tortured with red-hot bars; they had their eyes gouged out, their stomachs ripped open and their limbs and organs hacked off. The conditions of German prisoner-of-war camps for Russians were indescribably horrible, as were the trains in which they were transported. One train full of prisoners, made up of thirty trucks, had 1,500 corpses taken from it. Not one Russian had survived. For all this the Germans reaped retribution.

Nothing the Nazis did can be covered up; everything they did must taint the Wehrmacht. But in the succeeding chapters I have tried to paint an honest picture of the ordinary German soldier and to distinguish him from his compatriot—the Nazi beast.

Whether it is fair to regard Nazi aggression as a natural consequence of Prussian military tradition has historians, including German ones, sharply divided. Some regard Frederick as an eighteenth-century Hitler, while others profess to see no similarity. Despite what Frederick's detractors say he certainly was not like Hitler, but Hitler wanted to be like Frederick—military genius, conqueror, protector, a god. He believed that he was carrying Frederick's work to a logical conclusion—German domination of Western Europe.

Hitler was full of Prussian militarism and traditionalism; he gloried in it and shamelessly traded on it. In this sense Prussian military tradition was the root of Nazi aggression, but neither Frederick nor Prussian tradition can be blamed for Nazi excesses.

A full analysis of the means by which Hitler was able to bend the army to his will in the 1930s is beyond the scope of this book; it is a study in itself. However, Hitler's real control over the army began with the bloody purge of June 1934, when many senior S.A. leaders and other people considered dangerous were murdered by the S.S. on orders of Hitler, Goering and Himmler. Exactly how many people were slaughtered is not known. Hitler is reported to have said both eighty-three and seventy-seven. In 1957, at the trial of some of the executioners, the figure of 'more than a thousand' was given, but this has been labelled a gross exaggeration.

Two senior army officers, Generals von Schleicher and von Bredow, were cold-bloodedly murdered—for alleged treason— yet the Officers' Corps did not protest. Only two senior officers, the aged Field-Marshal von Mackensen and General von Hammerstein, aged fifty-six, spoke out against the murder of the generals. To their eternal honour they persisted in their protests until, in January 1935, Hitler, at a secret meeting in Berlin, admitted that the two generals had been 'killed in error'.

By condoning Hitler's gangsterism the officers had put themselves in an invidious position: they would find it difficult to oppose future Nazi terrorism. This did not bother them much in June 1934 for they had deluded themselves into thinking that the purge had ensured that the Nazi political movement would not now threaten army privileges and power. Just a little foresight would have told them that the S.S. would be much more dangerous than the S.A.

In August 1934 when Hitler became Führer and Reich Chancellor he ordered that all service officers and men swear an oath of allegiance—to himself.

> I swear by God this sacred oath, that I will render unconditional obedience to Adolf Hitler, the Führer of the German Reich and people, Supreme Commander of the Armed Forces, and will be ready as a brave soldier to risk my life at any time for this oath.

Until the moment that they took this oath the German generals could have effortlessly squashed the Nazis underfoot.

By taking it they tied themselves not to service of their country but to Adolf Hitler personally. Being spiritual or lineal descendants of the Junkers, being honourable men and honour-conscious, the officers felt bound to keep this oath. Even when very senior officers knew that Hitler was destroying Germany they honoured their oath. Later many of them used it as a convenient, dishonourable excuse for acts they had committed outside the normal bounds of military action.

Hitler may or may not have been mad; he was being brilliantly astute when he enforced the Hitler oath.

CHAPTER XXI

Blitzkrieg

Writing in the 1939 issue of the official *Militärwissenschaftliche Rundschau*, General Geyer noted that an offensive battle had four phases:
1. The preparation for battle, lasting up to ten months.
2. Artillery preparation, largely the duty of the Luftwaffe.
3. Encirclement of the enemy.
4. Annihilation of the encircled enemy.

Geyer believed that an offensive battle must be concluded in fifteen days. If unsuccessful it should be broken off with whatever gains had been achieved. But many German experts said that the battle must show decisive results within six days.

After war broke out decisive results did not always come within six days, but come they certainly did. First, German troops invaded and annexed Austria on 12 March 1938, as part of Hitler's stated plan to unite all Germanic people.

When Hitler marched into Austria a large number of tanks broke down on the road. This was seized on by foreign correspondents, some of whom managed to write a lot of foolishness about 'the German lack of mechanical aptitude'. But when the tanks rolled into other countries none of them broke down; the Germans had learned quickly from their earlier errors.[1]

After 'the assimilation' of Austria, Hitler declared now that he had no further territorial ambitions, but by 15 March 1939,

---

[1] They had learned in other ways, too. No longer were there complaints about disparity of treatment between officers and men. Officers received neither more nor better food than their men and all received the same subsistence allowance for food when on leave. A lieutenant was paid only about twice as highly as a private.

he had completed the occupation of Czechoslavakia. Hitler was now ready to wage war for the conquest of Europe and on 1 September German troops invaded Poland without a declaration of war. Within sixteen days—only one day longer than the period specified by General Geyer—the Polish armies, the fifth largest in the world, were broken.

German strategy was designed to annihilate enemy armies as fighting forces, not necessarily to wipe them out. In Poland the idea was to defeat the Polish forces in one decisive battle by a manœuvre known as the double envelopment. This has been the aim of all strategists but of none more than the German General Staff. In the Battle of Poland they applied it not once but twice; and the second double envelopment trapped forces escaping from the first.

New weapons gave Germany tactical power and speed to carry out the strategy. Planes and tanks supported the infantry in breaking through enemy lines and rolling up their flanks. Wherever Polish defences were weak, German infantry punched holes in them with tanks, then exploited by driving through and enveloping the flanks on either side of the gap. Fast moving infantry, often motorized, swept forward as much as forty-five miles a day. This was blitzkrieg.[1]

The German Panzer (armoured division) of 11,792 men, had 250–350 tanks and many other vehicles and was organized in three echelons, but it was infantry—mainly motorized infantry —which won the Battle of Poland. A division had immense fire power—516 machine-guns, 147 mortars, 75 tank-attack guns and 48 howitzers.

When Germany attacked Poland, Britain and France declared war—on 3 September—but it was almost a month before a small British expeditionary force took up positions in France. Cynics accused England and France of opposing blitzkrieg with sitzkrieg—the phony war—because no major actions occurred through the winter of 1939–40.

In April German troops overwhelmed Denmark and Norway, bringing in mortar and machine-gun troops by plane. In

[1] 'Blitzkrieg' was not a German word, but was invented by foreign newspapermen—probably Americans—to replace the original German word, Angriffsschlacht—meaning offensive battle. The word blitzkrieg was an unfortunate one, since it tended to give many people the impression that if the lightning war failed then Germany had temporarily shot her bolt. In reality, the blitzkrieg was merely a phase—admittedly a big one—of a tremendous effort.

these operations airborne infantry and parachute battalions weathered their first test.

The Germans did not take Norway without losses—probably about 45,000 of them. Some casualties were inflicted by British counter-attacks, which were repulsed.

Britain and France were still not ready for full-scale warfare when the German armies turned west to crush them on 10 May 1940. Within a month they had swept across the borders of Holland, Belgium and Luxembourg on a campaign which was to destroy France and which, Hitler told the troops, would decide the fate of the German nation for the next thousand years. The Germans planned to repeat the victory of the Franco-Prussian war, but on a grander scale, with the conquest of France and England.

To achieve it the Germans had mobilized an overwhelming force of nearly seven million soldiers, formed into 240 divisions, of which at least 12 were armoured. The French had mobilized 95 divisions; Britain had an expeditionary force of 13 divisions, the Belgians had 21 poorly trained divisions and the Dutch had, on paper, 400,000 men.

Not only lack of planes, tanks and guns made France weak. Her inept strategy and leadership, and class strife, were equally responsible. The French staked their safety on their supposedly impregnable Maginot Line.

German strategy, true to the teachings of Clausewitz, did not aim to capture Paris but to neutralize the opposing armies. The same attempt had been made in 1914 under the Schlieffen Plan. The Germans decided on central penetration to expose flanks. In the Great War such attacks had bogged down because infantry lacked the speed to exploit a breakthrough before it was closed. This no longer applied; German troops could now move frighteningly fast. They broke through at the hinge of the Allied line in the Ardennes along the Meuse, where the main Maginot works ended and lighter works ran north-west to the sea.

The psychological approach of the Germans to war was evident even in battle. Artillery drumfire of the Great War went out to some extent and protracted bombardment by aircraft and tanks came in.

Destruction was widespread, but the Germans were more concerned with the disintegration of morale than with destruction of material. This was the purpose of the screaming Stukas and the bombs with sirens attached—an idea suggested by army psychologists.

The acoustic novelties were effective. They engendered in many enemy soldiers not only acute fear neuroses but actual nerve paralysis. Previously untried troops were easy meat for this form of attack. Occasionally in the middle of a dark night the Germans dropped or fired flares of extraordinary colours and shapes which, while doing no physical damage, further played on the fears of already demoralized soldiers.

In the event of an enemy retaliating in kind—which they did not to any extent—the Germans were prepared. Officers had orders to keep men busy by playing music, singing, even telling stories. But the best antidote of all, the psychologists advised, was steady work.

During the 1940 fighting on the Western Front the Germans spread what they called emotional and symbolic superstition through secret agents. They also projected images onto drifting clouds during moonlit nights. Superstitions and magic lantern shows had no adverse effect on British troops, but probably they were effective against civilian populations.

During periods of waiting, too, everything was designed to keep the troops occupied. There was nothing new in this, but the Germans developed their concerts, unit newspapers and organized radio-listening to a degree unequalled until the Americans set out benevolently to brainwash their troops through every conceivable form of entertainment.

Before the war and even during its first year army psychologists deprecated the use of stimulants such as alcohol and drugs for fighting troops. Published references against such stimulation disappear after 1941, but I do not think this is conclusive evidence that the Germans then used drugs. There has been much discussion on this point and various people have claimed that the German paratroops in Crete and elsewhere used drugs. I think this is possible, but I have been able to find no evidence to suggest it. It would seem to be right against the German military ideal of manliness, but the Nazis being what they were perhaps they overcame army objections.

The army certainly had no objection to the Nazi idea of changing the system of war reporting. They did away with all photographers and correspondents appointed by newspapers and magazines and made them instead into soldiers, sharing all risks and progressing in rank like any other soldier. As early as April 1940 no fewer than twenty-three of these reporters had been killed in action. The total number killed throughout the war is unknown, but it probably exceeded three hundred.

These so-called 'front-reporters' produced some fine pieces of journalism and photographs. One official report puts the number of photographs taken at more than two million.

They were present when parachute troops seized Dutch airfields, bridges and highways and with reinforcements of airborne infantry secured the bridges over which German motorized troops quickly reached Rotterdam. In Belgium, where many bridges remained undemolished, the Germans reached the Albert Canal where they faced its chief strongpoint, Fort Eben Emael.

The fortress might be besieged and after a long time starved into surrender, the Belgians said, but it could never be taken by storm. Many foreign experts agreed with them. Within thirty-six hours of crossing the border the garrison of 1,400 marched out and surrendered.

It was said at the time that the fortress had been betrayed, that the Germans had used a paralysing gas, that third-rate troops manned the fortress. None of this was true. Fort Eben Emael, ultra-modern in design, commanded the approaches to the River Meuse and the Albert Canal and it was flanked by more than twenty smaller forts scattered over an area of a square mile. These forts were of steel and reinforced concrete, deeply embedded in rock and connected by deep tunnels. All were heavily armed and each fort, as well as the system as a whole, was protected by minefields and elaborate barbed wire entanglements.

But the Germans had been training assault parties, developed from those earlier groups of the previous war. To practise assaults on Fort Eben Emael they had used a full-scale model.

On 10 May, when the immensely large and powerful German Army smashed across the borders, one small combat-team had right of way on all roads—it comprised a battalion of demolition engineers, a company of infantry, a battery of tank-attack guns and a battery of small calibre anti-aircraft guns—neither of which was to be used for its normal purpose—and a small detachment of chemical warfare troops. The whole made up a skilled, efficient team.

That night the unit was at the base of the plateau on which lay the fort. During the day dive bombers had attacked the fort and about fifty paratroopers had dropped into shell-holes. That night when the combat unit reached the base of the plateau on which the fort squatted, these men established radio communication with the unit.

The Belgians were unworried; Eben Emael had been built to take punishment. At dawn on 11 May the German engineers crawled with difficulty up the slopes, using as cover craters made by the dive bombers. No time was wasted. The tank-attack and anti-aircraft guns fired point blank at the fort's gun slits. The chemical warfare troops blinded the smaller posts with smoke. The infantry company poured small arms fire at anything that might hide a Belgian. And the demolition engineers advanced.

Few men in any fight have faced such danger. They carried 7 lb. blocks of TNT; they carried long poles to which more TNT was attached; they were loaded with grenades, flame throwers and sub-machine-guns. Some of them fell; some were blown to pieces when a Belgian bullet set off their grenades and TNT. But many of the engineers reached safety—the small area just in front of the fort on to which the fortress guns could not be depressed.

With German thoroughness, quickly, but unhurriedly, the engineers went to work. Some fired flame throwers through the slits; others placed TNT charges at vital points such as turrets, doors and joints, or set a delayed fuse and went to ground while it exploded. Some charges were pushed into places with the long poles.

The noise was terrific, for neither the Belgians nor the more distant Germans had ceased firing. But the systematic attack slowly weakened Eben Emael; here and there a turret jammed, gun slits were filled with rubble, flames made it impossible for men to man certain points. And the Germans exploited these points.

It was only a matter of time and the Belgian commander knew it. Soon after noon on 11 May he surrendered. The Germans were satisfied; they had expected to have the fortress out of action by noon.[1]

The reduction of Fort Eben Emael was typical of efficiency and speed of the German thrust.[2] In eleven days in May

[1] Many years after the war I met a Belgian who had been a young lieutenant in Eben Emael. 'The Germans took the fortress because they used unfair tactics,' he said.

[2] Despite the great gallantry of many German soldiers in the attack on Eben Emael, the first award of a Knight's Cross of the Iron Cross to a rank and file soldier in World War II was to a lance corporal who fought against British units. He was Lance Corporal Hubert Brinkforth, from Westphalia who, near Abbeville, on 27 May 1940, was serving as No. 1 on a tank-attack gun in an advanced position. Here he 'smashed the attack of a powerful British tank unit'. His citation credited him with destroying eleven tanks in twenty minutes, which, despite heavy firing, he allowed to approach within 100 yards before opening fire. In June 1941 *Signal* published a full-page colour photograph of him.

armoured spearheads raced 220 miles through the enemy's rear to the English Channel. By the end of May it was clear that unless the British were to be annihilated they had no choice but to leave the Continent, which many troops were safely able to do both at Dunkirk and at other points farther south. But they lost their heavy equipment. The French Army was dismembered by fast-thrusting attacks that left French commanders bewildered. 'Generals are commanding battalions,' Paul Reynaud wrote to President Roosevelt when Paris fell. In the railway carriage at Compiègne, where Marshal Foch granted Germany armistice in 1918, Hitler had his revenge. France was divided and the rich industrial north, over three-fifths of the country, was occupied. The French were charged with the costs of occupation, at the rate of about £3,000,000 a day, while French prisoners-of-war remained in Germany.

All the Continent west of Russia fell under German sway. German military power overawed Fascist Italy, outflanked Sweden and surrounded Switzerland. Yugoslavia, Greece and Russia, the only nations which still resisted the New Order, soon felt the tramp of the jackboot. The Yugoslavian–Greek campaign was over in three weeks, with great losses to the British Imperial forces who had come to help the threatened country.

The German military machine seemed invincible. It next attacked Crete, planning to capture it in two days. Conquest took ten days and the Germans suffered 17,000 casualties—but victory was undeniable.

After the German victory in Crete the idea of the German 'all-round soldier' began to make its appearance in the British Press. The idea does not exist in the German language; it would be necessary to use several words to express it correctly. In spite of the differences between the various arms the German soldier was fundamentally the same.

The German soldier was trained to take the initiative under all circumstances. The doctrine that it was better to act wrongly than not to act at all was the basis of his training.[1] The guiding principle of all action was sound common sense and not any special regulations. The Germans regarded the German N.C.O. as a good example of the combination of sound common sense with love of initiative.

By now a vast variety of badges was playing a big part in

[1] A statement made in *Signal*, May 1942.

German army life and morale—the work of psychologists again, although there is some reason to think that the idea was put forward by Hitler himself.

The Germans, like the British, had always been keen on the trappings of military life, but under the Nazis symbols took on greater meaning. Service officers and military psychologists collaborated in their scope and design. Many hundreds of different badges, combat shields and emblems as well as medals were issued, all with the swastika as part of the design, and all most soldierly in appearance.

Apart from badges and insignia there were ceremonial daggers turned out in quantity and high quality by the famous steelworks of Solingen and Wuppertal. Those made by Carl Eickhorn were particularly impressive.

As a soldier saw more service he was awarded more badges —or bars to his badges. For instance, to the tank assault badges there were bars for 25, 50, 75 and 100 actions. Similar bars were issued to members of the Luftwaffe and the Kriegs-marine.

There were wound badges—black for one or two wounds; silver for three or four; gold for five wounds or more. And in the holocaust of the Russian Front gold wound badges were not uncommon. Hitler had a special wound badge struck for those officers wounded in the attempt on his life in July 1944.

The psychologists did their job well. German soldiers coveted the array of emblems. A German would do as much to win an Iron Cross in any of its many grades as a Frenchman of Napoleon's era would do to win the Legion of Honour.[1]

The very uniform the men wore, and their jackboots, were chosen with psychological bias. The field grey had a martial quality about it; the boots made a man feel like a man. There was nothing haphazard about a single thing the Germans of the Nazi period wore or used or did.

A regular occurrence was a parade in the Berlin Sports

[1] Nazi insignia has a strange fascination for many people, who collect it avidly. So great has been the demand, ever since the war, for badges, emblems, flags, daggers, swords, helmets and other souvenirs that in Germany enterprising businessmen are still manufacturing supplies. In fact, there is more genuine and counterfeit material outside Germany than inside, for every British and American soldier who ever served there brought away at least a 2nd Class Iron Cross. Added to this, for a long time it was an offence to own any insignia sporting the swastika and many German soldiers got rid of their medals and badges, even if only to exchange them for food in the grim days immediately after the war.

Palace for Hitler to address aspirant officers.[1] Hitler might have been eccentric but he was clever enough to know how to inspire these young men. And though young, they were not starry-eyed with the thought of high adventure. Every one of them had seen active service, had been intensively trained and had passed a stiff examination. Hitler told them what he, the Reich and Europe expected of them, what the dead heroes of bygone Prussian armies expected of them.

The salute was another symbol carried further than in the Allied armies. All German soldiers, off duty or on, saluted not only superiors but each other as well. The idea was to help build up the spirit of comradeship. The troops were told, and they believed, that it was a privilege to salute, not a mere duty. At least until 1942 members of the armed forces used the traditional military salute and not the 'Heil Hitler!' salute.

At a time when most other armies had given up the practice of taking bands to the front, the Germans were still doing it. And all regiments had drum ceremonies which were highly effective in rousing martial and fighting spirit.

[1] 'Every German with the privilege of bearing arms, who is physically and mentally healthy, and has not been punished by law, has all the qualifications necessary for becoming an officer,' he would tell them.

CHAPTER XXII

The 1,800–Mile Russian Front

But after German armies invaded Russia on 22 June 1941 bands became obsolete. The two strongest powers in Europe were now at grips, for Russia was also organized for total war. After nearly two years of conquest, the Axis commanded the population and resources of fifteen European countries. But Russia had a population of 192,000,000, more than Germany and her vassals combined, and the Soviet peoples were spread over a sixth of the earth's surface. That the Germans attacked her shows the extraordinary confidence which permeated the German Army at this time. There is no mystery about the German attack. Hitler had always looked on Russian Communism as his worst enemy and had long coveted the resources of the Soviet to make Germany self-sufficient.

Until the invasion of Russia the Nazis had never engaged in a campaign of longer than four months or fought on a front of over 300 miles. In their attempt to conquer Russia they had to spread their forces along a broken front of 1,800 miles from the Arctic Ocean to the Black Sea. Instead of bringing off another blitzkrieg they involved themselves in a grim, savage, relentless war which sapped their strength for three long years—but this was not obvious in June 1941.

When the Germans marched into Russia, Churchill said: 'Napoleon disappeared; that gives me confidence. . . .' The German propaganda department seized on this and published a long comparison between Napoleon's and Hitler's campaigns, under the heading HISTORY DOES NOT REPEAT ITSELF.[1]

[1] *Signal*, December 1941.

Part of the article read:

'Adolf Hitler marched very differently from Napoleon. The French Emperor advanced with a single army column; flanked by two side columns; Adolf Hitler attacked along a wide front reaching from the Arctic Ocean to the Black Sea. Napoleon had to look for the enemy for months till he made ready for battle at Borodin near Moscow, an ordinary frontal battle. Adolf Hitler began with a frontal attack and succeeded in the first week in resolving the frontal battle into individual encirclement operations. . . . So the sanguine comparison fails from the very first day. After six weeks there is only one fact which could justify the comparison—every town and every place taken by the Germans is on fire: the civil population of these towns are often left behind by the Soviets, starving and deprived of their wretched homes. . . .

'It is not necessary to entice the Germans forward, as the British and American debating societies say. The Germans push forward of their own accord into the great spaces. They carry out one battle of annihilation after another and are not afraid of the great spaces. The fireside astrologers and strategists who are so fond of comparing Hitler and Napoleon have left one thing out of account—the Germans have fought in the East before, in the Great War, and they were the victors . . . as at Tannenberg. This battle . . . taught the Germans a very useful lesson, namely that great battles of annihilation are best fought in wide spaces. Broad, undulating spaces are the best terrain for such operations, so General Space has gone over to the Germans and helps them in their strategy of annihilation. . . . Is not General Space an uncertain, even a malicious ally, onle waiting for the moment when he can turn and rend thy Germans? No!

'The organization of the German Army cannot be compared with that of any former army. Another army marches, sometimes almost alongside the fighting troops, mostly close on their heels. It consists of workmen and is led by engineers. This army, in which the Todt Organization, the Reich Labour Service and sections of the Pioneer Troops are combined, is inconceivably great. Every mile of conquered territory is at once examined and developed by this second army. In the first three months of the war against Russia this army, apart from much other work, converted 9,000 miles of Russian railway lines into the gauge of the German railways.

'The German soldier has broken the backbone of the greatest military power in the world . . . the soldiers wish to destroy Bolshevist rule. The German Army of 1941 cannot be compared either in its basic structure or in its equipment and armament with the motley, exhausted troops of Napoleon in 1812. Nor can the German generals be compared with Napoleon's generals and marshals . . . the only one who possessed any tactical genius, Jomini, never rose above the position of governor or adjutant and was never entrusted with a great command. How can one compare the brave old soldiers and mediocre tacticians whom Napoleon had assembled around him with the German generals, whose names continually appear in the Supreme Command's communiqués?

'Winston Churchill himself was apprehensive about his questionable comparison between Hitler and Napoleon and said that Liberty was marching with Napoleon's armies in 1812 while the Prussian jackboot reigns in Hitler's empire. Apart from the fact that it was Britain that waged war for twenty years against the Napoleonic "spirit of liberty", the only meaning that "the Prussian jackboot" can have in this connection is that Adolf Hitler has annihilated Germany's enemies. Every student of history knows that the jackboot originated in the time of Napoleon . . . However, after Napoleon had set his jackboot on Prussia's neck she shook off that boot and defeated Napoleon according to his own recipe for annihilation; she had then, as an aspiring and struggling nation, to realize that in military conflicts with other nations half-measures are of no use. . . . Germany has destroyed the enemy armies which opposed her, but has carried out this destruction in the spirit of reconciliation between nations: *she has "annihilated in such a way that it is possible for the enemy of yesterday to be the friend of tomorrow. . . ."* '[1]

The German Army was preening itself at this time. An army reporter wrote:

'Within two years the German Army has conquered a

[1] Author's italics.

series of opponents of whom a number were considered to be invincible. Every one of these opponents was equipped with the most modern means of technical warfare. Many of them had at their disposal not only the most modern tanks, the most modern armoured cars and planes, but even airborne troops and amphibious tanks. The German soldier during this fighting has captured fortifications which in the opinion of their constructors were stronger than the walls of Jericho. Numerically weak German units have not only defied the enemy, but also beaten him, as was the case at Narvik.

'The same dispassionate characteristics are typical of all these victories. The German soldier has not taken up the fight with any of his opponents with feelings of hatred or fury in his heart. He has fought against them all with the same spiritual calm and with the same precision in his superiority which has caused the opponents of the German Army to give it the name "the German war machine".

'The German Army regards this name as a title of honour, although it knows that the name does not come from any honourable intention. When the instrument of annihilation is compared to a machine, the intention is to belittle the spirit which leads to victory. Machinery is an aid to man but never takes the place of man himself. Man with his capacity to suffer and think and, even then, to act when the animal surrenders, is the triumphant victor of the battlefield. Will power and intelligence, soul and brain, are the essence of the art of war. Who has ever heard of a machine which had moral qualities? And if this title is to remain, what has Germany's opponent, Britain, to oppose to this machine? Only the tired arts of the "strategy of hanging on", of a policy of war extension at any price, of a seeking for new theatres of war. This art was successful only when used against an opponent in the way in which Rome used it against Hannibal, against the man who was fighting far from his home-land on foreign soil and cut off from the resources of his country. Britain should not forget this lesson of history. Germany is not Hannibal and the German people is fighting in Europe for Europe.'

The German soldier certainly knew a lot about war—more than any other soldier in the world. He had fought under a variety of conditions and was superbly fit and trained. His morale was as high as that of any soldier has ever been. He was well read in military history and he knew about Prussian campaigns of old. But in Russia he was to discover a new kind of warfare and a new kind of enemy.

The invasion of the Soviet Union fell into five phases, each an attempt at decisive victory which was never achieved. In the first phase—22 June–10 July 1941—the armies made good progress at forty miles a day. They overran Lithuania in the north, encircled Bialystok and Minsk in the centre and captured Lwow in the south.

In the second phase—11 July–8 August—the Germans penetrated deep into the Stalin Line, advanced to Leningrad, besieged Odessa on the Black Sea, pushed to Kiev in the Ukraine and fought the great battle of Smolensk. The main Russian force escaped destruction, although the Germans pressed them hard.

During the third phase—9 August–30 September—the weight of the German attack shifted south-east to Kiev. The central and southern armies joined in the encirclement of Budyenny's forces and spread into the Ukraine. In the north Leningrad held out in a siege that was to last for two years.

In front of Smolensk the Germans gave ground for the first time.

The fourth phase—30 September–15 October—was the largest tactical operation the Nazi Germans ever planned. It took the form of two enormous double envelopments of Vyazma and Bryansk to trap the forces defending Moscow. A violent battle followed and for the Russians the situation became critical along the whole front. The Germans took prisoners in their hundreds of thousands.

The fifth and final phase of the invasion was a series of three progressively furious battles—a violent attack on Moscow, a wild rush in the south to Rostov and finally, in November and December, a series of heavy attacks on three sides of Moscow. Hitler called the Battle of Moscow the deathblow of the Red armies, but Russian reserves saved the city and the bitter winter stopped the Germans from their usual vigorous offensive. The fury and size of these battles was extraordinary. No fewer than 5,000 tanks took part in the attack on Moscow. The Russians met the threat by massing guns of every type to support its infantry, but in the end it was Russian manpower rather than fire power which defeated the Germans.

One general who was killed in action—in November 1941—
was General von Briesen. At his formal lying-in-state, the Chief
of the General Staff of the corps Briesen led, made this address:

'Forty-eight hours ago General von Briesen fell at the
head of his troops—as the law commanded. The law within
him, the law of the incomparable Prussian soldier. The
tradition of his family taught him to live and die for Führer
and Reich. He was a leader with unusual creative power,
with an inspiring, irresistible personality, he was a soldier
of the highest calibre.

'At the head of the division which, during peacetime, he
had made into a first-class instrument of war, he took the
field. At a critical moment by his personal bravery he
turned the Battle of the Bzura into a victory and in spite of
a serious wound he remained at the head of his troops.

'General von Briesen was the first soldier whose action
the Führer and Commander in Chief of the German
people described as a model of exemplary heroism. He was
one of the first to be awarded the Knight's Cross. In the
west he led his division through Holland, Belgium and
France from victory to victory and with it entered Paris.

'In November last year (1940) he was appointed general
in command of the Corps, our leader, commander and
comrade. Five months ago our Corps took the field against
Russia. I wish to mention only a few landmarks along our
road of victory: Prem Przemsyl, the pursuit along the
Dniester, the breakthrough of the Stalin line south of Bar,
the crossing of the Bug near Ladyshin, the annihilation of
the Russian Sixth Army near Golovanievsk, the struggle
for the Dnieper, Poltava and Isium. These battles were
fought by his brave troops, but the general's rousing,
stimulating personality fired on to victory every soldier
who saw him—and he was always to be seen among his
men. He was the soul of battle for his Corps.

'But just as his will to act was irrepressible and compelling, so was his gentle and sympathetic manner when
his men suffered. . . . General von Briesen, the last of the
family, fell almost exactly 27 years after his father,
General von Briesen, killed in Poland in November 1914.

'The line is extinguished, but the martial spirit of
Frederick the Great, which he incarnated, still lives. The
inheritance he left us is the sacred duty to serve and fight in

his spirit until the final victory has been won by Germany. The General Command of the Corps bows in silent reverence before its great fallen hero.'

It is a revealing address, with its reference to the 'incomparable Prussian soldier'—not the German soldier; to 'the martial spirit of Frederick the Great; to 'the sacred duty to fight'. The very fact that von Briesen was accorded a formal lying-in-state and such an eulogy when the corps was in action is expressive of the veneration in which great soldiers were held.

It was at this time that an anonymous American writer—in the December issue of the American periodical *Fortune*—said that the German Army was 'undoubtedly the best in the world'.

The writer quoted a U.S. officer as saying, 'We have all read thousands of words explaining how the tanks or the Stukas or the infantry, or this or that, has been the cause of German military success. We have seldom read ten words saying that the German successes are largely due to tactics. The Germans have announced several times that they have no new weapons. We know this to be true—they have simply combined effectively the use of well-known weapons. In other words they have used effective tactics. . . .'

Tactics are only useful when well-trained troops are available to implement them. You can man a barricade with untrained men, but you cannot take a complicated enemy position with them. To turn civilians into trained assault troops as incredibly fast as Germany did there had to be a spiritual willingness in these civilians to become real soldiers. Willingness is as important as capacity.

The German Army of 1941 was really no more than five or six years old. The Germans would not have been insulted if anybody had suggested that the German Army was nothing but an improvisation.

In the German Army of the 'forties there were lieutenants aged forty-five; they had fought in the first war, but had retained the elasticity of mind and body necessary for a new war. The army had four kinds of officer:

—The former officers of the German Army from the time of the monarchy, who became active again after the reintroduction of compulsory service.

—The officers of the 100,000-man army.

—Officers who were formerly N.C.O.s in this and the new army.

—The new young officers.

At the beginning of 1940 most officers were chosen on the basis of demonstrated ability. Each candidate had first to obtain promotion to non-commissioned rank in the field, after which he was sent to officers' school. The period, of course, was shortened—to four or six months. When officer casualties became so plentiful in Russia, commanding officers were empowered to recommend privates and corporals for training as officers. If a man was especially capable, the commanding officer could give him a commission on the spot. Most of the men so appointed were highly successful.[1]

But the Germans, capable as they were, could not fight 'General Winter'. German troops in summer clothing perished. Soviet guerrillas cut their supply and communication lines. The bitter cold froze the lubricating oil and cracked the cylinders of tanks, planes and trucks.

[1] In 1942 the army had more than forty officers of colonel and above who had risen from the ranks.

CHAPTER XXIII

Gallantry and Gore; Courage and Carnage

No German Army ever suffered as much as that which fought on the Eastern Front in winter—with the thermometer sometimes recording 100 degrees of frost. Separated from Germany by many hundreds of miles of roads deep in mud, they feared the winter more than they feared the Russians.

The mud sea was a great and distressing enemy. Beneath German boots and wheels and tracks Russia turned into a great morass of mud-porridge. Lorries floated about like boats, sliding to the side of the road, then planting themselves diagonally across it. In the midst of this slimy quagmire upon which heavy rain still fell incessantly, pools appeared, for the ground was unable to soak up any more moisture.

As the troops pulled their boots out of the mud—each one five pounds heavier because of the stuff—they plunged them into water a foot deep. Real ponds formed, then small lakes. Everything the men wore was covered with a thick coating of mud; lorries were plastered with mud to the roof. Stones and pieces of wood and the faggots of sunflowers went into the mud to try to hold it reasonably firm. Horses and pack animals which had been killed or had floundered into mud and been drowned lay like grotesque sculptures.

Then snow fell. A bitterly cold wind brought flakes as big as a man's hand. As the snow reached the ground the mud soaked it up and turned it also into mud, which now became granular and dirty white and more sticky. Men and machines could often do no better than a few yards an hour. At one dangerous time Italian horsed cavalry, the only part of the Axis force which could make progress, was pushed in to hold a gap the Russians were trying to exploit.

Eventually the cold defeated the mud by freezing it, but this brought new problems. Tanks had to rest on masses of twigs and bracken or their tracks would freeze to the ground, burial parties had to use explosives to dig graves.

The photographs taken by Front Correspondents at this time show the scene more vividly than words can possibly describe; soldiers and animals and vehicles floundering hopelessly and helplessly in the mud . . . the ruins of burnt-out buildings . . . the rubble of those knocked down . . . German publicity did not play down the rigours of the Russian campaign; the reporting was honest, full and frank. Censorship no doubt eliminated military information, but the Front Correspondents obviously suffered less from censor-frustration than did their enemy counterparts who were often exasperated by idiotic restrictions.

Soldiers instinctively avoided front-line houses in the Great War and such avoidance was later preached as a tactical law, because they provided enemy artillery with good targets and therefore increased casualties. But faced with the choice of being exposed to Soviet fire or the cold, they accepted the cold as the greater danger—and entered the houses.

The village houses were made of clay and they were one-room hovels. For the Germans, who were generally content to share the house with the owners, the roof and the stove were the important parts. The stove had to be kept going at all costs and after the fences, barns and furniture were all burnt they used straw. Anything more than a mile away was unreachable and coal was virtually unprocurable. When the wind whirled up the snow into great drifts supply columns could not get through and sometimes troops were out of rations for days on end. When no tobacco came through many soldiers smoked the dried stalks of sunflowers.

The Russian towns through which the Germans passed and in which they were billeted often held 100,000 people—two or three families to each small house. With three or four Germans also inhabiting the house the crowding can be imagined. There were no shops, no restaurants, no public houses. Wherever possible the retreating Soviet Army took away with them or destroyed all supplies and all industrial plant. The Russian civilians could only stand about in gloomy silence, killing time, or offering to do any conceivable kind of job in exchange for a piece of bread or a few shreds of tobacco.

But the Germans dug in as if to stay. Typically, they began repairs on the great power plants, got mines working again, distributed steam tractors throughout the Ukraine to speed food production, altered the railway gauge for German trains. Conscript Poles and prisoners-of-war were put on to building defence lines in the rear.

Russia had by now acknowledged casualties of 2,122,000; they were probably more. The Germans claimed they had 3,806,000 prisoners. Moscow claimed that they had killed 3,500,000 enemy invaders, also untrue, but even after the winter the Germans admitted to a death loss of only 251,291. This was absurd. Their probable loss was 1,200 a day. The point is, however, that their morale held.

In 1942 the Russians made counter-attacks and fighting was continuous, but in the Crimea many Russians were trapped. The Germans claimed the annihilation of nineteen divisions and seven armoured brigades and the capture of 150,000 prisoners.

Many Russian regiments were hurriedly formed and poorly trained and at night often ran onto the field of fire drunk, yelling and waving their rifles above their heads.

German mobile assault guns often joined in battles being fought by the infantry. This modern weapon enabled the general to get near to the dream of Napoleon who wished for direct participation of the artillery in the front line as decisive for the outcome of the battle. So that the men inside the armour-plated gun could do their duty they were accompanied by a machine-gunner who lay on the topmost plate. His only protection was his gun and the cold-bloodedness with which he used it. It was a dangerous job and casualties were high, but as we shall see the assault gun could be devastatingly effective.

The Russians were left with only one position in the Crimea—the great naval base of Sebastopol, said to be the strongest single fortress in the world. It probably was. The Russians had strengthened its ancient and its natural defences. It had nineteen modern forts hewn out of rock, four levels deep, with 11-inch guns in battleship turrets, all protected by hundreds of pill-boxes and thousands of landmines. It had a garrison of 125,000 soldiers and marines under General Petrov and its entire civilian population apart from two hundred had been evacuated.

On 2 June General Manstein attacked the outer fortifications from the north and east with 200,000 troops while Richthofen's air fleet and heavy artillery concentrated on a narrow sector to pierce the defences and reach the inner forts quickly. After two weeks the Germans blew up the magazines at the vital point of Fort Maxim Gorki; they then occupied the northern shore of the harbour, while others took the hills of Inkermann east of the city. A night landing led to the capture of Fort Malakoff and Sebastopol was occupied. Seventy thousand troops were trapped into surrender.

Too little is known about this great battle, in which German planes made 25,000 sorties and dropped 125,000 heavy bombs. Above all, heavy artillery fired 30,000 tons of shells on the fortress, that is, fifty tons every hour of the day and night for twenty-five days. After being thus pulverized the Russians were in no state to repel the ultimate infantry attacks. Sebastopol was a battle of annihilation in typical German manner.

The German rifle was heavier than the Russian rifle, took only five rounds against the Russian's fifteen and was slower to use. But the Germans, who could certainly have produced better rifles than the Soviet effort, were content. They were more concerned with accuracy than with rapidity. The German soldier was not taught to eject the cartridge like lightning after each round, but to expel the air from his lungs before firing each round. He was never allowed to shoot until he could aim. The rifleman was trained to be calm and precise. 'When you have fired five rounds,' the recruit was told, 'it is time to take the rifle from the shoulder and take a deep breath.'

At home martial psychology had built up to impressive proportions. Perhaps the General Staff now realized the intensity of the ordeal through which German soldiers would have to pass and wanted to make sure they were conditioned for it. By mid-1942 the army psychological activities were controlled by the High Command Central Psychological Laboratory, with twenty departments, plus seventeen army and two naval testing stations; and special staff for psychological campaigns and a psychological intelligence service.

At this time German propaganda was moralizing about war. In June 1942 Colonel E. Moravec, obviously under the influence of Clausewitz, wrote of war as a 'social phenomenon'. Moravec's article was a metaphorical-philosophical piece and its importance is that it shows that after nearly three years of war the Germans still saw war as a holy mission.

'The German artist Franz von Stück painted war in the shape of a dreadful knight. Armed with a huge sword dripping blood, War rides across a field strewn with corpses. Anybody seeing this picture realizes that peace is the great benefit conferred upon us by life.

'Then came the Great War with the hard life in the trenches and afterwards the equally hard peace which was really only an armistice lasting twenty years. Now, however, another two and a half years of a fresh war have passed, of a war for a new Europe longing for permanent peace.

'In view of this long struggle a realization grows up in us which we might easily have failed to notice in other and calmer times: The aim of war is peace, the aim of the struggle is the life of the coming generations, the safeguarding of their lives. War is a touchstone of the vital capacity of nations just as in a disease a patient's temperature is the touchstone of a sound heart.

'War is unpleasant, painful and grim, but when there is no other choice but complete annihilation then it forms a way to new life. Man is by nature a creature disliking submission and disliking sacrifices. The desire for liberty and property has made man, thanks to his intelligence, the most terrible beast of prey. There have always been serious reasons when mankind has voluntarily submitted to a leader and been prepared to sacrifice life and property for a higher aim.

'The aim of war is not destruction but the construction of permanent peace. Peoples understanding war in this way are capable of founding indestructible empires lasting for centuries as well as great and valuable civilizations.

'War is a social phenomenon. The leader, who is at the same time a great general,[1] is usually the incarnation of social forces which for reasons of self preservation have set the masses moving and placed weapons in their hands. Such a war is a bold leap across the chasm to the firm ground on the other side when on this side the ground

---

[1] The 'great general' hardly needs a label. In 1943 *Signal* published this fulsome note about Hitler. 'The character of the attitude of the army to Adolf Hitler seems to be unknown abroad. His bravery and his knowledge are not the only distinctive features of a good soldier. The good soldier also has a very fine instinct for military leadership. The good soldier intuitively feels the qualities of an N.C.O. just as clearly as those of the highest commander. The instinct of the German soldiers has declared itself in favour of Adolf Hitler. They cling to him as their highest commander, because instinctively they feel that that is what he is.'

has turned into a bog under our feet into which we would gradually but irresistibly sink and in which we would perish if we looked on inactively or merely indulged in self-pity.'

Whatever Colonel Moravec thought, it is fairly certain that many German soldiers indulged in self-pity on the Russian front. Fighting never stopped for long and the lines were never stabilized. The Russian armies had turned blitzkrieg into a war of attrition. But still German Army morale held and the fighting spirit of the troops never flagged. Assault gun commander Sergeant Primozic proved this. Sergeant Primozic is worth studying, for he was one of the most outstanding German soldiers of the Second World War and in some ways the most outstanding.

A big, strong, neat, intelligent-looking man, Primozic lived in Backnang, Württemberg, where he worked as a locksmith. His father had been killed in action during the Great War. At the age of twenty, in 1934, Primozic joined the regular army—he was one of only three men accepted from sixty applicants the day he enlisted.

Originally he served in the horse artillery, but when the army became more mechanized and men were being tested for service in armoured units, the psychologists soon saw that Primozic was qualified—he would never lose his head and would not allow others to do so. He became an instructor in armour, then was appointed commander of one of the first assault guns.

The assault guns were as heavy as tanks but were flatter and had no turret. The Germans used them as Hannibal did his elephants to spread terror among the enemy. But until that moment came the assault artillerymen had to wait long, bitter hours while they saw the enemy artillery improving its range. When the hail of shellfire died down and the first enemy tanks approached, the assault guns went into action, often driving forward over trees and bushes to fire their single heavy gun at practically point-blank range.

In 1942 Sergeant Primozic went to the Russian front without any decoration on his tunic. Five months later he had fought his way through German decorations to win the Oak Leaves to the Knight's Insignia of the Iron Cross, after some of the most outstanding personal gallantry of the war. He was the first N.C.O. to win the Oak Leaves.

At Rshev in September Primozic almost every day destroyed Soviet tanks which were launching persistent attacks. He bagged five on each of three consecutive days. On the fourth day he was given the task of covering the division's flank. The fighting was severe and Primozic used all his ammunition; he was alone and defenceless in open country with his assault gun. Then he saw another German assault gun which had been hit and put out of action; in it were four defenceless Germans. Russian troops were only 100 yards away but Primozic drove up to the other gun, slammed to a stop, jumped out and grabbed up two wire cables. Under heavy fire he fastened them to the crippled assault gun and dragged it away, eventually reaching German lines, though he was under fire all the time.

The battle of Rshev was developing into a stalemate when the Russians launched their most furious attack with tanks and infantry preceded by heavy artillery fire. Under the barrage Primozic and his crew waited—they and the crew of one other assault gun. They were the only two the Germans could bring into action that day.

Then the second assault gun was hit by a Russian shell. Primozic faced the enemy tank onslaught alone. First of all he destroyed stray tanks, usually with one shot at a range of 100 or 150 yards. Then came the crisis—the *élite* Stalin Tank Corps attacked with nearly fifty machines. During the early part of the battle Primozic's gun knocked out seven tanks; now, in one hour, he destroyed seventeen more—twenty-four for the day, thirty-nine in all during the battle.

The German High Command credited him with having won the battle of Rshev single-handed. If, under analysis, this seems too sweeping a statement, it is certainly true that his gun alone was responsible for preventing the Russian breakthrough. By February 1943 he had destroyed sixty Russian tanks. Many of these victories were not gained by a single shot. On some occasions a duel lasted for a long time and Primozic would have to fire seventeen or eighteen rounds before destroying a Russian tank. There were many hazards. Once the caterpillar track of the gun broke while it was under fire. The driver, Corporal Braun, and another crew member climbed out and repaired it while Primozic and the fourth crew member—the top machine-gunner—gave covering fire.

Primozic and his crew were given a lot of publicity and Primozic, in addition to his several decorations, was commissioned. In February 1943 he and his crew were interviewed by Radio Berlin, but Primozic, in answer to questions, could not define courage and would not say if he had been courageous.

Both then and in later interviews he merely said, 'You have to keep calm.' He probably never thought how these words justified the psychologists' assessment of him.

Primozic was lucky; he came back from the Russian front and survived the war—the most decorated German soldier of the war, apart from senior officers.

German field artists painted some magnificent impressions of Primozic's gun in action and many photographs were taken of him and his crew, but all trace of these records disappeared later in the war and survive now only in the pages of *Signal* magazine.

In September 1942 when Sergeant Primozic was busy at Rshev the Germans laid siege to Stalingrad. Not since Madrid in the Spanish Civil war had a great city become a battlefield. For sixty-six days—14 September–19 November—the German Sixth Army under General von Paulus smashed at Stalingrad with everything it had. German infantry actually conquered most of Stalingrad and occupied four miles along the western bank of the Volga around the Barricade Factory, but they never swept the Russians entirely out of the city.

This is how Front Correspondent Lieut. Benno Wundshammer described it:

'An acrid smell of burning greets us. The carcasses of horses, their bellies swollen, fill the air with the stench of putrefaction. Prisoners and fugitives totter towards us. Then we enter the town. I have already seen many towns gutted by the fires of war, yet I have never seen such great destruction. The complicated technical installation of a modern industrial town lies a chaos of burnt and broken ruins. Whole railway stations are only a tangled confusion of rusting iron. A dead soldier is lying by the roadside. Even in death he still holds his sub-machine-gun tightly in his grasp and I cannot bring myself to take it from his rigid hands. German soldiers have established themselves in cellars and vaults under a heap of ruins. . . . Every house is a fortification. The enemy fires from the storeys of the houses and cellars. They are usually in parties of fifteen men under the command of an officer or commissar. They will not come out of their holes at any price. We crawl up to them and throw hand grenades at them as they fire. then they lie down and die. . . .'

Von Paulus refused the Russian demand to surrender because

Hitler had ordered him to resist to the last man. The German soldiers suffered. They froze, they starved, they died of wounds, they were blown to pieces and ground under the treads of tanks. Wounded men were pushed back into the fight to try to hold the rapidly shrinking perimeter. Out of ammunition, they met advancing Russians with grenades and when they ran out, with bayonets. Mercilessly, the Russians, under Rokossovsky, annihilated the German Army. If ever the German soldier showed that he could take punishment this was it. The old indifference to death came back to them. They threw corpses into deep holes with no more outward emotion than if burying rubbish. Many a man did enough to win an Iron Cross—and died, his heroism unwitnessed.

Some men harnessed themselves to their gun and dragged it for twelve miles through the snow to Stalingrad.

One particularly brave group, remnants of the 11th Army Corps under General Strecker, established itself in a tractor works. The Russians worked forward to within twenty yards of the fitting shop, the hub of the defence. In subterranean passages and pits the Germans met Russians in bloody hand-to-hand fights and killed hundreds of them with the bayonet and with shovels. Men suffering from severe frostbite passed ammunition to those still able to fire.

The Red Army found the Germans as difficult to pin down as rats. The Russians had to storm every building. Shock squads of six to eight men, each armed with ten grenades, a tommy-gun and a dagger, rushed each enemy post. Fierce fighting followed. Eventually the German Army was sealed off, but even then, short of everything, von Paulus counter-attacked on all sides.

The whole continued defence was military madness and every man in the Stalingrad pocket knew it, from von Paulus down, but they fought as best they could. The end came when Paulus, recently promoted Field-Marshal, was captured. With Paulus, 23 generals, 2,000 officers, 90,000 other ranks and 40,000 non-combatant soldiers and civilians surrendered. About 34,000 sick and wounded had been evacuated during the campaign and more than 100,000 were killed, died of sickness, starvation and cold and left sick and wounded in Stalingrad.

These men were massacred by the Russians, who threw explosive charges into the hospital shelters. On 3 February thousands were buried alive when the entrances to the great Timoshenko bunker were dynamited. Of the 90,000 prisoners about 45,000 are believed to have died of starvation within the first six weeks of captivity. Only a few thousand eventually returned to Germany—years after the war ended.

The Russians took 60,000 trucks, 6,700 guns and 1,500 tanks among other booty. It was the greatest defeat ever administered to a German army in the field but on its memory clever German propagandists will one day raise a rallying banner.

CHAPTER XXIV

Inch by Inch Retreat

Bitter fighting took place for a long time after the Stalingrad débâcle. The Germans had not lost heart and though they were pushed back they contested every foot of the way. They made some desperate counter-attacks which were often successful. At the end of two years of the war, Russia, according to Stalin, had lost 4,200,000 men killed in action. At that time the Axis had about the same number of effective men in Russia, but the Russians were better able to withstand heavy losses.

Germany still saw herself as 'Europe's shield'. In the March 1943 issue of *Signal* magazine, published almost immediately after the defeat at Stalingrad, Major Dr. Wilhelm Ehmer wrote an article with precisely this heading and with the sub-title 'Concerning the spiritual foundations of German Army traditions'.

The author made no reference to Stalingrad but the timing of the article, being circulated throughout Europe in a dozen languages, is significant.

> 'The battles of material during the last two years of the Great War had played a large part in establishing the view that the individual soldier was once and for all doomed to disappear from the battlefield. Mechanical war, the war machine crushing everything in its path, was supposed to have taken its place. This opinion was held by many foreign military writers. It also made itself felt in the measures adopted by the General Staffs.
>
> 'For example, when the German Army was disarmed in 1918 particular care was taken to ensure that it possessed

no heavy weapons, no heavy guns, no tanks or planes. It was believed that this prohibition more than anything else would render Germany defenceless.

'The Maginot Line was another example. If mechanical war was going to decide the victory in the future it was only necessary to establish a tremendous wall of heavy weapons to be invincible for all time.

'It would be interesting to investigate whether the Germans, too, would have adopted this view if they had not been forced at Versailles to do without the most important weapons. We doubt whether the German theorists and practical experts would in such case have recognized the superiority of war material over the soldier. The spiritual foundations of the German military tradition had always been too firmly established in the nation itself for that. Had not, too, the individual German soldier, by defying the material superiority of his enemies for so long, proved that determined men scornful of death are superior to blind material?

'The Treaty of Versailles forced Germany where her army was concerned to rely upon that strength which no dictate could forbid—the spirit. Where there was lack of external means the internal ones were mobilized and where the employment of material was restricted the abundantly flowing spring of ideas was exploited.

'The "victors" of the World War clad themselves in a heavy coat of armour and dug themselves in behind lines of fortifications built with the greatest cunning and bristling with weapons, while the tiny German Army of 100,000 became the guardian of the great spiritual German soldierly tradition and at the same time developed this tradition by drawing the necessary conclusions from the experiences of the World War.

'The difficulties of the situation did not cause it to throw in its hand or to despair. On the contrary they aroused all the soldierly virtues, strength of character, determination, inventiveness and courage, all of which are foundation stones on which the German soldierly tradition has been built from its beginning.

'Peoples which have to fight for and secure their existence on a poor soil under hard conditions regard soldierly virtues as the expression of an attitude forced upon them by necessity. The two German races, which were the first to develop a genuine soldierly spirit, had to carry out tasks of a warlike character. The Prussians were obliged to wrest from their country, which had been so ungenerously treated by nature, the foundation for a modest existence as a nation. Moreover, they had to defend themselves against strong and more favourably placed neighbours.

'The Austrians,[1] being the inhabitants of the frontier, were forced to become soldiers to defend themselves against the south-east. In both cases, therefore, it was not the whim of a despot which established an army and imbued the people with soldierly conceptions, but their historical fate, nature itself, which stood as the god-parents at the cradle of both the Prussian Army and the old Austrian Army. After again covering their colours with immortal glory during the First World War both have been organically incorporated into the young Nationalist Socialist German Armed Forces.'

Giselher Wirsing, writing in the same issue, pointed out that the war was not only a German war, but a European Holy War to save the countries of Europe from the stranglehold of Soviet-Asiatic Imperialism.

When the propaganda machine had had time to digest the Stalingrad defeat *Signal* did have something to say about it—after some interesting preamble.

'The amazing German victories won since 1 September 1939 must not be interpreted only in the light of technical progress or material organization. . . . They must be ascribed to the mental and spiritual strength of the rejuvenated German Armed Forces. Ever since the democracies so despicably threw away the magnificent chance they had in Versailles of carrying out a really just reorganization of our Continent, Germany has undertaken to provide tortured Europe with new possibilities of existence. It is in this sense that the German Army feels that it is, indeed, the executor of a political will.

'It was not the lust for conquest which caused Germany to take up arms; this war has been forced on her by the destructive aims of her enemies. The German soldier is

---

[1] This is one of the few occasions on which a German writer has deigned to recognize the Austrians as having Germanic qualities.

convinced of this to the innermost depths of his being; this is why the Army is invincible.

'It is, moreover, inspired by the belief in the high mission of protecting the Reich and thereby also the whole of Europe against the attacks of the Capitalist Powers in the West and above all against the horrors of Bolshevism.

'The German still fights chivalrously as he always has done and does not employ cruel methods of a brutal mercenary with which he has become acquainted during this war from his antagonists, such as the shelling of military hospitals and attacks on planes engaged in rescuing men in distress at sea, air raids on open towns carried out by the British in order to terrorize the population, and the terrible maltreatment of prisoners by the Bolshevists. The populations of all the territories occupied by the German Army are unanimous in their praise of the exemplary conduct and discipline of German soldiers.

'The most sublime example . . . is the sacrifice of the troops fighting at Stalingrad which enabled the Allied armies on the Eastern front to hold up the raging Bolshevist torrent and continue to preserve Europe from the annihilating rule of the Soviets.'

The summer was no kinder than the winter to the Germans. An army reporter painted a vivid picture of infantry on the march.

'When a German infantryman speaks of his experiences in Soviet Russia, the first thing he says is that all the roads there go up hill. The country is flat but the roads go up hill irrespective of the direction in which they run. It is only the curvature of the earth's surface, the old footslogger says, which makes all the roads go up hill in that flat country. This may be so, but it may also be an illusion. The important thing is that this is the impression you have, this is what you feel when marching through a country where all the roads lead up hill. The sea is a force of nature but that the earth can also be a force of nature is realized only by the German infantryman and his European comrades who are marching with him in the east.

'A pace measures 60 centimetres. There are, of course, both shorter and longer paces, but 60 centimetres is the average. You have to take 84,000 paces in order to cover

50 kilometres, 84,000 paces in hard hob-nailed boots and up hill all the time. Swaying to their own rhythm, bathed in their own sweat and topped by brown and blond hair blowing in the breeze, that is the picture of a German infantry column on the march. The greatest efforts are not made during the battle. The German soldier knows that he must fight and is able to fight. But the tremendous spiritual effort is made in overcoming distance. A comrade tires, his feet drag, he begins to stumble and finally he is exhausted. With pale face and clenched teeth he tries to march on. His comrades carry his rifle and the rest of his equipment, but he cannot carry on. He stumbles out of the ranks and falls in again at the end of the column. His weapons are passed back, two comrades support him, a third carries his equipment for him. Others join him. A heavy burden drags at the end of the column. Yet one pace measures 60 centimetres and so they move on. The head of the column is filled with the urge to advance. The company commander's will carries the column farther and farther forward, one after another of the 84,000 paces is overcome, the gleaming sun grows black in front of the men's eyes and whenever there is an engagement with the enemy, it comes as a relief.

'But afterwards, they go on again. Their feet ache and burn, but at last they have reached their objective. It had seemed impossible and yet they have managed it all the same. Those who had faltered smile and overcome their fatigue when they hear the company commander say: "The General saw you and praised your marching. Well done again, boys!"'

But no German general said, 'Well done, boys!' after the gigantic tank battle which developed at Orel and Belgorod in July 1943; losses were estimated at more than 1,000 machines on each side. The Russians knocked out German tigers and Ferdinands with massed artillery fire and mobile anti-tank reserves. With superior air power and almost equal numbers of troops, the Red Army maintained the flanks of the salients the Germans had punched, absorbed enemy tank attacks without giving much ground and crippled the Nazi armour.

Once the Germans had committed their reserves above Belgorod, three Soviet armies in the north attacked fifty German divisions on the Orel salient. Rokossovsky pounded it with the greatest artillery preparation of any war. He fired 2,950 guns on every mile of his nineteen-mile front, a barrage ten times heavier than that at Verdun. This and the fighting that followed was the most severe that the Germans had ever encountered. That they were able to hold formation and keep the front from being broken is an indication of German tenacity. But they could not stop themselves from being pushed back and in that summer offensive the Red Army liberated an area 700 miles long by up to 180 miles wide.[1]

The retreat inevitably continued, but there was no rout. The German armies retreated in good order at all times. At the end of 1943 they were still capable of an offensive. They counter-attacked around Kiev and reconquered much territory.

Nevertheless, they were on the retreat much of that year—an aggressive, fighting retreat. They had fought well in Africa, winning ground, losing it, winning it, losing it. All the many races of soldiers who fought them respected them—Australians, British, New Zealanders, South Africans, Indians, Poles, Americans.

Pushed into the hills of Tunisia, the Germans used interesting defensive tactics only possible with well-trained, well-tried troops. They seldom held the crest line or the forward slopes in any strength but dug themselves in strongly on the reverse slope. The only positions on the forward slope were a few well-sited, well-protected light machine-guns and observation posts

[1] In 1943 the Russian propaganda department sent to Britain much corre-spondence allegedly collected from German prisoners and taken from bodies on the Eastern front. It comprised letters to and from German soldiers and extracts from diaries. They were published in England under the title *True to Type*. It is possible that some of the collection was genuine, particu-larly the letters from relations and friends in Germany telling of the damage caused by British air raids. It is probable that a lot of it was not genuine. Much of it reads as if painstakingly prepared by Russian pro-paganda experts. For instance, extracts from the diary of Major Reich, assistant chief of staff of the 25th German Motorized Division, include such entries as: 2/7/41: Jews shot. 3/7/41: Twenty-two Russian soldiers, some of them wounded, shot in peasant farmyard. A lieutenant in the 185th Regiment is quoted as writing, 24/11/41: . . . we look into the future with alarm . . .

The Russians supplied very long letters supposedly written by soldiers while 'the infernal death-dealing symphony of battle goes on and on'. And there are such naïve editorial comments as: *Here the diary breaks off*. There is much praise for the Russians and much criticism of inept German leader-ship and of 'cowardly comrades'. The book was intended to prove that the German troops were callous sadists, and in 1943 it probably served its purpose.

for artillery and mortars. As the British troops advanced up hill the Germans brought heavy direct fire from the machine-guns and observed fire from artillery and mortars. If the Germans on the forward slope could get out safely, they did so; if not they surrendered. The British troops would then reach the crest, where they were ideal, silhouetted targets on which every available gun would open up. Then, whenever possible, the Germans launched strong infantry counter-attacks to push the British down the slope they had just ascended. These tactics were difficult to beat and the Allies did so only with great difficulty and at great expense. Eventually, they were pushed out of Africa altogether.[1]

In July 1943 the British and Americans attacked them in Sicily, where the campaign lasted thirty-eight days and involved fierce and continuous fighting in most difficult country at the hottest season of the year. Twenty-four thousand Germans died in Sicily, but they died hard. They showed particular intelligence in the way they blew up mountain roads, passes and bridges to delay the Allied advance.

They contested the Allied invasion of Italy and fought a series of savage delaying battles at one defensive line after another as they were pushed northwards. One of their greatest triumphs was the holding of Cassino for so many bitter winter months. From this natural fortress they fought off attacks by American, British, French, Indian and Polish troops; they even bested the élite New Zealand Division. Outnumbered, outgunned, outtanked and without air cover, they held on with such courage that Field-Marshal Alexander wrote to Churchill, 'The tenacity of these German paratroops is quite remarkable. I doubt if there are any other troops in the world who could have stood up to it (the incessant assaults) . . . and then gone on fighting with the ferocity they have.' At this time the defenders were men of the 1st Parachute Division, probably the most outstanding formation of the German Army.

Ernie Pyle, one of the greatest war correspondents, sat with a group of American soldiers one night in Italy while they discussed whether or not it was a good idea to yell when making a close-in attack. An officer thought it was good psychology because the Germans were afraid of night attacks, and a good barrage of Indian yells would further demoralize them. 'But

[1] The Axis campaigns in Africa cost Italy and Germany 950,000 soldiers killed and captured, nearly 2,400,000 tons of shipping and 8,000 aircraft, 6,200 guns, 2,550 tanks and 70,000 trucks.

the soldiers mainly disagreed,' Pyle reported. 'They said Jerry didn't scare as easy as all that, and when an attacker yelled he just gave his position away.'

The Germans liked night attacks no more than any other soldier likes them, but noise did not bother them. They were experts in noise. At this time they were using the *nebelwerfer* against the Americans—a six-barrelled rocket rack which fired one rocket after another with a bloodcurdling, vicious swish.

The beginning of the end for the Germans was 6 June 1944—D-Day—when the British and American forces fought their way ashore in Normandy. Even after the fantastically furious pre-invasion bombardment they had to claw their way ashore because never before in the history of warfare had a more deadly array of defences been prepared for an invading force. The finishing touches to these defences were the work of Field-Marshal Erwin Rommel.

The Germans, though shocked by the intensity of the attack, fought back well, especially on 'Bloody Omaha' beach where the landing dissolved into carnage and chaos, until somehow the attacking Americans pulled themselves together for a forward movement. As the invasion gathered momentum some Germans surrendered; others held out in small groups and died to the last man—often because they had no choice with a do-or-die officer or sergeant standing over them. But generally the withdrawal was orderly and controlled enough to slow down the invasion.

During the first twenty-four hours of the invasion they inflicted 12,000 casualties on the British, Americans and Canadians. The German losses were not more than 9,000 and were probably much less, possibly only 5,000. D-Day and a foothold on the Continent were dearly bought, though most Allied commanders expected heavier casualties. They certainly won a much larger area of territory for fewer casualties than was the case in World War I.

In the Mortain-Falaise Pocket of Normandy the Wehrmacht suffered its greatest disaster since Stalingrad, but a third of the Seventh Army escaped the trap.

On only one part of the Western front could von Rundstedt's troops meet the Allies on more or less equal terms; this was in the area of the Upper Moselle. Elsewhere, as a British Intelligence officer commented, 'Both as regards quality and diversity the enemy force opposing us shows the effects of the recent measures in Germany to step up the national effort.

Paratroops and pilots, policemen and sailors, boys of sixteen and men with duodenal ulcers—all of these have been through the Corps cage during the last few days. And now we have some deep-sea divers.'

In the autumn of 1944 Germany's military position was hopeless and steadily first at one point and then at another her armies were driven inwards towards the heart of Germany. But the Germans were not finished—not by a long way. Numerically, the Wehrmacht still listed 10,000,000 'men' under arms, although 4,000,000 had been killed since the beginning of the war and although it had suffered 1,200,000 casualties in the previous three months.

Many German generals at this time were all for pulling back to the Siegfried Line and settling in to a defensive battle of attrition that nobody could win—except on the terms of 1918. Field-Marshals von Rundstedt and Model—the most competent of the German leaders—had other plans. Rommel by now was dead, having been forced to commit suicide. Hitler had another plan—one that was entirely his own.

Von Rundstedt and Model met Hitler on 27 October 1944, and he listened impatiently but fully to all their objections to his campaign, which he labelled Watch on the Rhine—also called 'Christrose'—and to their own plans for saving Germany. The Field-Marshals' plans were at least practical, but Hitler brushed them aside.

'Don't you remember Frederick the Great?' he asked. 'At Rossbach and Leuthen he defeated enemies twice his size. By a bold attack. Study history . . . History will repeat itself, for the Ardennes will be my Rossbach and Leuthen . . . the Alliance against the Third Reich will split apart!'

All Hitler's senior officers must have known that his plan was doomed to failure. The Germans had neither the strength nor the petrol to recapture Antwerp and his boast that he would 'Dunkirk' the Allies north of the Ardennes was mere wishful thinking. All the Germans could gain in the Ardennes was time —but time for what? Only one German general—Hasso von Manteuffel—had the courage to challenge the NOT TO BE ALTERED Operation Orders handed down from Hitler's H.Q. So Christrose went forward—to flare into dazzling success and then to fizzle out.

CHAPTER XXV

The Last Great Fight—The Battle of the Bulge

Before dawn on 16 December fourteen German infantry divisions moved through the misty trees of the Eifel mountains and forests towards the American line. The noise of the tanks, assault guns and transport moving with them was drowned by salvoes of V.1.s which screamed towards Antwerp and Liège. At 5.30 a.m. 2,000 guns began shelling the American positions between Monschau and Echternach. Under cover of this bombardment the infantry advanced to attack and five Panzer divisions moved up close behind them for quick exploitation. The German force amounted to nearly 400,000.

In one of the waiting armoured columns an Untersturm-führer of the Hitler Youth Division wrote a last letter to his sister. 'I write during one of the momentous hours before we attack, full of excitement and expectation of what the next days will bring. Some believe in living but life is not everything! It is enough to know that we attack and will throw the enemy from the homeland. It is a holy task. Above me is the terrific noise of the V.1.s and artillery, the voice of war.' On the back of the envelope he added: 'Ruth! Ruth! Ruth! WE MARCH!'[1]

That a German soldier, late in 1944, could strike this magnificent note of soldierly exaltation and exultation is astonishing. Certainly the writer was probably in his first action, but he must have heard of the many German disasters and the suffering on the Eastern Front. Yet here he was engaged in a 'holy task' and keyed up to the ultimate pitch of excitement.

[1] This letter was found, unposted, by the U.S. 1st Infantry Division. It was not unique; many other letters said much the same thing.

That night officers read to their men a message from von Rundstedt: 'Soldiers of the Western Front! Your great hour has come. Large attacking armies have started against the Anglo-Americans. I do not have to tell you more than that. You feel it yourself. We gamble everything. You carry with you the holy obligation to give all to achieve superhuman objectives for the Fatherland and our Führer.'

The main thrusts were to be made by Sepp Dietrich's Sixth S.S. Panzer Army, for Hitler believed that only the S.S. divisions had the fanaticism to ensure success. For the sake of Nazi prestige he wanted them to win the glory for the victory. But for complex tactical reasons, ordered by Hitler, Dietrich's army was committed on the northern wing, not in the centre, where the Field-Marshals wanted it. In any case, neither Dietrich[1] nor his troops could carry out the tasks Hitler gave them. Von Runstedt said later: 'The decision to use the Sixth S.S. Panzer in the north unbalanced the whole offensive.'

The point for the assault had been well chosen. It was the same hilly and wooded Ardennes across which the first blitzkrieg had been launched. Here, because Eisenhower had divided his main forces between the Ruhr and the Saar, four American divisions were guarding nearly a hundred miles of front—a 'ghost' front where nothing had been happening.

The Ardennes is rolling forested country, broken by steep, twisted valleys of mountain streams. Many roads exist, but few at that time were good and most passed through narrow, awkward defiles where they crossed rivers. The best routes run south-west, and as the Germans wanted to advance north and north-west, they would not only be running against the grain of the country but would have to use secondary roads.

It was a much better defensive country than offensive—unless the defenders could be taken by surprise, which the Germans had achieved in 1940.

Model, the commander in the field, saw clearly that the campaign would be a series of battles for road junctions. He had no doubt that he could break through the American front for he knew exactly what units opposed him. They were newish, mostly untried units, being broken in to active service conditions, which in an Ardennes December were very cold.

The massive bombardment aroused the Americans but few

---

[1] Dietrich—a sergeant in World War I, later a butcher and a street brawler—was highly regarded both by Hitler and the S.S. men, but as a commander his limit was as a brigade commander.

appreciated its significance until German troops emerged from the morning mist. They were as surprised as many Frenchmen had been at Auerstadt more than a century before.

The Allied commanders were amazed and incredulous at the offensive. They had become so used to thinking that the Wehrmacht was about to collapse that they simply could not believe it could mount such a major attack.

The attack was spectacularly successful. For instance, on the River Our sector the U.S. 28th Division, spread over a front of twenty-eight miles, was crushed by five German divisions. That evening armoured columns used searchlights to continue the advance into the night. Spearheads, exploiting a fifty-mile gap, were twenty miles inside Belgium. They had not taken all their objectives and in places they were checked but they had reason to be happy with the day's fighting. Most of the American troops fought well, but some units flew in broken confusion before the German onslaught.

Coincidentally, at one point the right wing of the force led by Sepp Dietrich ran head-on into American divisions heading towards the Ruhr dams.

Communications broke down everywhere and the German plan for spreading confusion and alarm succeeded more than even Hitler's expectations. The Kommandos of Colonel Otto 'Scarface' Skorzeny created much of this confusion. More than forty jeep-loads of his American-speaking Germans got through the lines on the first two nights. They cut telegraph wires, intercepted and shot despatch riders and liaison officers, destroyed radio stations and shot military policemen directing traffic at vital junctions. One German sergeant calmly took over traffic direction and sent an American regiment down the wrong road. All but eight of the German teams returned safely to their own lines.

Rumours flourished. German paratroops and saboteurs were reported everywhere; German tanks were firing into the rear of American lines. Germans in American uniforms were creating havoc behind the lines and suicide squads were searching for Eisenhower. Skorzeny men dressed as nuns and priests were said to be among the killer-groups out to get him. The only American not in a panic about it was Eisenhower himself.

Among the already jittery Americans these incidents caused near hysteria. They imposed security measures so strict that they threatened to slow down the whole American reaction. At one time General Bruce Clarke was arrested and imprisoned for many vital hours because some military policemen thought he was a German.

An American historian, present at the battle, reported that 'retreating troops clogged the roads and blocked reinforcements on their way to the front. At times complete panic gripped some units as rumours of approaching Germans were heard. . . . Much equipment was jettisoned in perfect working order. . . .'[1]

Here and there, in the general retreat, a bastion stood. One such was Bastogne, where the garrison, though surrounded, refused to yield. On 22 December General von Lüttwitz sent two German officers with a polite and formal note calling on the American commander, Brigadier General A. C. McAuliffe to surrender. McAuliffe, after glancing at the paper, dropped it on the floor said, 'Aw, nuts,' and went out to some routine duty.

Later, when he returned to his command post, a colonel told him that the two German envoys were still present and wanted an answer to their formal military communication.

'What the hell should I tell them?' McAuliffe asked.

An operations officer suggested that McAuliffe's first reaction would be a good answer—Nuts.

McAuliffe wrote:

> To the German Commander
> Nuts!
> The American Commander.

Naturally, the Germans needed the reply explained to them. Neither they nor other Germans were amused by it and perhaps they were justified in feeling irritated. Even in total war there are times when good manners are necessary.

In no fewer than twelve main thrusts, many of which fanned out into more minor stabs, the Germans pushed an alarming bulge in the American line, which was hastily, almost frantically, bolstered by further American and British forces.

On the Schnee Eifel, just north of the centre of the front, the Germans hemmed about 10,000 American troops into a few square miles of wood near the town of Schönberg. Artillery and mortar fire concentrated on this small area and the mass of trapped men were thrown into absolute confusion. Then tanks took up position and fired air-bursting shrapnel from their 88s. Casualties were great. Inevitably, reluctantly, the two senior

[1] R. E. Merriam, in his book, *Dark December*.

officers, Colonel George Descheneaux and Charles Cavender, decided on surrender to save total slaughter. Next to Bataan, in the early days of the Pacific War, it was the greatest surrender of Americans in history.

Colonels Descheneaux and Cavender were bitterly criticized for surrendering but their decision was sane and right. The well-placed Germans would have kept on pounding until the area had not an unwounded man in it. As the American prisoners filed to the rear the Germans grabbed souvenirs—watches, rings, equipment.[1] Young German officers shook hands and congratulated one another.

The Germans did not have it all their own way. In the north-east a group led by Colonel Joachim Peiper—one of the most dashing German officers of the war—after a galloping break-through had been surrounded and now held only two villages—Stoumont and La Gleize. The key to Stoumont was a fortress-like sanatorium which the Americans pounded to fragments. But the Germans held it until only twenty survivors remained, then they sneaked out to the second village, where Peiper himself was.

Peiper, with time on his hands, explained to a captive American officer how the French, Belgians, Dutch, Norwegians and Finns had accepted Hitler's idea of one Europe. Even the Russians had welcomed the Germans in the early days of the war, he said. 'We're fighting your fight against the Communist menace,' he said. He meant what he said. Leading his 800 survivors, Peiper pulled out of La Gleize on 24 December.

Despite all their commitments in this campaign-battle—for action was ceaseless—the Germans made yet another and different attack. This was launched on 1 January 1945 south-ward from the Saar. But it was an abortive adventure.

On this day, too, the Luftwaffe made its last major attack—when more than 1,100 aircraft made a slashing attack across the Ardennes, destroying 300 Allied aircraft and laying waste to twenty-seven Allied bases from Eindhoven to Brussels. It was the Luftwaffe's attempt to help the Wehrmacht. The price was high; 300 German fighter pilots were lost.

But the bigger the bulge became the bigger became the Germans' problem of supply and defence; the lengthening front

[1] Just as the Americans stripped captured Germans of watches, wallets, medals and Lugers. In one disgraceful exhibition on 29 December an American officer could not get his men to follow him in a critical attack because they were too busy fighting one another for souvenirs.

of the bulge had to be defended against attack, which meant that fewer men were available for the actual pushing-ahead. In effect, they had created an enormous salient—and a salient is always terribly vulnerable to flank attack. Inevitably the pace of the push slackened and then the front became static. Finally, the Germans reached a maximum penetration of seventy-five miles, to within five miles of the Meuse at Dinant—with a maximum north–south breakthrough of fifty-five miles.

About this time an *unteroffizier* of the 167 Volksgrenadiers somehow found time to write a field postcard to somebody at home—probably his brother. 'This is glorious,' he wrote. 'We are bitterly cold, but it will be warmer on the Channel. God must be with us this time.' And he underlined 'us'. Americans and British were writing letters, too, but I doubt if any of them described what they were living through as 'glorious'.

Hitler knew he would not reach the Channel. In fact, he realized that further advance was impossible and he decided to turn the operation into a deadly battle of attrition. But clearly Allied pressure would not permit this and on 9 January, following a frank appraisal of the situation from von Rundstedt, Hitler gave the order to pull back. Panzer units at the tip of the bulge turned round and headed east.

By 20 January the great retreat was on in earnest. All the Germans were on the way back, except for a few picked infantrymen—picked not because they were especially efficient, but because they were very young, old or useless. They were posted in lonely foxholes, in heaps of rubble, in cellars, in pine trees and told, 'Stay here and hold up the Allied advance'.

These 'picked men' knew they were being abandoned in order that the best fighting men might escape back behind the West Wall where they could turn on their pursuers. They fought gallantly—and great gallantry is needed to fight alone, knowing that death is almost inevitable.

The Americans found boys of fourteen and fifteen, rifles frozen to their hands; they found men in their late fifties who had done what they were ordered and then died from exhaustion; they found men crippled from earlier wounds. Nearly all these soldiers killed at least one enemy before they were themselves killed. It was significant that they were all killed in some definite position, never in the open as if they had been running away. The Germans will never forget these heroes; they will never be allowed to forget.

The men of Watch on the Rhine, the survivors of one of the

great battles of history, struggled back to the Fatherland.[1] They were exhausted, cold and hungry; they were wounded and dying. Some men struggled along with intestines hanging from mangled stomachs; some were blind, many were clotted with frozen blood; ghastly, ill-bandaged wounds were exposed to the cold through rents in tattered uniforms. Thousands of men had dysentery, and others vomited and retched. Napoleon would have recognized the sights.

An able historian of the Battle of the Bulge[2] has said that 'the will of the German soldier was broken'. It was not. This time, unlike 1918, he knew he was beaten. But his will was intact; the will of a man worthy of the name of soldier is never broken. Had a leader said, 'We will form a line here and die here,' these men would have obeyed. The order *was* given and they *did* obey.

They checked the advancing British, Canadians and Americans as they were pushed back to the Rhine, but by 23 March Hitler had lost more than a third of the forces which had been guarding his western frontiers six weeks earlier, for 293,000 men had been taken prisoner and at least another 60,000 killed or seriously wounded since the start of the Reichwald offensive.

Still the Germans were not finished. On Montgomery's left the German garrison in Holland was still holding fast; remnants of the First Parachute Army were preparing to fall back from one water line to another so as to deny the north German ports to the Allies; on Montgomery's right, Model's Army Group was standing firm in the Ruhr with orders to defend it as a fortress. But the Germans had lost their defences in the centre—the way to the Elbe.

Further south, the Americans were moving forward relentlessly and on 28 March joined battle with the Germans in what was perhaps one of the most symbolic battles of the war. On that day American armoured columns covered fifty-five miles to reach Paderborn, the cradle of Hitler's Panzer divisions. On to this famous German training ground now came the real thing. For forty-eight hours Panzer instructors and officer cadets,

---

[1] According to SHAEF records, the casualties suffered by the First and Third U.S. Armies in the Ardennes were: killed, 8,407; wounded, 46,170; missing, 20,905. Total, 75,482. No directly comparable German figures are possible, but von Rundstedt's H.Q. estimated that the Wehrmacht's casualties came to 'not less than 120,000', of which 12,652 were known to be killed. In all, 75,000 men died in the Ardennes.

[2] John Toland.

specialists and tank trainees, manned guns and armour in a way that even the Americans had to admire. Paderborn was sacred ground to the Wehrmacht and they could not have given it up without being crushed, which they were, on 1 April. Tactically, this defeat also meant that Model's entire Army Group, about 250,000-strong, was trapped, and with it another 100,000 men of the Flak Command.

Under relentless pressure, the Ruhr 'fortress' broke up, largely because the German troops were reluctant to prolong a battle which could only inflict more suffering on the already much-battered civilians of the Ruhr. Model managed to resist for eighteen days but in the end 325,000 of his men became captives—a bigger haul than Stalingrad. Model was not among them; he committed suicide.

By now the winter campaigns of 1944 had restored most U.S.S.R. territory to Soviet peoples and the Germans were back where they had come from, badly mauled, much reduced in numbers but holding their lines. What reserves they had they needed in France and Italy to oppose the British and Americans.

It is pointless to go over the many campaigns in the south and west. The Germans stubbornly resisted at line after line, all the time aware that their own country was being systematically reduced to rubble and that their families were in even greater danger than they were.

When the Russian armies broke on to German soil Ilya Ehrenburg urged them to ravage and ruin. 'Kill! There is nothing that is innocent that is German. Neither in the living nor in the unborn. Follow the directive of Comrade Stalin and trample into the ground for ever the Fascist beast in his cave. Break by force the racial haughtiness of German women. Take them as your lawful prey! Kill you brave advancing Red soldiers!'

At various times Hitler blamed his own generals for his defeats but they had served him well—too well for their own good. 'Generals think wars should be waged like tourneys of the Middle Ages,' he had said. 'I have no use for knights. I need revolutionaries.' This was slander, for his generals waged war as German generals always had done. But the German Army had always been short of revolutionaries. Hitler had generals of great competence; he should have left them to their competence. It was his own impatience which frustrated his designs.

The German generals were proud professionals and many of them were disinterested in Nazism as such, though very few took any step to curb its excesses. The great majority held them-selves aloof from politics and even from quasi-military activities. The treatment of Jews and captured peoples, the oppression and the cruelty, this was not their business.

The vanity of the German generals persisted to the end. They knew that Hitler was leading the nation to destruction, but even while he wounded their honour and insulted them they paid lip service to him. They accepted the promotions, the decorations and the gifts he handed out because in their supreme, historic egotism they could not help themselves. A few genuine rebels existed but even some of these were half-hearted. Such ideas as a 'general strike of generals' were pure fantasy, for no German general could stomach the idea of being deprived of a command and the power and the glory it was supposed to bring. The generals were victims of a system that had gripped generations of commanders before them.[1]

Whatever Hitler thought of his generals and senior officers, he had no reason for criticizing his junior officers and the men in the ranks. Professionals, volunteers and conscripts, they had fought hard, consistently and loyally, though not mainly, I think, because of Hitler, but more because they were the inheritors of a unique military tradition.

In the spring of 1945 the life of the German Army was ebbing fast and the final act of surrender was signed in Berlin by Field-Marshal Keitel on 8 May 1945, although fighting continued until 11 May, when 374,000 German troops in Czechoslovakia surrendered to the Americans and Yugoslavs. The German Army casualty list for the war was more than 4,500,000, of which number about 2,000,000 had been killed.

The military psychologists were as responsible as the fighting qualities of the German soldier for the army's being able to hold out for so long against overwhelming odds. It is largely because of the psychologists that the Germans do not even now consider themselves to have been beaten—not fairly, at least. They consider themselves brutally crushed, not militarily defeated. Alien minds might not be able to see the difference, but this is not important. The Germans *know* there is a difference.

---

[1] Between the autumn of 1939 and the spring of 1942 more than twenty-five generals died in action. About eighty in all died in action. It is doubtful if any army has had a higher casualty rate in general officers. There was no leadership in the German Army without life being continually at stake.

POSTSCRIPT

Peace Is Ignoble

One writer has said that after the war 'the great military myth
... lay shattered in ruins'.[1] Germany was in ruins, the army was
a shambles—but neither it nor its prowess had been a myth. In
any case, within a few years both country and army were
prosperous and efficient.

There is a naïve idea that Germany's new army is safely in
the hands of senior officers who were anti-Hitler. Even if this
were true, it would make no difference, for the army can hardly
be put under command of generals who are anti-German.

The stated official policy to provide a sort of 'citizens in
uniform' army was intended only as a smokescreen for Germany's former victims. Such an idea is wholly contrary to
German tradition and character.

True, the psychologists are busy again. Appointments to the
position of colonel and above are studied by a massive board of
forty members, all supposedly anti-Nazi and presumably anti-
militaristic. Junior officers are put through 'the forty questions',
devised by a German psychologist retained by the Americans.

Since the applicant knows what answers he is expected to
give, he gives them. 'No, I have no Nazi leanings; no, I have no
feeling of revenge for the defeat of Germany; yes, I realize that
Germany could never again hope to dominate Europe; no, I
would never obey an order to execute unarmed civilians.'

Germany has more than 700 ex-servicemen's groups, all
active, many militant and neo-Nazi. A Major Ewart, at a
meeting in Krefeld in 1956, spoke for many men when he said,
'We are playing about with democracy and forgetting the

[1] Brian Connell in *Watcher on the Rhine*.

conception of German patriotism. Our youth must be taught to obey and feel as Germans, ready to make any sacrifice for the sake of the Fatherland. Many a civilian will be licking his fingers once he can shake the hand of a real soldier again.'

The Army of the Federal German Republic today has real soldiers, despite the alleged serious defects found during NATO exercises. An assessment following the 'Fallex' manœuvres, for example, relegated German forces to the lowest category of all, that is, 'suitable in certain circumstances for defence'. I do not know by what yardstick this estimation was made, but it is faulty. It is possible that the officers commanding the German troops involved were under secret orders to make the army appear to be second-rate, so as to deceive both Allies and potential enemies. The German High Command would be quite capable of such deceit, as it has proved many times before. Morale in the Officers' Corps is said to be not as high as it might be and that good N.C.O.s are scarce.

The German Army today is small by Russian, U.S., Turkish and French standards, but I believe that it is as efficient as any of them and that its *esprit de corps* is as alive as that of the British Army. Its leaders are ambitious, too.

No German soldier is ashamed of the defeats of World War II. On the contrary he is proud of them, for he is being fed on the theme that only heroic German troops could have held out so long against such odds. Regimental museums are flourishing again—a sure sign of high spirit. The Germans do not question the fact of defeat; they say that they were unfairly defeated.

Today's armies, the world tells itself, exist to keep the peace. The Germans know better; an army exists to make war.

The German Officers' Corps has not changed a scrap from what it was in 1900, in 1923 or 1939. The Corps, by a thousand and one devices, circumvented all effort at Allied control after the Great War; it is doing the same today. But subtly, very subtly. 'Antagonize nobody,' the German officers—some of them former S.S. men—are warned. 'Our day will come. If not in this generation then the next.'

East Germans are also sure that their day will come for here, even more than in West Germany, Frederician and Nazi traditions are surviving strongly, if not exactly openly.

Let me take you back to that fortress at Tobruk, to that day when I met the former German soldier. He said two things I shall never forget. They were not original, for he was only expressing what many Germans have said before him and what all Germans have thought. He did not say these two things together, but they should be put together, for they form a sort of creed.

'Germany must triumph,' he said. 'Peace is ignoble.'

Sources

I have referred to many sources to write this book, to numerous histories, memoirs, biographies, official documents, private letters, magazines. To list them all would require an entire chapter, hence I am naming only those which have been especially helpful. One of my most significant and revealing sources was *Signal* magazine, which the Nazis produced as a semi-propaganda medium between 1940 and 1944. It was published in many languages, the smallest edition being that in English—for sale in the Channel Islands. With great trouble and some expense I have been able to build up an almost complete set of *Signal* in English. The material in *Signal*, though informative, must naturally be treated with great caution and cannot be swallowed whole. The magazine's greatest value lies in the picture it gives of the Germans *as they saw themselves*. Treated analytically, the articles in the magazine are historically valuable, and it must be admitted that *Signal*'s accuracy of war reporting stands up to comparison with Allied accounts of similar actions and campaigns. To those who might feel that a propaganda magazine could not be a reputable source of information I recommend a closer study of *Signal*; the military content is easily sifted from the political idealogy.

The chief books from which I have drawn material—I used many others for checking and cross-checking—are:

Atteridge, A. Hilliard, *The German Army in War*, Methuen, 1915
Battles of the Nineteenth Century, Seven volumes by various historians, Cassell, *c.* 1900
Bernhardi, F. von, *Germany and the Next War*, Arnold, 1914

Bismarck, Otto von, *New Chapters of Bismarck's Autobiography*, Hodder & Stoughton, 1920

Black Book, The (by various editors), Duell, Sloan and Pearce, 1946

Bonnal, H., *Sadowa*, General Hugh Rees, 1907

Brinitzer, Carl and Grossbard, Berthe, *German Versus Hun*, George Allen & Unwin, 1941

Clausewitz, Karl von, *On War*, first published 1832

Collier, Price, *Germany and the Germans*, Duckworth, 1913

Connell, Brian, *Watcher on the Rhine*, Weidenfeld and Nicolson, 1957

Coole, W. W. and Potter, M. F. (joint editors), *Thus Spake Germany*, George Routledge, 1914

Creasy, Edward, Sir, *The Fifteen Decisive Battles of the World*, Macmillan, 1902

Dane, Edmund, *Secrets of Success in War, A Comparison of the British and the German Systems*, Hodder & Stoughton, 1914

Denison, G. T., Colonel, *A History of Cavalry*, Macmillan, 1913

Dodd, Martha, *My Years in Germany*, Gollancz, 1939

Dodge, Theodore A., *Frederick the Great*, Houghton Mifflin, 1896

Erlam, Denys, *Ranks and Uniforms of the German Army, Navy and Air Force*, Seeley Service, 1942.

Farago, Ladislas (editor), *German Psychological Warfare*, Putnam, 1941

Felstead, S. Theodore, *Under the German Heel*, Newnes, 1930

Field, Cyril, *Old Times Under Arms*, Hodge, 1939

Fuller, J. F. C., Major-General, *Decisive Battles of the Western World*, Eyre & Spottiswoode, 1957

Gerard, James W., *My Four Years in Germany*, Hodder & Stoughton, 1917

German Army From Within, by 'a British Officer who has served in it', Hodder & Stoughton, 1914

German War Book, The, issued by the German General Staff

Hammerton, Sir John (editor), *The Great War: I Was There*, 3 vols., Amalgamated Press, 1934 (extracts from many books)

Harsch, Joseph C., *Pattern of Conquest*, Heinemann, 1942

Hart, George H., *Great Soldiers*, Grant Richards, 1911

Hart, W. E., *Hitler's Generals*, Cresset Press, 1944

Hooper, George, *The Campaign of Sedan*, G. Bell, 1914

Hutchinson, J. R., *The Romance of a Regiment*, Sampson Low, 1898

Igra, Samuel, *German's National Vice*, Quality Press, 1945

Infantry in Battle, various contributors, published by the Infantry Journal, Washington D.C., 1939

Jünger, Ernst, *The Storm of Steel*, Chatto & Windus, 1929

Karski, Jan, *Story of a Secret State*, Hodder & Stoughton, 1945

Ludendorff, General, *My War Memoirs, 1914–18*, Hutchinson, 1920

Ludwig, Emil, *The Germans*, Hamish Hamilton, 1942

Martin, A. G., Lieut.-Colonel, *Mother Country—Fatherland*, Macmillan, 1936

Miksche, F. O., *Paratroops*, Faber & Faber, 1943

Miksche, F. O., *Blitzkrieg*, Faber & Faber, 1941

Moltke, Helmuth von, *Franco-German War*, Harper & Brothers, 1907

Morgan, J. H., Brigadier General, *Assize of Arms*, Methuen, 1945

Morgan, J. H., Professor (translator and critic), *The German War Book*, John Murray, 1915

Morrison, Michael A., *Sidelights on Germany*, Hodder & Stoughton, 1918

Nicolai, G. F., *The Biology of War*, J. M. Dent, 1919

Rauschning, Hermann, *Makers of Destruction*, Eyre & Spottiswoode, 1942

Reide, Thomas, *Military Discipline*, published in London, 1795

Rosinski, Herbert, *The German Army*, The Hogarth Press, 1939

Russell of Liverpool, Lord, *The Scourge of the Swastika*, Cassell, 1954

Schellenberg, Walter, *The Schellenberg Memoirs*, André Deutsch, 1956

Shirer, William L., *The Rise and Fall of the Third Reich*, Secker & Warburg, 1960

Shirer, William L., *Berlin Diary*, Hamish Hamilton, 1941

Taylor, A. J. P., *The Course of German History*, Hamish Hamilton, 1945

Tetens, T. H., *The New Germany and the Old Nazis*, Secker & Warburg, 1961

Toland, John, Battle, *The Story of the Bulge*, Muller, 1960

True to Type, A Selection from Letters and Diaries of German Soldiers and Civilians collected on the Soviet-German Front, Hutchinson, 1943

Vagts, Alfred, *A History of Militarism*, Meridian Books, 1959

Wedd, A. F. (translator), *German Students' War Letters*, Methuen, 1929

Wilmot, Chester, *The Struggle for Europe*, Collins, 1952

I have referred also to official histories of the 1914–18 and 1939–45 wars relating to Britain, Australia, France, Canada and Germany.

Index